KNUT SAMSET

PROJECT EVALUATION

MAKING INVESTMENTS SUCCEED

FOR MAI, MAX AND LIVE

© The author/Tapir Academic Press, Trondheim 2003

ISBN 82-519-1840-5

This publication may not be reproduced, stored in a retrieval system or transmitted in any form or by any means; electronic, electrostatic, magnetic tape, mechanical, photo-copying, recording or otherwise, without permission.

Printed by Tapir Uttrykk
Binding: Grafisk Produksjonsservice AS

This book was published with support from the Norwegian Non-fiction Literature Fund

The Concept program
http://www.concept.ntnu.no

Knut Samset
Norwegian University of Science and Technology
Department of Civil and Transport Engineering
N -7491 Trondheim, Norway
Tel.: 73594640
Fax.: 73597021
knut.samset@bygg.ntnu.no

Tapir Academic Press
N–7005 TRONDHEIM

Tel.: + 47 73 59 32 10
Fax: + 47 73 59 32 04
E-mail: forlag@tapir.no
http://www.tapirforlag.no

INTRODUCTION

Organisations use projects increasingly to carry out major as well as smaller tasks. Projects help target and delimit activities, place the responsibility and transfer risk from the financing to the implementing party. Still, projects occasionally turn out terribly wrong. There may be different reasons: it was the wrong type of project from the very start, the design was inadequate, mangement failed to implement it as planned, or unforeseen events caused major problems during its lifetime. To avoid such problems some corrective interventions are needed at different stages of the project. It could be to explore alternative concepts before the project is agreed, to assess the feasibility when it is designed, and to review performance when it is implemented. This is what evaluation is used for. It has become popular as a tool to control, guide and draw lessons of experience from projects.

Project evaluation involves comprehensive studies of the progress, outputs and impact of projects. Evaluations take a broad view of the project in technical terms as well as considering the needs and interests of all stakeholders and affected parties. This helps secure success of the investments involved. Evaluation is a profession bordering on a range of skills including research and communication. The evaluator is supposed to produce relevant and reliable information for decision makers rapidly and often under difficult working conditions.

This book is intended both as a textbook for students and a handbook for practitioners. It provides hands-on easy to comprehend lessons about evaluation as a phenomenon, its design, preparation and methods of implementation – as well as the project as a management tool. The book consists of a sequence of 70 concise, self-contained chapters on key topics, accompanied by illustrations, examples to demonstrate their application, and checklists.

The book was written as input to the *Concept program*, an on-going Norwegian research program on front-end management of projects. The focus is on major public projects and the aim to help improve the chance that projects passing Parliament will be a success. The means to do this is to strengthen front-end management so that the best concept is chosen, and strengthen government's requirements and procedures to ensure quality-at-entry.

The approch to evaluation described in this book centers round what is known as the logical framework approach or project cycle management. Since the 1970-ies this methodology has been promoted by the UN and national governments, later also by the OECD and the European Commission. It is used widely both in international development and national projects. The work comes out of years of practical experience with evaluation, teaching and inspiration from colleagues and clients. A special thanks to Basil Cracknell, Jarle Haarstad, Bjoern Lunoe, Erik Whist, Erik Berg, Vegard Bye, Niels Dabelstein, Hans Lundgren, Kim Forss, Claus Rebien, Yuriko Minamoto, Naomi Okada and Ken Fujimura, and Kristin Ingstad Sandberg who also happens to be my wife.

Trondheim, February 2003

Table of contents

Chapter 1 The project

1.1	Introduction – topics covered in this book	3
1.2	The project as a means to achieve an aim	5
1.3	Uncertainty affecting projects	7
1.4	Internal and external uncertainty	9
1.5	The project's main stakeholders	11
1.6	The stakeholders' interests in the project	13
1.7	The project in a time perspective	16
1.8	The project's design	19
1.9	The project strategy	22
1.10	Successful projects	25

Chapter 2 What is Evaluation?

2.1	What is evaluation?	31
2.2	Documentation to improve performance	34
2.3	Evaluation: a tool in quality management	37
2.4	How to make evaluations useful	39
2.5	Drawing lessons from evidence	41
2.6	Two main approaches to evaluation	44
2.7	Purposes and focuses of evaluation	46
2.8	The quality of evaluations	48
2.9	Evaluability assessment	50

Chapter 3 Evaluation, step by step

3.1	The main parties to an evaluation	55
3.2	Carrying out the evaluation	57
3.3	The decision to evaluate	59
3.4	Preparing the mandate	61
3.5	Initiating the evaluation	63
3.6	Implementing the evaluation	65
3.7	Preparing the report	67
3.8	Finalisation and follow-up	69

Chapter 4 The Focus of Evaluation

4.1	Measures of success	73
4.2	Evaluation criteria	77
4.3	Measuring efficiency	79
4.4	Measuring effectiveness	81
4.5	Assessing impact	83
4.6	Assessing relevance	86
4.7	Assessing sustainability	88

Chapter 5 The Cross-sectoral View

5.1	An integrated evaluation model	93
5.2	Policy support measures	96
5.3	Economic and financial issues	98
5.4	Socio-economic aspects	101
5.5	Environmental impact	103
5.6	Institutional aspects	105
5.7	Technological aspects	107

CHAPTER 6 DESIGN AND METHODOLOGY

6.1	Deductive versus inductive research	111
6.2	Reviewing the strategy	113
6.3	The problem of attribution	115
6.4	The information process	118
6.5	Study design	121
6.6	Quantitative and qualitative analysis	123

CHAPTER 7 DATA COLLECTION METHODS

7.1	Collecting information	129
7.2	Using existing data	132
7.3	Key informant interviews	134
7.4	Direct measurements	136
7.5	Direct observation	138
7.6	Focus group interview	140
7.7	Informal survey	142
7.8	Case study	144
7.9	Extensive observation	146
7.10	Formal survey	148

CHAPTER 8 ENSURING QUALITY

8.1	Knowledge and evidence	153
8.2	Quality of information	155
8.3	Securing validity and reliability	157
8.4	Securing credibility	160
8.5	Triangulation to establish facts	162
8.6	Securing resources for evaluation	165
8.7	Evaluation ethics	167

CHAPTER 9 REPORTING AND USING RESULTS

9.1	Making reports that are used	173
9.2	The use of evaluation	176
9.3	Using evaluation as a learning arena	179

CHAPTER 10 PROJECT CASES

10.1	Evaluating a project	183
10.2	Three strategies assessed	192
10.3	Four cases reviewed	198

ANNEXES

1.	Glossary of evaluation terms	216
2.	Relevant literature for further studies	228
3.	Evaluation sites and sources	231
4.	Index	232

CHAPTER 1

THE PROJECT

ADVENTURE IS THE RESULT OF POOR PLANNING.
COL. BATCHFORD SNELL

Chapter 1 – The project

1.1 INTRODUCTION - TOPICS COVERED IN THIS BOOK

This book focuses on evaluation of projects – or more specifically on how to systematically assess the extent to which a project is or will be successful. To this end, it is necessary to identify the different stakeholders involved in or affected by the project. Projects constitute a meeting place for project owners, financers, contractors, users, opponents and public authorities. These can have shared or conflicting interests – often a combination of both. Their interests will depend on their particular perspectives on the project. For instance, the society's perspective will usually be much broader than the perspectives of the bank manager, the contractor or the user. Much of media's discussion of projects is limited to the implementation of the project itself seen in a short-term perspective, notably with regard to delays and expenditures over budget. One reason is that these aspects can easily be measured and are usually the first criteria against which the project can be assessed. The effects of the project and whether it attains its goal can only be verified at a later stage. It is a much broader issue and therefore difficult to measure.

> During the so-called "International Water Decade" before the turn of the century, the international community spent much resources on projects aimed to produce clean domestic water for the rural poor in developing countries. The projects were initiated on the assumption that clean water is a high priority for all people. However, it turned out that many of the projects failed in the sense that the facilities were not maintained, they broke down, were not repaired and were abandoned. Numerous evaluations were carried out, and many of these looked at people's needs and priorities in a broader perspective. Such studies made it clear that the initial assumption did not hold for the poorer segments of the beneficiaries. Their highest priority was food, jobs, certain commodities, etc - while clean water was not at the top of the list. With their limited resources they were not able to maintain the facilities. As the result, enormous resources that could have been used better on agricultural or industrial projects were wasted.

Despite the difficulties, it is essential to take a broad perspective on projects from the very start when the project is conceived and formulated – and throughout its implementation. Much of the failures in a project can in fact be attributed to the problem that it has been designed and implemented without taking into account some of the broader and long-term effects. Also, evaluations are frequently conducted late in the implementation process. In such cases, their impact on project management will be limited – since it is too late to change the project strategy.

Applying a broad perspective when projects were analysed is what project evaluation is all about. This book takes as its point of departure the project as a phenomenon, and focuses on the stakeholders to the project and their particular interests, since this is the reference for measuring success. Chapter 1 discusses how success can be interpreted in different perspectives, and presents an analytic framework that is used to formulate and assess projects. In chapter 2, evaluation as a phenomenon is discussed. A major part of the book is devoted to the application of the so-called integrated approach to evaluation, which is used in target-oriented project evaluation worldwide. This evaluation model is described in chapter 3. The integrated approach is concerned with taking the long-term perspective as described in chapter 4 - as well as a cross-sectoral view on the project, as described in chapter 5. When an evaluation is initiated, what should be considered the long-term and short-term objectives of the projects need to be clarified. There is a need to make explicit the measurements that would be used as indicators of achievement of the project's objectives. In chapter 6, the analytical process and the methodology applied in evaluation are described. Chapter 7 and 8 provide an overview of methods used in collecting and analysing data. Finally, in chapter 9, reporting and how to make use of evaluation results are discussed.

1.2 THE PROJECT AS A MEANS TO ACHIEVE AN AIM

A project is a fairly recent phenomenon in history. Earlier, most tasks in society were handled by designated permanent organizations – be it the construction of a bridge or a road, arranging a cultural or a sports event, developing a new industrial product, solving a research problem or testing a new drug.

Over the last decades, however, projects have become increasingly important as a way to organise work. More than ever before, projects are used to solve big tasks of public utility. They operate across organisations, and are terminated when the planned task is completed. There has been a significant increase in the amount of such major projects – not least in sectors such as offshore, infrastructure and information technology. But projects are also organised within individual organisations. This means that their value added and profitability increasingly depend on successful projects.

> A project is a temporary endeavour undertaken to create a unique product or service.
> (Project Management Institute, PMI)

Organizations perform work. Work generally involves either *operations* or *projects*, although the two may overlap. Operations and projects share many characteristics; for example, they are performed by people, and planned, executed, and controlled. They differ primarily in that operations are ongoing and repetitive while projects are temporary and unique. Temporary means that every project has a definite beginning and a definite end. Unique means that the product or service is different in some distinguishing way from all similar products or services.

Projects are undertaken at all levels of the organization. They may involve a single person or many thousands. They may require less than 100 hours to complete or sveral million hours. Projects may involve a single unit of one organization or may cross organizational boundaries as in joint ventures and partnering. Projects are often critical components of the performing organization's business strategy. Examples of projects include:

- Developing a new product or service.
- Effecting a change in structure, staffing, or style of an organization.
- Designing a new transportation vehicle.
- Developing or acquiring a new or modified information system.
- Constructing a building or facility.
- Running a campaign for political office.
- Implementing a new business procedure or process.

The tasks that projects are assigned to solve are defined in terms of more or less precise and realistic *goals*. Being a temporary arrangement, and also because the undertaking is more or less unique, uncertainty is often greater than what is common in permanent organisations. Because of the uncertainty associated with planning and implementation, the extent to which the project will attain its goal is also uncertain. This is one of the reasons why improved know-how and tools that can better the planning and management of projects are of great and increasing economic significance. It is also one of the reasons why there has been an increasing tendency to evaluate ongoing and completed projects.

There are numerous examples of projects that have caused high additional cost for the society both during and after they have been implemented. A comprehensive study of major projects, *Morris and Hough (1991)*[1], concludes that the track records of projects are fundamentally poor, particularly for the larger and more difficult ones. Overruns are common. Many projects appear as failures, particularly in the public view. It seems therefore that there is a contradiction between the increasing use of projects and the fundamental problem of projects often overrunning their budgets and exceeding their set limits.

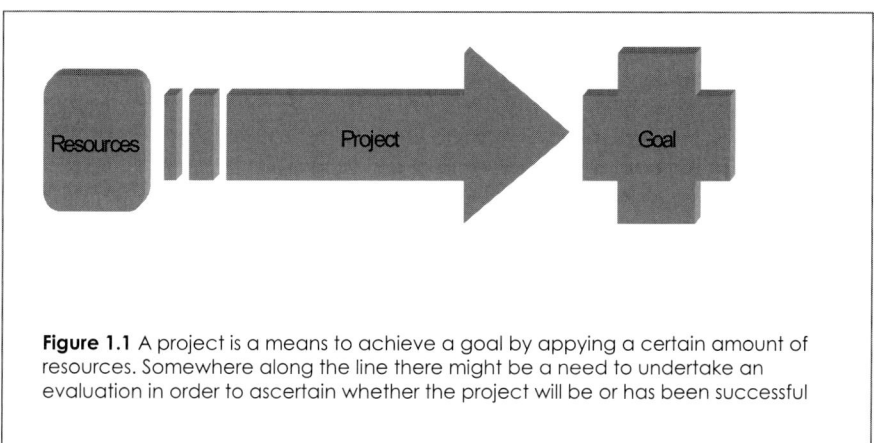

Figure 1.1 A project is a means to achieve a goal by appying a certain amount of resources. Somewhere along the line there might be a need to undertake an evaluation in order to ascertain whether the project will be or has been successful

However, in reality, most projects attain their objectives in one way or another, even if too many are made too expensive or are delayed. There are several reasons for the increasing use of projects today. One answer is that many tasks in society are so enormous and complex that individual organisations lack the competence or capacity to carry them out alone. This is particularly the case in small countries. Another answer is that the project focuses and visualises the task, and therefore has a motivating effect on all stakeholders. In projects, responsibilities are clarified and the different parties are made accountable. Moreover, the project is an expedient way of transferring risk from the financing to the implementing party. The project is also a conducive way of organisation, which allows participants to pool resources and co-operate towards a common goal.

---

[1] Based on 31 separate studies from the period 1959-86 covering more than 4000 projects

1.3 UNCERTAINTY AFFECTING PROJECTS

Because projects are unique undertakings, they involve a degree of uncertainty. Uncertainty characterises situations where the actual outcome of a particular event or activity is likely to deviate from the estimate or forecast value. It follows that decision-making becomes more difficult as uncertainty grows. Further, that the availability of relevant information increases predictability and reduces uncertainty seen from the decision maker's point of view.

This is illustrated in Figure 1.2. In general, uncertainty would be highest at the earliest stage where the project concept is conceived and will reduce as time passes and information accumulates. A reasonable suggestion is then that the potential to *reduce* uncertainty and risk is largest in the outset and that it could be achieved by adding more information. Obviously, there are limits to this. Also, the illustration suggests that an evaluation conducted late in the implementation process would be of limited use to help reduce uncertainty.

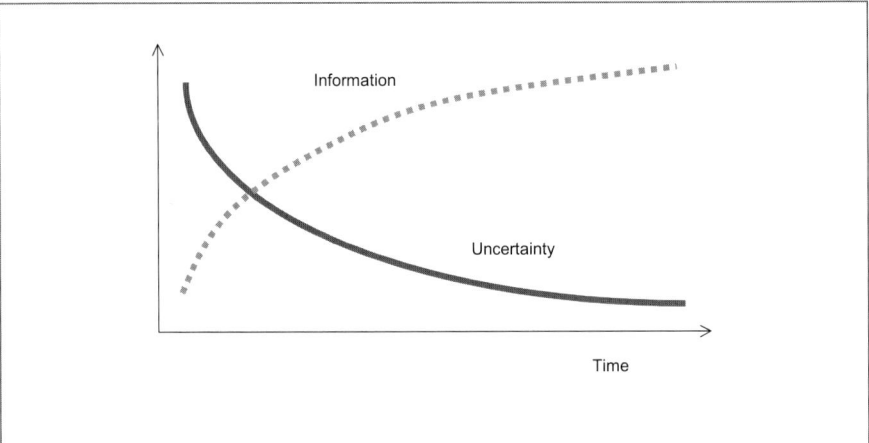

Figure 1.2 Uncertainty vs. available relevant information in a project. In general, uncertainty would be highest in the outset and reduce as time passes and relevant information is generated.

Usually, the distinction is made between the value-neutral term *uncertainty*, and the *subjective* effect of uncertainty which may be either negative or positive seen from the point of view of different parties, usually termed *risk* or *opportunity*, respectively. Uncertainty can therefore also be seen as a source of motivation. For instance, a strictly pre-defined and predictable routine job provides few challenges and the motivation will frequently be low. Increasing uncertainty may represent a challenge which motivates for improved performance. However, if uncertainty increases beyond a certain level where major parameters become unpredictable and the understanding and control over the project is lost, the motivation is commonly reduced.

Uncertainty may have many various causes, related to the situation itself, the design of the project, the time perspective, available information, the implementation of the project, etc. *Ritchie and Marshall (1993)*.

The presence of opportunity and risk is of course a key to whether a project will succeed or fail. People's understanding of these concepts doesn't necessarily correspond with the definitions. There is a tendency to value not only risk but also uncertainty in negative terms. This is because more people are risk-averse than risk seeking, and tend to highlight the negative aspects of uncertainty more than the positive. They become uncertainty-averse and may therefore put themselves in a position where they may avoid risks, but at the same time cannot take advantage of the possibility to explore and exploit the impending opportunities in an uncertain situation.

This suggests the necessity to strike a balance in handling uncertainties and risks. Too often, managers focus on elimination of both uncertainty and risks. Failure is punished even if it is caused by unforeseen events and not by bad management. This, foster a culture of uncertainty avoidance which could mitigate both against motivation and realisation of the positive potential in uncertainty. The challenge therefore is to create an environment, which also rewards the managers that look for opportunities in uncertainty and try to make projects perform better than planned.

Uncertainty

- Unceratinty characterises situations where the actual outcome of a particular event or activity is likely to deviate from the estimate or forecast value

- Different stakeholders tend to view uncertainty differently, i.e. in terms of
    - risk – negative effects
    - opportunities – positive gains

- In general, people tend to view uncertainty negatively – and be risk-averse rather than risk seeking.

- The challenge is to systematically consider the opportunities inherent in an uncertain situation judged against the possible risk

1.4 INTERNAL AND EXTERNAL UNCERTAINTY

In analysing uncertainty in a project, a useful distinction is between *operational* uncertainty and *contextual* uncertainty. *Christensen and Kreiner, 1991.* Operational uncertainty is basically associated with the implementation process itself and considered relatively independent of the context in which the project operates. It is characterised by such features as the quality of plans, management, staff qualifications and experience, project design, funding problems, etc.

The operational uncertainty may be high in an innovative development project which explores new ground, and low in a routine type project with many repetitive elements, extensive experience from similar processes and where the outcome is largely predictable. A characteristic with operational uncertainty is that it will be reduced as the process develops. To some extent it can therefore be reduced by increasing the amount of information available. It can also be reduced by establishing operational objectives at a realistic ambition level and through systematic, realistic planning.

> Uncertainty is the combined effect of the initiating events and all processes that cause and affect the outcome. Each of the initiating events and processes may be predictable to varying degrees. Their combined effect is usually considered to be less predictable. Uncertainty is determined to some degree by the type of and number of such processes involved.

Contextual uncertainty is associated with the surroundings or the context of the project. The contextual uncertainty would be high in projects operating in an unknown environment. Contextual uncertainty is linked to conditions or circumstances beyond the scope and authority of the project, for instance political processes, decisions and responses in affected institutions, demands and responses in the market, technological development, price changes, etc., The possibility to influence contextual uncertainty is often limited. It is often the result of complex processes to a degree, which causes the information gap to be maintained despite effort to generate relevant information. The causes and effects of contextual uncertainty are more difficult to predict than for operational uncertainty.

Clearly, uncertainty is a key parameter in project evaluation. In assessing the success of a project we combine the assessment of perfomance and the effect of uncertainty, precicely as explained above, in terms of operational and contextual factors that will have to be identified and broken down into operational indicators that can be measured.

There is a widespread belief that success and uncertainty is related. Projects therefore go to great length to explore, understand, reduce or overcome uncertainty in decision-making. To this end, the most common means is to:

1. Generate and analyse as much essential information as possible
2. Take a broad view to understand the factors that affect the project
3. Reduce the level of ambition
4. Reduce the planning perspective in time, etc.
5. Improve planning, for instance by using stochastic analysis, etc.

However, as illustrated above, reality, at least outside the physical laboratory, is in constant change, and therefore more or less unpredictable. The reason for this is the in-built dynamism in social and administrative systems, particularly their self-adjusting abilities. There are obvious limitations to what can be achieved in terms of reducing uncertainty. As the result, minute plans developed at an early stage may be less effective in achieving objectives than successive interventions to influence the dynamic process as it unfolds. Systematic assessment of uncertainty at different stages could therefore be seen as an alternative or supplement to planning. It would also be an essential part of evaluation, both in the front-end when the viability of basic project concepts as assessed, and later when performance and effect are scrutinized.

   Operational and Contextual uncertainty

- **Operational** uncertainty is associated with the implementation process itself and usually considered:
    - relatively independent of the project's context
    - high in innovative projects which explores new ground
    - low in a routine type project with many repetitive elements
    - likely to be reduced as the process develops
    - can to some extent be reduced by increasing the amount of information
    - can also be reduced by establishing realistic objectives and plans

    ♦

- **Contextual** uncertainty is associated with the surroundings or the context of the project, and usually considered
    - high in projects operating in an unknown environment.
    - beyond the scope and authority of the project
    - with limited possibility to influence its effect
    - that causes and effects are difficult to predict

1.5 THE PROJECT'S MAIN STAKEHOLDERS

Projects are implemented by project operators in accordance with a given budget and schedule. What is commonly termed the *project perspective* is often the perspective of the operator. However, this is misleading as there are several stakeholders that are parties to a project. Assessment of the success of a project must necessarily be associated with the interests of the project's stakeholders.

Project stakeholders are individuals and organizations who are actively involved in the project, or whose interests may be positively or negatively affected by the project. The key stakeholders are the *financing party*; the *operator,* and the *users*. Their roles and interests are described in chapter 1.6, below. The outline is simplified and does not take into account that there in many cases might not be a clear-cut distinction between the three groups. The financing party can, for instance, represent the society's perspective in a project to construct a power plant, or could also represent the users in a residential housing project initiated by a housing association. In many cases, it is not possible to distinguish between the financing party and the operator in, for example, a project which is internal to an organisation. In other cases the operator may also be the key user of the project's result.[2]

Example.

Projects are often designed without an adequate analysis of the key stakeholders' interests and needs: A tunnel project was implemented in order to connect a community on a small island with other islands in the region based on a rather diffuse motive of the financing party to promote economic development in remote areas. Important aspects such as the users' ability and willingness to pay for the new infrastructure, or its usefulness for local industry were not properly assessed.

The project was successful from the contractor's perspective, being built on time and with costs considerably below budget estimates. However, because of the island's small population, it became apparent that the financial basis was insufficient and user toll correspondingly high. Also, that the connection to the mainland was not decisive for the industry. The size of the investment, combined with low revenue from toll fees made the project a heavy burden for local district authorities,

An analysis of how to interpret "regional development" could have restricted the project goal to the priorities of industry and uncovered that the real need was not for a road connection with the mainland, but for improved harbour facilities – which would have been economically viable.

---

[2] In some cases, each of these parties might be represented by several individual stakeholders, who, in certain cases, are also legally or financially independent of each other. Therefore, not only do conflicts of interest arise between the different groups, but also within the groups themselves. In exceptional cases severe problems might occur just because of internal changes of personnel. It is easy to forget that we deal not only with organisations, but the representatives of these organisations, and that these not always act in a co-ordinated manner.

The operator will not automatically be concerned about the project's possible effects on users and the society - unless explicitly defined in his contract. The operator is not likely to follow up on such aspects at his own initiative – and in any case if this might adversly affect cost, progress or other key management criteria. Equally, usage and effect criteria are notoriously difficult to follow up directly when the implementation is under way, because one can only measure the true effects after the results are in use.

A project is not necessarily successful in a broad societal perspective - even if the implementation is successful from both the perspectives of the operator (in terms of time, cost, and quality) and the user. Also, we cannot automatically assume that a project with major overruns in terms of time and cost and also with major quality flaws will come out as a failure when seen from the users or the society's perspective. There are many examples of projects that have failed in the implementation phase have proven successful at a later point in time, when assessed in a wider perspective. One example is Sydney Opera House, which started out with a six year time-frame and a budget of 7.2 million Australian dollars. In reality, it took over 16 years and 102 million Australian dollars to complete! Afterwards, the building has become an international attraction and has brought enormous financial gains both directly and indirectly and placed Sydney on the world map.

Experience from project management suggests that in order to succeed, one has to try to see the bigger picture, and strike a reasonable balance between the narrow and broad perspectives. In other words, to keep in mind the interests of both the operator, the user and the financing party. In project management, the focus has traditionally been on the contractor's perspective. One of the characteristics of evaluation is that it attempts to maintain the three perspectives in an broad, overall analysis.

☑ Main stakeholders

KEY STAKEHOLDERS	ROLE	FOCUS	COMMON TERMS USED
OPERATOR	Responsible for implementing the project, either by contract or on their own behalf	Project outputs	Implementing party, contractor, project manager
USER	Primary user of the (first-order) results or services of the project	Project goal	Target group, customer, beneficiary
FINANCING PARTY	The initiating party with an interest in the long-term effect of the project	Project purpose	Developer, project owner or financier

1.6 THE STAKEHOLDERS' INTERESTS IN THE PROJECT

The operator's perspective

Project operators have their attention directed, first and foremost, towards the production of project outputs – focusing on the cost, time-frame and quality produced. In other words: the concern is the *tactical* completion of the project within the *strategic frames* which are laid down by the financing party.

This is often misleadingly termed as the project perspective. It is the most restricted and short-sighted perspective one can use when assessing projects. It refers to the lowest level in the project's hierarchy of objectives, see figure 1.3. Take, for example, a road project, where the focus is narrowed down to the road itself, and the extent to which it is built according to the agreed quality standard, budget and schedule. The project outputs for a school construction project might correspondingly be restricted to constructing and outfitting the school buildings.

If focus is placed on the operator's perspective alone, a number of problems can develop. Too much emphasis on the agreed time schedule, budget and so forth, could divert attention away from possible adverse side-effects of the project, which can, in the long run, bring about considerable negative reactions in society. Paradoxically, this can result in a much more costly solution, or reduced long-term economic gain as the result of the project.

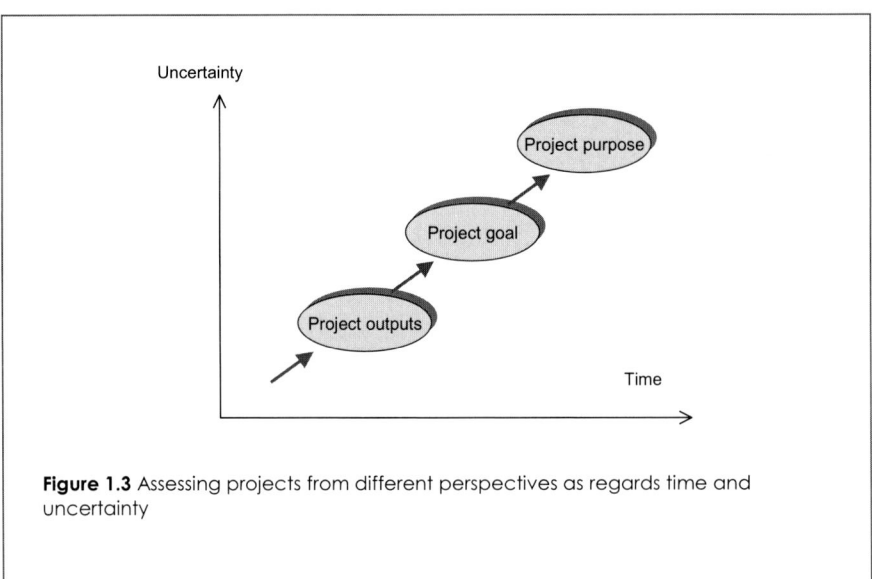

Figure 1.3 Assessing projects from different perspectives as regards time and uncertainty

The user's perspective

Users are more concerned with the utility of the project seen from their point of view, and less with the actual implementation. They tend to assess the project from a broader perspective, with reference to the *project goal*. The parameters used to assess the extent of success are associated with the project's first-order effects. Assessment, thereby, concerns how the project's application and financial aspects affect the user. In a road construction project, such assessment to a certain extent concerns the technical quality of the road, but primarily whether the road makes it easier and quicker to travel from A to B, e.g: the distance and the flow of traffic. For a school construction project, the user's interest goes beyond the suitability of the school buildings, and to the learning and teaching that takes place in the buildings. This, obviously, falls outside the operator's sphere of responsibility. The user's perspective is therefore more ambitious as regards both time and uncertainty, as is illustrated in Figure 1.3. The chance of success is correspondingly more limited in relation to assessing the project from the perspective of the operator alone.

The financing party's perspective

The financing party normally has a perspective beyond the user's perspective, or what is seen to be the immediate effect of the project. Society in general has a perspective that tends to include the collected effect of the project on society as a whole. This is what is termed the project's *purpose*, which is the highest level and expresses the long-term consequences of the project. Private investors will normally place greater emphasis on the value added or profitability, while public investors would emphasise public utility.

In a road construction project, one is concerned with the positive economic effect on society, for example, as the result of reduced travel time, yielding more productive time, the establishment of new settlements or enterprises near the road and so on. In a school construction project, the long-term aim would focus on the effect of education in terms of employment, the economic effect of provision of goods and services, and so on.

In principle, the assessment is similar to that of the user, but now related not only to the primary "user-group" but also to the interests of other parties that are affected by the project, directly or indirectly. Such assessments are ambitious; since the time horizon is extended and uncertainty is higher than is the case of the other perspectives, see Figure 1.3.

Stakeholders' perspectives

PERSPECTIVE	ROAD CONSTRUCTION PROJECT	SCHOOL CONSTRUCTION PROJECT
OPERATOR: project outputs	Road constructed	School buildings built/furnished
USER: project goal	Improved traffic flow	Education
FINANCING PARTY: project purpose	Value added as the result of improved transport	Provision of services as a result of education

1.7 THE PROJECT IN A TIME PERSPECTIVE

As discussed above, people's perspective on a project is related to their roles and responsibilities. The financing party usually has a broader perspective on the project than the contractor, which is in turn broader that the sub-contractor's perspective. If the broad perspective is lacking at the highest level, one cannot expect that it will be present at lower levels. However, all parties need a comprehensive and precise picture of the project strategy that explains in precise terms what is expected to be achieved by realising the project outputs. This will make it easier for all concerned parties to help produce relevant information for managers at higher levels.

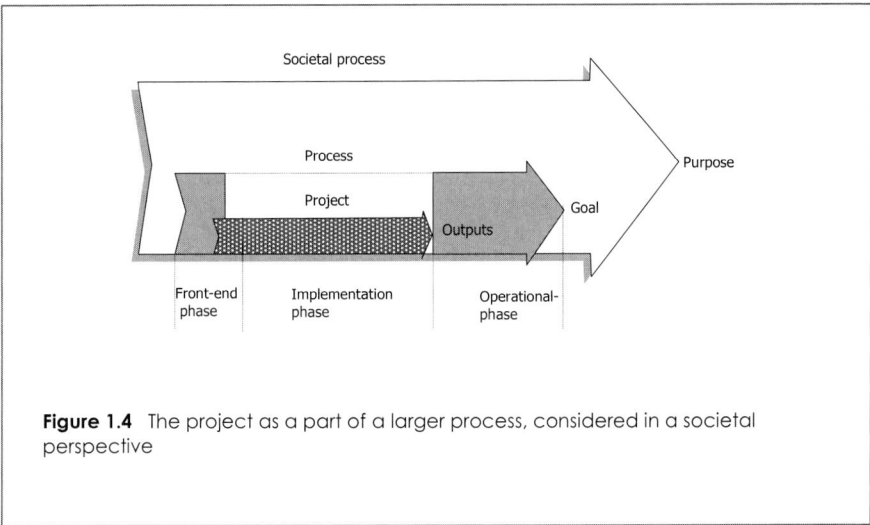

Figure 1.4 The project as a part of a larger process, considered in a societal perspective

Figure 1.4 illustrates the project over time as seen in relation to the three planning perspectives outlined earlier. The idea is that the project represents a focussed undertaking where the primary objective is to produce a number of agreed outputs within a specified time-frame. Commonly, the project can be seen as a time-restricted part of a *process* with a wider purpose and a time perspective beyond that of the project. This process can be characterised by what is termed the project goal. The process in turn contributes to a broader and more long-term societal process, which in this context is characterised by what is termed the project purpose. This objective gives a concerted strategic perspective both for the project and the process that the project is part of. It is often the case that the process presupposes that several projects run concurrently or in sequence. The process, in turn, will be one of many processes that contribute to the long-term objective, here called the project purpose.

The project is planned in a *front-end phase*, which ends when the final decision is made to appropriate funds for the purpose. It is executed in an *implementation phase*, which ends when the project outputs are realised. Commonly, there is an *operational phase* of the project, which follows when the project outputs are realised, that is when the building is built, the road is constructed, etc. As shown in Figure 1.4, it can perhaps be more appropriate to view this phase as a part of the process which the project is part of. As discussed earlier, it is essential to distinguish between the project and the process, since both the objectives and the implementing responsibilities usually will be different in the two cases.

It follows from the illustration in Figure 1.4 that the time perspectives vary for the different parties. The operator could possibly have a time perspective of three to four years, and would wish to delimit his commitments to the period of the guarantee. The financing party could have a much wider time perspective equal to the pay-back period or beyond, and will want to restrict his obligations to this period. For large infrastructure projects, the period could be between 15 and 20 years. The lifespan for that which has been constructed can be much longer. The socitey can thereby be obliged to maintain the built object for generations.

Economically, the front-end phase deals, to a greater extent, with the organisation of who bears the uncertainty and risk involved in the project. When the financing party has established the strategic framework for the project and the main terms that should guide planning and implementation, and has identified a qualified party to take on the responsibility for implementation, then it is implicit in the arrangement that he does not wish to manage the project in detail but hand the responsibility for the project and the risk over to the operator.

His concern would rather be to ensure that the project moves in the right direction. He should monitor the project and detect as early as possible which amendments would be neccesary to secure that the project has its desired effect in a strategic perspective. The division of responsibilities between the financing party and the operator is commonly regulated by contracts to ensure a certain flexibility for the operator within the strategic framework laid down by the financing party.

The operator will, in the front-end phase be concerned first and foremost with estimating the right price in order to be able to carry out the work to a satisfactory level without too great risk and, at the same time, seeing a profit. What makes this transaction viable is that the transfer of risk comes at a price. A core part of the contract between the two parties implicitly concerns how to share and price the risk. This forms the basis for the sharing of responsibility, such that both parties can attain their goals either fully or in part.[3]

---

[3] The division of responsibility should have reference to more than just the disribution of risk.

Chapter 1 – The project

Project phases

FRONT-END PHASE	❑	From the initial concepts are concieved until funds are appropriated to the project
IMPLEMENTATION PHASE	❑	From detailed planning until agreed outputs (operational objectives) have been produced
OPERATIONAL PHASE	❑	The pay-back period until the results of the project (buildings, roads, software, etc) are no longer in use

1.8 THE PROJECT'S DESIGN

The point of departure for the evaluation team, is the project design including the key elements in the project as well as the most important influencing factors in its surroundings, i.e. the contextual uncertainty, see Figure 1.5.

An adequate design of a project is built on a sequence of causes and effects, which starts with an amount of resources to be exploited by the project (the inputs) in order to produce a number of project outputs. Clearly, the resources need to be sufficient for the purpose. The project outputs should be defined such that they are close to one hundred per cent attainable. In some projects, outputs in formally agreed plans are hypothetical and therefore outside the scope of the project in relation to its mandate and the available resources. The possibility to succeed within the framework of the project is thereby not formally available.

The design should encompass the three planning perspectives. This would include a *project purpose* or a long-term objective, explaining the rationale behind the project, and a *project goal* which specifies in an exact manner the desired state that the project is intended to contribute to in the short-term. Project goals and project purposes are hypothetical because the project at hand is just one of several factors that must come into place for these goals to be realised. The likelihood that this will happen is thereby less than 100 per cent. As is mentioned above, a road construction project should, for example, contribute to the solution of a traffic problem. This should, as a follow-on, lead to reduced accident frequency, and to people using less time on travel, leaving more time for productive activities such as work or leisure. The building of a school ought to provide education for a community, which thereby leads to a higher level of competence in that community. The road and the school are project outputs, movement of traffic and education are project goals, and productive use of time and higher levels of competence are project purposes.

In the design of a project, the project goal ought not to be more ambitious than that which is realistically attainable within the time-frame associated with the goal. The same is true of the project purpose. These objectives need to be as precisely formulated as possible. The project should have only one goal; this will act as clarification when planning, deploying resources, managing the project and checking the work. One can often see that projects have several independent goals, which often represent causal chains of objectives with differing levels of ambition. In some cases, the same project can have several conflicting goals. This confuses the allocation of resources in the project and it leaves room for interpretation and misinterpretation, such that different parties can understand the aim of the project in differing ways. Good project design requires, therefore, that the project has only one concerted goal, see the project goal-structure in Figure 1.5.

The project structure provides a broad, comprehensive description of the project. Such a hierarchy, weeded of details, is most decisive for all parties involved, and a good point of departure for the assessment of the whole, as regards realism and design. This can be contrasted with the much more restricted but more detailed picture, which is usually presented when using the most common project management tools. In such cases, the assessment is limited in its most essential aspects to the realisation of the project outputs on the basis of a detailed underlying plan of activities.

Chapter 1 – The project

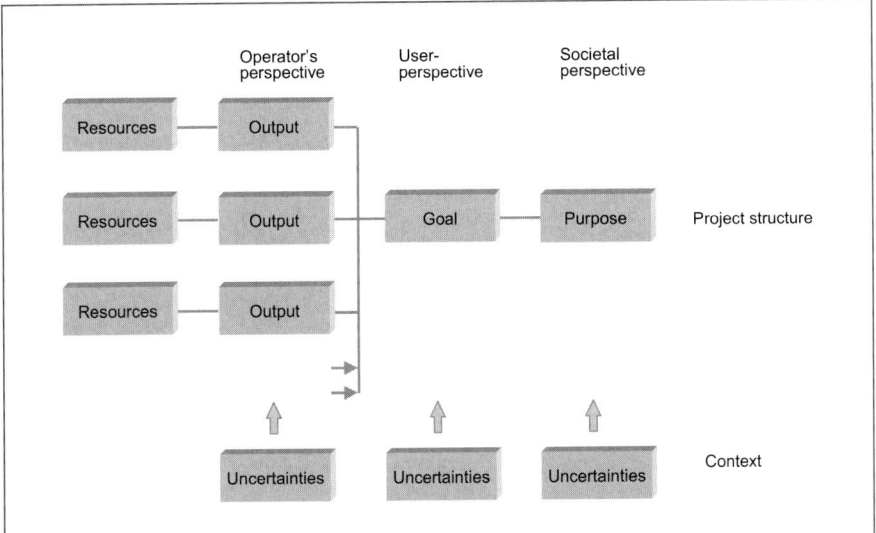

Figure 1.5 The project structure and the project's context. The project structure describes the logical linkage between the use of resources and project outputs, as well as the overriding objectives that the project is intended to contribute to. In a realistically designed project, the conditional probability of realisation on each level should be acceptable, while taking into account the probability of realisation of sub-ordinated objectives as well as the effect of uncertainties in the project's context.

It obviously makes sense to establish and analyse such a broader, overall project hierarchy before the details are described.[4] The level of ambition should be clarified in the outset on the basis of systematic assessment of the probability of realisation. This is often not done properly. Projects are planned without an initial assessment of the priorities involved as seen from a user perspective. The broader societal perspective is often only applied in major publicly funded projects where there is a legal requirement that a comprehensive impact assessment is carried out.

---

[4] This is a simplification. The processes constituting and affecting a project is a dynamic system of inter-linked events rather than a one dimensional chain of causes and effects as is commonly used in planning. Discussing uncertainty in a narrow cause-effect perspective meets with severe theoretical and methodological difficulties. What should be seen as causes and effects would depend on sequence, strength of connection and scope of impact. In the real situation, every event in the dynamic system of a project is affected by a complexity of trends, patterns and structures

Chapter 1 – The project

The project's design

PROJECT PURPOSE   The long-term objective, which explains the rationale behind the project

♦

PROJECT GOAL   The first-order effects of the project - the desired state that the project is intended to contribute to in the short-term

♦

PROJECT OUTPUTS   The specific agreed results that should be produced when the project has been implemented.

♦

RESOURCES   The financial, material and manpower resources necessary to produce the project's outputs.

1.9 THE PROJECT STRATEGY

Project designers tend to be ambitious. One reason may be that ambitious objectives provide motivation for those involved to improve performance, another that ambitious objectives help justify proposed projects at an early stage. The dilemma is that high ambitions tend to reduce the probability of success, since success is determined by performance relative to ambition.

Planners may start with an idea of the amount of funds available and stipulate an objective to match the resources. Although this is a perfectly rational approach in planning, the result is often a mismatch between objectives and resources. Often, objectives are ambitious beyond what available resources can support, since people have a tendency to underestimate costs. Availability of resources, however, does not necessarily guarantee project success. The critical factors affecting the project may be insensitive to the amount of resources available, for instance if they are related to the market response, carrying capacity of the environment, the availability of technology, etc. The assessment of realism at the planning stage would usually have to consider a large number of such factors.

Laying a realistic strategy is a question of deciding the ambition level rather than laying out the sequence of events and stipulating achievements in detail. A systematic analysis of the *probability* and *utility* associated with each ambition level in the project is probably more significant than the detailed analysis. It is also much less expensive. And still, systematic analyses of probabilities and utilities are not always done in projects.

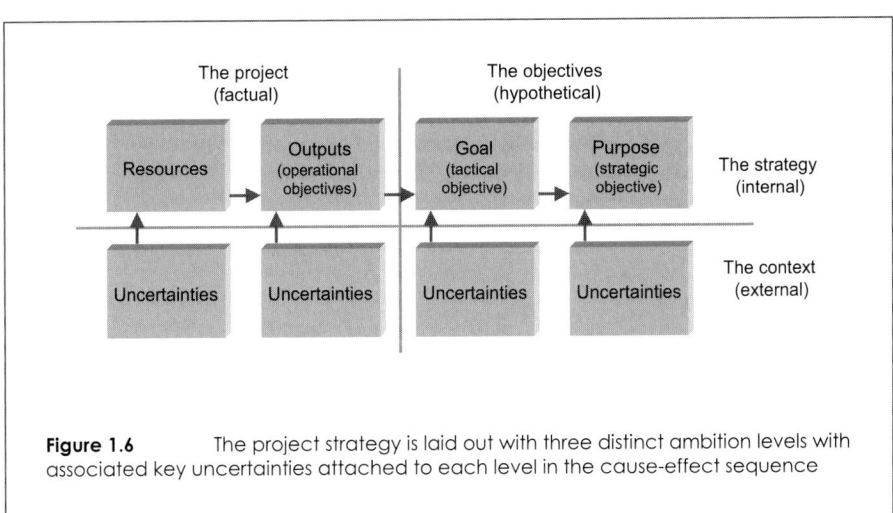

Figure 1.6 The project strategy is laid out with three distinct ambition levels with associated key uncertainties attached to each level in the cause-effect sequence

In figure 1.6, the key elements in a project have been structured in a logical sequence including an operational, tactical and strategic level, with the main contextual uncertainties influencing the strategy linked to each level. A realistic strategy needs to provide a description of the main elements in the project and the main influencing factors or uncertainties in its surroundings. It should have a strategic objective which provides the justification for the project, a tactical objective which is explicit regarding the preferred situation that the project is meant to contribute to, and a number of operational objectives that are explicit regarding what the project should produce. The operational objectives should be *factual* in the sense that the project is expected to fulfil these objectives with a high probability. The tactical and strategic objectives are *hypothetical* in the sense that the project is only one of several conditions that have to be fulfilled in order for the objectives to be realised.

A realistic strategy is built on a cause-effect chain, which starts with an amount of resources to be used within the project to fulfil a number of operational objectives. The resources must be sufficient to ensure the realisation of objectives. The operational objectives must therefore be defined so that the probability of realisation is close to 100 per cent. If the operational objectives are hypothetical, the project is not formally designed to succeed.

Projects are often designed with several independent objectives at the tactical and strategic level, sometimes involving different ambition levels. In some cases the same project can have conflicting objectives. This creates internal uncertainty, which opens up to different interpretations of the objectives by different parties. A successful strategy requires that the tactical objective should not be ambitious beyond what is realistically achievable within the time frame associated with the objective. Also, the objectives must be defined precisely and as singular objectives. Agreeing on only one tactical objective will facilitate planning, allocation of resources, project management and control. The same requirements apply for the strategic objective.

The project's strategy is established by the main normative elements in the upper row in the matrix in figure 1.6. Below are the main uncertainties affecting the strategy and linked directly to the fulfilment of the different levels in the strategy. A realistic strategy requires that as many as possible of the major uncertainties are identified in the outset. The matrix provides room for the information necessary for an overall description of the fundamental characteristics of the strategy. Such a strategy, without details, will provide useful insight for all parties involved in or affected by the strategy and will be a good point of departure for the assessment of realism and a subsequent more detailed design of the project. The framework provides a fuller perspective than the much narrower but more detailed picture presented by common project management tools. It is therefore also the point of departure for evaluators when the project is evaluated, see chapter 3.1.

A realistic strategy

- It should be built on a consistent cause-effect chain, which starts with an amount of resources to be used within the project to fulfil a number of clearly specified objectives

    ♦

- Objectives should not be unclear or conflicting, which opens up to different interpretations by different parties, in order to avoid internal uncertainty

    ♦

- The operational objectives or outputs should be 100 percent achievable

    ♦

- The tactical and strategic objectives should not be ambitious beyond what is realistically achievable in their respective time frames

    ♦

- The major uncertainties likely to affect the project should be identified in the outset

    ♦

- None of the uncertainties should represent a risk that would threaten the realisation of the associated objectives

1.10 Successful Projects

Projects are evaluated more frequently than institutions and other more permanent initiatives. This is because projects are temporary undertakings that are implemented in a confined period of time, where there is a desire to evaluate the outcome before the project is formally terminated.

A key issue in evaluation is to establish the degree of success of the project. However, success is a highly aggregated parameter. There are large variations in how it is defined and interpreted. A meaningful comparison of success rates in different projects can only be made if the definition and application of the concept is carefully explained in each individual project. This is often not the case.

> The concept of project success has remained ambiguously defined both in the project management literature and, indeed, often within the psyche of project managers. Projects are often rated as successful because they have come in on or near budget and schedule and achieved an acceptable level of performance. Other project organisations have begun to include the client satisfaction variable in their assessment of project success. Until project management can arrive at a generally agreed upon determinant of success, our attempts to accurately monitor and anticipate project outcomes will be severely restricted.
>
> *Pinto and Slevin, 1988*

However, assessing success is not only a question of choosing the right parameters. It will also largely depend on which ambition level is used as reference when the project is evaluated.

A restricted interpretation of the concept is to look at success in an *operational* perspective where it is measured according to whether (1) the project was completed on *time*, or (2) the *costs* did not exceed the budget, or (3) the *quality* of its outputs met with expectations. These are the most commonly applied measures of success. A more compound measure of success in the operational perspective would be an aggregate based on these three (or more) parameters. Obviously this would narrow the chance of success considerably, as indicated with the shaded area in Figure 1.7.

A broader interpretation of the concept would encompass the *tactical* perspective and focus on the extent to which the project (1) has achieved its formal *goal*, or whether (2) the *impact* of the project is predominantly positive, or whether (3) the project is *relevant* in relation to people's needs. Clearly, these measures are more ambitious and there is more uncertainty involved. Realisation of these measures can only be expected at a later stage. The aggregate of the three components would measure the usefulness of the project rather than its performance during implementation, and hence more ambitious. Therefore, the chance of success would also be less, as indicated by the shaded area.

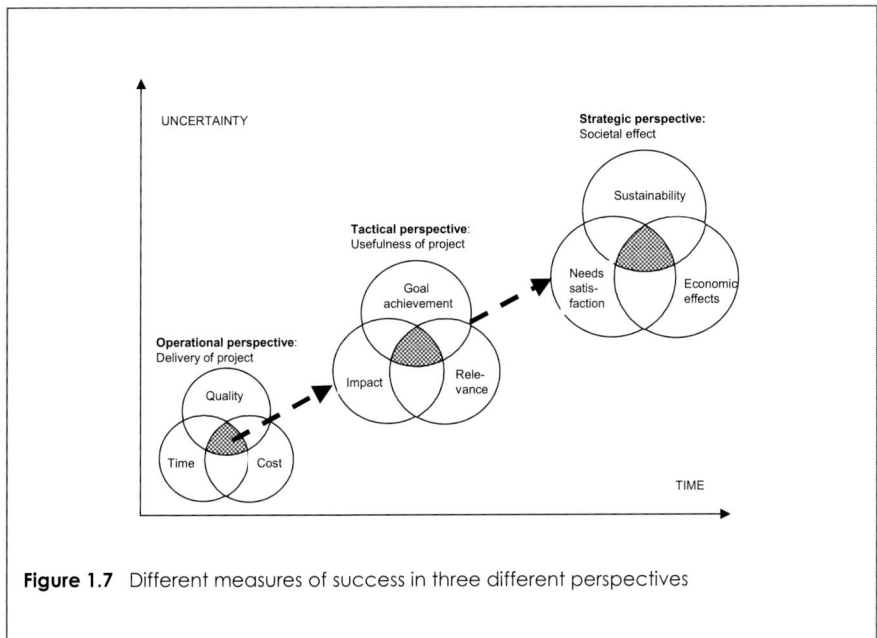

Figure 1.7 Different measures of success in three different perspectives

The broadest interpretation of project success is associated with the *strategic* perspective, which could be based e.g. on measures of (1) the long-term economic effect in the broadest sense, (2) the extent to which it can be *sustained* in the long term, and (3) whether is satisfy *needs*. This is the society's perspective. Obviously these are even more ambitious and aggregated measures with a correspondingly lower chance of realisation. By combining these measures as indicated by the shaded area in Figure 1.7, the chance of success is even more restricted.

It follows from figure 1.7 that the chance of success of a project is highly dependent on what time in the project cycle the evaluation takes place. During implementation it is usually possible to establish with some confidence whether the project will succeed in the operational perspective; more so the closer we get to the completion date. A reliable assessment of success in a tactical or a strategic perspective will have to be made at a later stage.

To confuse the picture further, projects have a tendency to change both ambitions and performance over time. In such cases, its success as measured against operational, tactical and strategic objectives may change considerably. In literature, success rates are often discussed and even compared without any reference to what stage in the project cycle the projects have been evaluated. This problem further limits the possibilities to make valid comparisons of success between projects.

Chapter 1 – The project

✓ Measuring success

- Success is determined by performance relative to ambition

    ♦

- Success is a highly aggregate parameter and needs to be precisely defined in order to warrant comparison between projects

    ♦

- The chance of success is highest in a limited restricted perspective at a low ambition level

    ♦

- The chance of success is more limited in a broad perspective at a high ambition level

    ♦

- The time factor is essential when measuring success

CHAPTER 2

WHAT IS EVALUATION?

IT IS EASIER TO SOLVE PROBLEMS THAN CRISES.
JOHN GUINTHER

2.1 WHAT IS EVALUATION?

Generally speaking, evaluation is used to establish the outcome of processes and activities with some accuracy. It ranges from the formal examination of students to the broad and in-depth studies of public programs. Over the last couple of decades, public institutions as well as industry have used evaluations increasingly.

Evaluation can be defined as systematic, analytical studies conducted occasionally to answer specific management questions about performance. Project evaluations may assess and explain any of a variety of project performance issues, as discussed further in chapter 4. They are often conducted by experts external to the project, and independent of other key stakeholders. However, some may be self-evaluations conducted by project managers and/or have participation by stakeholders such as the financing party or the users.

	LEVELS OF INQUIRY
First order effects	Project performance and production of outputs
Second order effects	Benefits for users
Third order effects	Impact in society
Fourth order effects	Long-term return on investments

Evaluations tend to be in-depth analyses that examine and explain performance in their broader contexts. They not only present evidence about results achieved, but they interpret, explain, and make judgements about performance in light of the conditions that influence the outcomes and impact of the project. Evaluations typically provide recommendations for actions to be taken that flow from the analysis. In other words, evaluations may draw their findings from performance data, but go well beyond simple presentations of results, by drawing conclusions, interpretations or judgements based on an understanding of the broader context, and then making recommendations. Without such understanding of underlying causes, management may take inappropriate actions.[5] Moreover, evaluations often draw broader lessons for future project designs and/or for formulation of overall strategies and policies.

Scope of evaluation

Evaluations may focus on smaller or larger parts of the process that the project is part of, or look at the project from the perspective of one or several of the key stakeholders, see chapter 1.5. Usually, an evaluation takes a perspective beyond the production of the

---

[5] Just knowing that a project has fallen short of its targets does not necessarily tell managers whether to terminate it or increase efforts.

agreed outputs. It could include impact studies beyond the first and second order effects of the project. Evaluations would usually not restrict the focus only to the positive effects but also take the negative effects into account. Evaluations are carried out at different levels of activities, from project level to policy level.

- Evaluations of *individual projects* focus on performance issues and effects in order to verify achievements or improve management. Project evaluations may address one or more of a variety of project performance issues. Via in-depth analysis, project evaluations answer specific performance questions raised by management. They may, for example, investigate early warning that performance is falling short of expectations.

- *Program level* evaluations will focus more on the combined effect of a group of related projects and less on performance of individual projects. Such evaluations may attempt to compare and assess the relative effectiveness of the different project strategies aimed at the same objective, their synergies and potential conflicts/tradeoffs.

- *Sector or company* level evaluations usually focus on selected policy issues. Several methodologies and data sources may be used in such evaluations. They may, for example, review and synthesize findings from a series of existing evaluation reports on related projects or programs in a given sector or theme area. From these case studies an overall synthesis report is then prepared.

Two main types of evaluation

In some cases, evaluations are used to establish performance or achievements, for instance at the end of a project. Such evaluations are called *summative* evaluations. In other cases the aim is to examine and change processes as they are happening. This is called *formative* evaluations.

A well-known analogy is the following: When the cook tastes the soup – it is formative. When the guest tastes the soup – it is summative. The use of the two types of evaluation is discussed further in chapter 2.2.

Stages of evaluation

Evaluations are carried out at different stages of the project cycle:

- Evaluations of ongoing projects are called *interim evaluations*, and usually take place mid-term in the implementation period or at the end of a distinct phase. Interim evaluations will typically focus on operational activities, but will also take a wider perspective and possibly give some consideration to long-term effects.

- *End-evaluations* aim to establish the situation when the project is terminated and to identify possible need for follow-up activities.

- *Ex-post evaluations* are carried out after the project is terminated. The main purpose is to assess what lasting impact it has had or is likely to have and to extract lessons of experience.

The role of evaluations in the projects cycle is discussed further in chapter 2.3.

Two types of evaluation

	SUMMATIVE EVALUATION	FORMATIVE EVALUATION
AIM	Finding out about the past	Improving future performance
EMPHASIS ON	Degree of success or failure	Reasons for success or failure
EVALUATORS	Impartial and independent	Including stakeholder representatives

Source: Cracknell, 2000

2.2 DOCUMENTATION TO IMPROVE PERFORMANCE

Evaluation is a management tool that is used to find out about the past in order to improve upon future performance. The challenge for the evaluator is to provide credible documentation of project performance and effects, and to generate sound advice based on lessons of experience.

Documentation purpose

Evaluations are analytical assessments of the results of private and public investments. The amount and quality of information may vary in projects. Part of the information generated in the course of a project relies significantly on judgement. Evaluators are expected to help improve information and reduce uncertainty. In this respect so-called *documentation evaluations* aim specifically to account for the use of resources through making operations and results transparent. A main concern is to produce reliable information. Evaluations are therefore expected to be impartial and carried out by professionals who are independent of the project activities under study.

Documentation evaluations are summative and usually based on a mandate or *Terms of Reference* that specify the issues on which to focus. The Terms of Reference is a key document to guide the evaluation, and is part of the formal agreement between the evaluators and the commissioning party. However, the Terms of Reference commonly state that evaluators are obliged to include other topics not covered if the analysis indicates that this is important.

Evaluation is often carried out as a means to help ensure accountability for the results both at the financing and implementing side. In such cases the formal aspect of the evaluation and the disciplining effect it would have on the involved parties might be equally important as the information produced by the evaluation team.[6]

Documentation of performance (summative)

Providing decision makers and the general public with professional documentation as to the use and results of resources and contribute to a better understanding of a project, its potential and limitations

Lessons of experience (formative)

Contributing to the improvement of projects by the collation, analysis and dissemination of experience from current and completed projects. Evaluations focus on the causes and explanations as to why activities succeed or fail and produce information that helps make future projects more relevant and effective.

---

[6] Take the auditor's role as an example: The main purpose of a formal audit is not the audit itself but its disciplining effect on accountancy. The auditor's report is just a formal tool towards this effect. Correspondingly, a formal evaluation is expected to have a disciplining effect on management both at the financing and implementing side. Its main significance is to set a standard for reporting which can be applied by the parties involved.

Evaluations to improve performance

An evaluation designed to draw lessons from experience and improve performance needs to be interdisciplinary and comprehensive enough to generate the necessary perspective and insight for learning. Such evaluations will often be thematic. The perspective could be narrow, looking at a specific aspect of a project or programme - or wide, focussing on a group of projects or a programme.

External, independent evaluators would typically be used to manage this type of evaluation. However, since the purpose is to generate experience more than ensuring accountability, representatives from different stakeholders need to participate more actively than in documentation evaluations. Such broader participation is essential to ensure that experience generated through evaluations is applied in the formulation of policies and strategies, and in the design and initiation of future project activities.

Such *formative evaluations* therefore often start with a process to determine which areas or topics would be relevant, and provide an overview of possible topics and angles. This could involve a series of workshops designed to identify topics and focus the evaluation. Such workshops could be internal with participation from stakeholders and with external expertise. Based on the recommendations from this process, the Terms of Reference for the evaluation can be formulated, and the evaluation set in motion. The evaluation itself could be an intensive study resulting in a final document, or an open-ended process over considerable time where evaluators would interact with stakeholders to improve performance and effects at different stages of the process.

Chapter 2 – What is evaluation?

☑ Two main types of evaluation

	Summative **DOCUMENTATION AND CONTROL**	*Formative* **IMPROVING PERFORMANCE**
AIM	Produce reliable information for visibility and accountability	Draw lessons to improve current and future projects.
TARGET GROUP	The financing party, key decision makers, public authorities, etc.	All stakeholders, affected parties and the public
EVALUATORS	External, impartial, independent team of specialists	Interdisciplinary team of external evaluators and representatives of key stakeholders
BASIS	Data collection and analysis according to an agreed Terms of Reference	Open ended process or workshop to identify topics and focus the evaluation

2.3 EVALUATION: A TOOL IN QUALITY MANAGEMENT

Evaluation can be seen as part of a wider quality management system, complementary to other measures to improve quality. It has traditionally been an instrument for in-depth analysis to provide insight in the complexity of projects and processes.

Organizations performing projects will often divide each project into several project phases to provide better management control and appropriate links to the ongoing operations of the performing organization. Taken together, the project phases are known as the *project life cycle*. The project life cycle serves to define the beginning and the end of a project. For example, when an organization identifies an opportunity that it would like to respond to, it will often authorize a feasibility study to decide if it should undertake a project. The project life cycle definition will also determine which transitional actions at the end of the project are included and which are not.

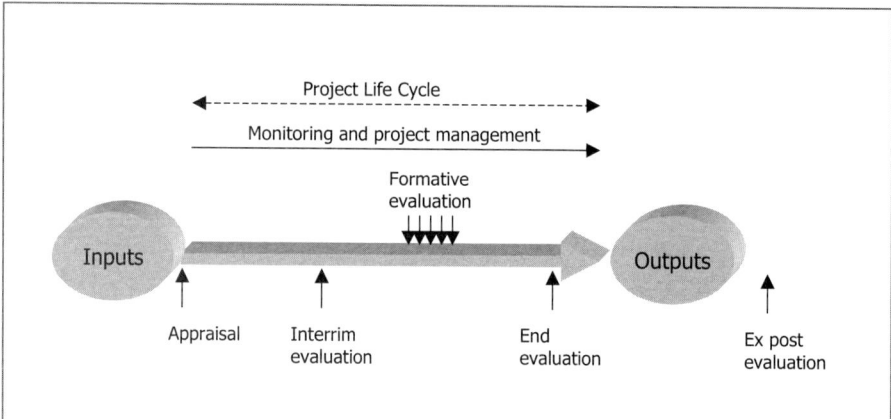

Figure 2.1 Evaluation applied during the project life cycle. Evaluation is done as individual studies before, during or after the project – or as a formative process during parts of the project's life cycle.

Both implementers and financers strive to improve quality of the projects they are responsible for. Over the years, a repertoire of tools has been developed to improve performance. These could be seen as elements in larger quality management systems.

In this perspective, it is appropriate to make the distinction between evaluation on the one hand - and performance management on the other. The distinction would be that performance management focuses on performance issues, is mandatory and largely based on self-assessment – while evaluation tend to look deeper on fewer issues, is selective, and more commonly involve external evaluators.

While performance management is an integral part of the project/program, evaluation is an ad-hoc exercise that is undertaken at certain stages and for certain purposes, either during implementation to provide guidance (interim evaluation), at the end to verify achievements, or some time after the project/program has been terminated to explore the longer term effects (ex post evaluation). In addition, formative evaluation may be applied during parts of the project life cycle in order to strengthen project management.

The role of evaluation during the project life cycle could be described as illustrated below:

1. **Appraisal.** This is an early assessment of the project concept. It is done in order to decide whether or not to finance the project and go ahead with it. The appraisal should take a broad view of the project much in the same way as subsequent evaluations, in order to ensure that it is economically viable, relevant in relation to user needs, and is likely to be sustainable.

2. **Monitoring.** This is a management function aimed to collect and analyse information on a regular basis in order to check performance with budgets, work plans and objectives. Monitoring data is indispensable as basis for evaluations, particularly since it has the advantage that it provides the basis for trend analysis.

3. **Interim evaluation.** This is usually done to guide management or in response to request or pressure from stakeholders or the public. The reasons could be that it has been programmed initially, that the project is entering a new phase, that the project is considered problematic, that there is a need to analyse impacts, etc.

4. **End evaluation.** This is done as a formal exercise to establish achievements at the end of the project life cycle. It focuses essentially on the production of project outputs in terms of quality, timing and cost - but also the extent to which formally agreed objectives have been or are likely to be achieved.

5. **Ex post evaluation.** This is done to determine the longer-term effects of a project and the extent to which it has contributed to the achievement of formally agreed objectives. This may require analysis in a wide social or socio-economic perspective. The motive could be to draw lessons that could be useful for similar projects in the future. In most projects ex post evaluations will not be done.

In many cases there may be good reasons for not doing or postponing an evaluation, for instance in routine projects which are performing as foreseen, and where the possible impact are well understood. However, too often this is used as an excuse for not doing an evaluation. After all, independent evaluations have often proved essential to initiate necessary changes in management and strategy – and get such changes underway.

2.4 How to make evaluations useful

In the end, the worth of evaluation is judged by its utility. What is considered useful in this context could be the extent to which the evaluation contributes new insight, its impact on decisions, or its relevance in a making or changing policy. The actual outcome of an evaluation largely depends on the way it is designed, conducted, distributed and used. Evaluations can and do make a difference.

Most people think of the outcome in terms of the quality and distribution of the evaluation report. Others claim that it is the evaluation process itself that is the most useful: it offers an opportunities for main stakeholders to prepare essential information, thinking through objectives and strategies, and getting inputs on essential matters from external specialists.

Another view is that the "threat" of a formal evaluation may be more effective than the evaluation itself, since it tends to have a disciplining effect on the management of projects, much in the same way as the threat of an audit will have a positive effect on accountancy within a company.

In general terms, it is common to distinguish between whether evaluations are of *direct* or *indirect* use. By direct use is meant that decision makers and other stakeholders use evaluation findings directly, for instance by making specific decisions about immediate courses of action in the project that has been evaluated. By indirect use is meant that the use of evaluations influence thinking in a general way, for instance by sensitising individuals to certain problems or by indirectly having an impact on policy or procedures. Clearly, evaluators have a responsibility to optimise the direct utility of their work. But they also have a more difficult task to maximise the indirect utility, for instance by assessing their findings in a broad perspective.

In order to make evaluations useful there are a number of measures that need to be taken by the commissioning party as well as the evaluators at different stages of the evaluation process.

Evaluations need to respond to stakeholders' interests. In the quest to make evaluations useful, it may be necessary with broad participation in the evaluation design process to ensure sensitivity to various stakeholders' interests. This will also help sorting out differences in values and perspectives between stakeholders and evaluators at the outset to avoid conflicts when the work is presented.

Prior to, or as part of evaluations it might be useful to include an assessment of utilization. Evaluators and decision makers need not only to share an understanding of the purposes for which a study is undertaken but also agree on the criteria by which its successful utilization may be judged. An effort should be made to judge the extent to which the uses of findings are likely to meet these expectations.

There should also be a plan on how to use and disseminate evaluations. The purpose of evaluation needs to be clarified at the outset, to identify the main target groups. This will in turn affect the design of the evaluation as discussed above. Also, a plan needs to be made on how and when to distribute the report, what type of follow-up would be needed, seminars and workshops to be held, how to reach a broader audience, etc. This is discussed further in chapters 9.2.

However, the single most important aspect that determines to what extent an evaluation will be used is the stakeholders' assessment of whether the findings can be trusted. Therefore, the quality and credibility of the study should be ensured. This clearly depends on the selection of evaluators and the participatory process involved, But it also depends on the quality of the evaluator's work, which is discussed in more detail in chapter 8.

It is also essential that reporting is adapted to the cognitive styles of the users. For instance, presenting complex analysis may represent a barrier to understanding for non-specialists and the public. Clearly, reports and oral presentations have to be tailored to the intended audience, which is often a mix of specialists, decision makers, politicians, and the public. See chapter 9.3.

Finally, evaluation results need to be timely and at hand when needed. This is a question of the ability to select the right type of evaluation at the most appropriate time. But also to minimize the time it takes from the decision to evaluate is taken to the mandate is formulated and agreed, evaluators selected, field work carried out and the report has been produced. Evaluators therefore have to balance thoroughness and completeness of analysis with timing and accessibility of findings.

✓ Ensuring usefulness

REQUIREMENTS	MEASURES
RESPONDING TO STAKEHOLDR'S NEEDS	❑ Identify stakeholder's needs ❑ Involve stakeholders in evaluation design ❑ Agree on criteria to assess utilisation
BEING TIMELY AND AT HAND WHEN NEEDED	❑ Initiate evaluation at an appropriate point in time ❑ Plan and implement evaluation without delay
BEING CREDIBLE AND WITH ACCEPTABLE QUALITY	❑ Ensure qualified and experienced evaluators ❑ Set quality requirements ❑ Ensure that quality standards are applied
BEING USED	❑ Plan how evaluation should be distributed ❑ Agree on how to follow-up and use evaluation report

2.5 DRAWING LESSONS FROM EVIDENCE

To draw lessons from evidence that is produced in evaluation require that it is possible to generalise to some degree on the basis of the material at hand. Generalisation is the issue of making predictions based on a recurring experience. If something occurs frequently, we expect that it will continue to do so in the future. With enough evidence we can make predictions about development patterns. For instance, a training program that has produced excellent results time and again for years, may be expected to do so also in the near future. However, our assumptions are based on statistical probability and we do not expect the generalisations to operate the same way in every circumstance. For instance, a training program in one organisation might be a complete failure if used in another setting, for instance in a different country or company.

In research, the issue may be whether an observed phenomenon can be generalized to a population outside of the original study. In projects the issues are rather (1) whether a project can be *replicated* in other settings, and (2) whether specific lessons of generic nature are generally applicable.

Replicability

This typically is a matter of comparing success rates in similar projects in different settings. To the extent that evaluations of very similar projects yield convergent results, it demonstrates replicability. The problem seen from a methodological point of view lies in defining essential parameters to classify different interventions and their setting. This problem is in itself formidable. Standardisation of parameters would help, since this would make the comparative study of similar projects easier and more accurate. The problem is that in most cases parameters are not standardised.

Whether lessons can be applied successfully in another setting, may depend on for instance:

1. The nature and complexity of the project. The same aims can commonly be pursued in many different ways and similarity is important.

2. The contextual setting. The same type of project is not likely to perform in the same way in entirely different economic, geographic, political or social settings.

3. The timing. Lessons from one period may be obsolete a few years later because of changes in technology, attitudes, etc.

The problem of demonstrating replicability is even larger. Findings based on samples, however large, are commonly stripped of their context when generalisations are made – particularly generalisations across time, space and contextual settings. Yet all projects are heavily mediated by the context in which they occur. The problem is that in order to compare different projects, the evaluator will have to focus on a few, common characteristics. Thus there is a danger that multiple cases are analysed at high levels of inference, aggregating out certain patterns of causalities and ending with a smoothed set of generalisations that do not apply to any single case.

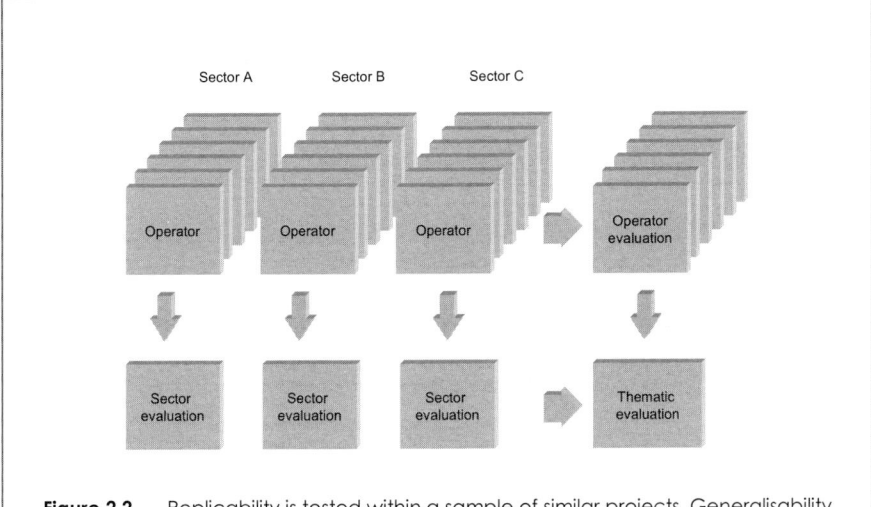

Figure 2.2 Replicability is tested within a sample of similar projects. Generalisability would typically require thematic studies of key variables in a wide range of projects

Generalisability

This issue is more challenging but also more rewarding. It typically involves the identification and study of key parameters in larger samples of projects. To the extent that similar effects are found over a range of different projects, settings, sites, etc., generalisability is demonstrated.

It may be possible to identify certain features of different types of projects based on a sufficiently large number of cases. Thematic evaluations, for instance, deal with selected aspects or themes in a sample that could include different types of projects carried out by different operators in different sectors, as illustrated above. In such evaluations, key variables are coded along with descriptive parameters. This information can then be compiled in a database and analysed in various ways. Such studies can show both the degree of convergence, and can examine the relationship between parameters.

Evaluations are systematic studies of considerable quality. Over the years the body of evaluation reports that is available worldwide represents a wealth of information. Thematic evaluations based on such material have proved to be useful as a basis for generalisation and in providing experience and recommendations at the highest level of aggregation, i.e. the policy level.

Chapter 2 – What is evaluation?

 Drawing lessons

REPLICABILITY

DEFINITION	❑ The extent to which evaluations of similar projects yield convergent results
METHODOLOGICAL CHALLENGE	❑ Selecting projects that are similar ❑ Selecting the essential parameters ❑ Compare convergence at a dissagregate level

GENERALISABILITY

DEFINITION	❑ The extent to which similar effects are found in different projects, sites, etc.
METHODOLOGICAL CHALLENGE	❑ Selecting a wide range of projects ❑ Selecting a few key variables and appropriate descriptive parameters ❑ Examine relationship between parameters

2.6 TWO MAIN APPROACHES TO EVALUATION

In management textbooks, a common distinction is between "management by objectives" and "process management". In the former, planning is directed towards a pre-determined objective; in the latter, emphasis is on adjusting the direction being taken in the light of experience gained on the way. Likewise, in evaluation there is a distinction between the "goal model" (based on deductive testing of hypotheses) and the "process model" (based on inductive research). (Almaas, 1990.)

With the *goal model*, the main principle is to formulate hypotheses, as to the assumed positive and negative consequences of the project. These are then tested against observable reality when the evaluation is carried out. The advantage is that it, to a large degree, takes as its point of departure existing experience. This makes it easier, in the course of the evaluation, to choose data and interpret findings.

The main criticism against this approach is that it may restrict the focus so that important aspects of the conditions under analysis may be overlooked. Project objectives will often be unclear or inadequately formulated; moreover, projects may have many unforeseen impacts - both positive and negative - which may well be overlooked if evaluation focuses only on what has already been identified as the objective of the project. The results of such evaluation are therefore highly dependent on the evaluation team's ability to define frameworks for investigations, which can capture some of major impacts of the project in question.

> **Goal evaluation:** Assessment of the effects of the project seen in relation to its given objectives
>
> **Process evaluation:** Assessment of the way the project functions and its consequences in the widest sense

By contrast, the *process model* does not build on set theories or hypotheses but is open-ended. Through observation and investigation, themes arise that in turn demand new knowledge, gradually leading to new insights. The process model is frequently applied when the investigator has little advance knowledge of the field in question.

The approach is time-consuming and demands a lot of the evaluator. One main objection is that, in order to avoid subjective biases, it often becomes necessary to place special emphasis on the selection of data, perspectives and methods, and to explain this in detail.

The goal model and the process model are two approaches which in practice may well complement each other. In planning and implementation of projects this can be done by re-assessing and if necessary redesigning the project underway, as new experience is gained. This requires a certain degree of flexibility in project management. Here process studies can be of considerable value.

Chapter 2 – What is evaluation?

> **Example:**
> A training project is aimed at a group of immigrants to assist them setting up their own businesses. Evaluation shows this project to be highly successful in relation to the pre-defined goals and objectives (economic and social). However, it also turns out that the project has created considerable conflicts in the local community since it benefits only the immigrants, and produces certain negative economic effects for local residents. To get a picture of the overall effects of the project, the evaluation team needs a mandate to see beyond the fulfilment of the intended objective and a more process-oriented approach in the selection of methods.

A project is defined as a planned undertaking, designed to achieve certain agreed changes within a given time through the use of specified resources. The scope of a project is limited in relative terms, which makes it relatively easy to focus the evaluation. That is, if the objectives against which the project should be evaluated are specifically expressed and in quantifiable terms.

The success of projects is usually measured in a restricted perspective. The main issue is whether *outputs* have been achieved quantitatively in time and within budgetary limits. However, project evaluation will usually go beyond what is planned and desirable and attempt to judge the project also on the basis of its foreseen and unforeseen effects in society.

It is therefore essential to make the distinction between what the project is formally expected to produce and the broader perspective applied in an evaluation. The former perspective is important for accountability, and the latter for extracting experience for the future. In many projects, formally agreed objectives are unrealistic and in some cases not established at all. In these cases the judgement should be based on what can realistically be expected with the available resources, rather than ill-defined objectives, in order to give the project a fair trial.

In evaluation, the goal model and the process model can be combined by expanding the perspective beyond the planned framework to also include various less easily predictable effects. This is further discussed in chapter 4. The evaluation format presented in this textbook suggests that goal evaluation and process evaluation can be combined.

2.7 PURPOSES AND FOCUSES OF EVALUATION

Those preparing the evaluation mandate must have a clear idea of what purpose the evaluation is meant to serve. This will influence the level of detail and precision chosen, and thereby also the choice of methods, sample size, team composition, involvement of stakeholders, etc.

Generally speaking, the purpose of evaluation is threefold. The intention is that it should contribute to efficient *control, management* and *learning*. In some cases the focus is on all aspects simultaneously, in other cases the focus may be restricted to one purpose, foe instance the control aspect, in which case the exercise comes close to what is normally termed an *audit*. The control aspect is the most restricted, focusing on expenditure in relation to budget, progress in relation to plans, outputs in relation to standards, etc. The management aspect is broader, looking at performance, organisational issues, processes, etc. The learning aspect of evaluation is even broader and requires a more open-ended mandate in order to focus on and get a deeper understanding of causes and effects, achievements seen in relation to experience with similar projects, etc. It is often necessary to study groups of several projects simultaneously in order to draw lessons for the future.

Examples:
- Where the management aspect is in focus, professional knowledge is important, and the evaluator's mandate should specify the extent to which alternative strategies need to be considered. Project implementation tactical choices will commonly be considered in detail.
- Where the learning aspect is especially important, the evaluation team will need to be inter-disciplinary. Here emphasis is on understanding project impacts in a broad sense, which could in some cases require wide-ranging societal analyses.
- Referring to the control function, it is important for the evaluation team to be independent of the financing party and the implementing party. Another requirement concerns precision, especially in assessing the use of resources.

Evaluation is used at different levels in the administration of projects. For the financing party or a contractor responsible for a portfolio of projects, co-ordination of resources is essential. Individual programmes and projects therefore need to be viewed in a larger overall context of policy or a major strategy. At national level, in order to be able to draw general lessons from experience, it may be useful to analyse several projects or programmes within the same sector within and even across nation-state borders (sector evaluation).

At the upper - *strategic* - level, evaluation is concerned essentially with the realisation of the overall, long-term strategic objectives or the purpose of the project, see chapter 1.6. If the evaluation were carried out during the project's implementation period, it would typically challenge the chosen strategy in view of developments and seek to improve the strategic focus of the project. It would question whether the project is consistently

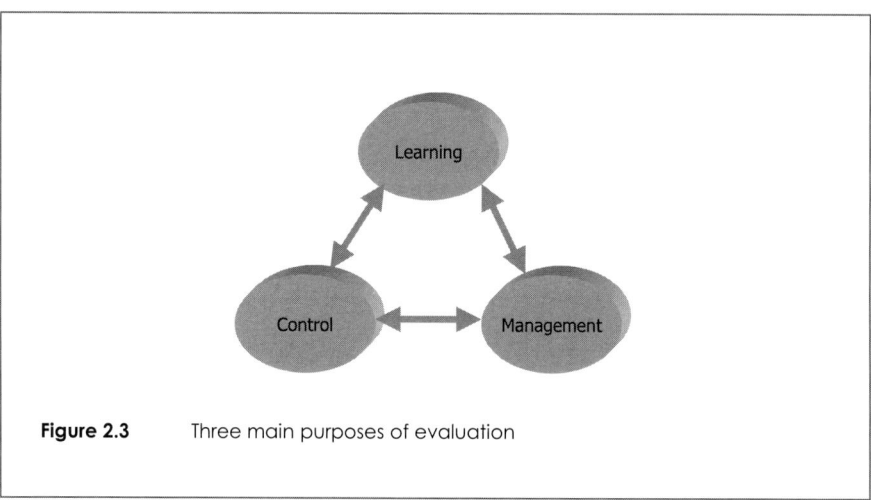

Figure 2.3   Three main purposes of evaluation

designed so as to support the chosen strategy. And it would be concerned with uncertainties affecting the project, which could cause the project to deviate from its strategy, or take a toll on available resources. Evaluations with a strategic focus are commonly initiated be the financing party or public authorities.

At the *tactical* level the focus is on the immediate objective and how to get there. The mandate would be more limited and put its emphasise more on resources and whether they are being employed in such a way as to have the desired effect in achieving the project's goal. Assessments at this level also concern such aspects as cost-efficiency and unforeseen impacts of the project. The party that has commissioned the project or has the overall management responsibility will normally carry out evaluations of this type.

At the *operational* level, evaluation is carried out in connection with the implementation of individual projects and programmes, viewed in relation to time schedules and budgets. This has traditionally been done in the form of regular, often annual project reviews, and as part of the implementing party's management procedures.

2.8 THE QUALITY OF EVALUATIONS

Various stakeholders, who would tend to use their own set of criteria in their individual assessment, often judge the quality of evaluations differently. Some of the most commonly used criteria are credibility, impartiality and independence, as well as cost effectiveness. These are briefly described below. Quality is discussed further in chapter 8.

Credibility

The credibility of evaluations depends on the expertise of the evaluators and the degree of transparency of the evaluation process. It requires that the evaluation not only report successes but also failures.

What is required is the right type of expertise and sufficiently qualified evaluators. In complex evaluations expertise in different fields will be needed. One way to ensure professional expertise is by applying a tender process, provided that a sufficiently large resource pool of professional evaluation staff exists to ensure a certain degree of market competition among evaluators.

Credibility also requires transparency of the evaluation process. This applies both to the planning and implementation of the evaluation itself, as well as making the results of the evaluation widely available. Stakeholders and informants need to know why and how the evaluation is carried out, how information will be available and the results be used.

Impartiality and independence

Impartiality contributes to the credibility of evaluations and particularly to avoid biases in findings, analysis and conclusions. Independence provides legitimacy to evaluations and reduces the potential for conflict of interest, which could arise if policymakers and managers were solely responsible for evaluating their own activities.

The evaluation process should therefore be impartial and independent in its function from the process concerned with policymaking, the delivery, and the management of the project. The requirement for impartiality will also apply to all stages of the evaluation process, including the planning of the evaluation programme, the formulation of the Terms of Reference, and the selection and approval of evaluation teams.

Involvement of internal staff as resource persons in evaluations will normally not compromise the requirement on impartiality and independence, since the members of the evaluation are external and independent, and the evaluation report is issued in the name of the authors. Involving internal staff in the evaluation will assist the team in getting useful insights in the project. At the same time it will help communication and increase the chance that the conclusions and recommendations from the evaluation are accepted and adopted

Cost effectiveness

What justifies an evaluation in the end is that it may have considerable positive effect on management of project activities and a substantial cost saving potential in terms of improved performance. A key value of evaluations is that they allow for in-depth study of performance and independent assessment of the effectiveness of other performance management instruments. Potential benefits are the greatest for large policies and programmes.

The cost of evaluations is usually very limited compared with the overall budget of the project or program under study. Still, experience shows that evaluations have often been too costly and time consuming compared to their real use and effect. There is also a risk of evaluations being used to slow the process of decision-making and justify inaction.

As a principle, benefits of evaluations should out-weigh their costs. Both costs and benefits can be improved by careful focusing of evaluations and by choosing the appropriate evaluators and the best-suited evaluation methods.

✓ Ensuring quality

CREDIBILITY	☐ The right type and sufficient expertise
	☐ Transparent evaluation process
IMPARTIALITY	☐ Independence of commissioning and implementing parties
	☐ Unbiased assessments.
COST EFFECTIVENESS	☐ Cost in relation to project budget
	☐ Cost in relation to real use
	☐ Cost in relation to potential savings/benefits

2.9 EVALUABILITY ASSESSMENT

Before the decision to evaluate is made, there is a need to ensure that it is appropriate or at all feasible – in other words to conduct an assessment of *evaluability*.

In essence, this is an examination of the coherence of project objectives to find out whether a goal-based evaluation is possible, while at the same time exploring the stakeholders' and program managers' information needs and the practicability and cost of meeting those needs. Moreover, an evaluability assessment may serve the important function to probe whether there is support for the evaluation amongst the project's stakeholders, or that the climate is such that it facilitates the planned evaluation.

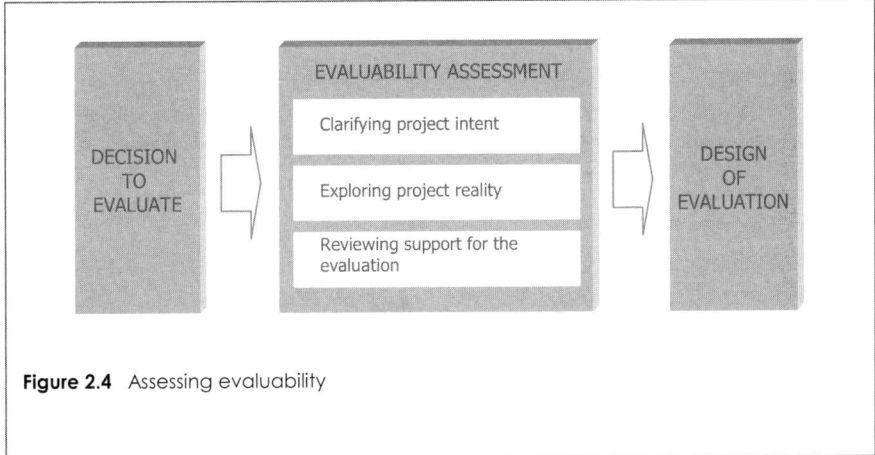

Figure 2.4 Assessing evaluability

The scope of such an assessment will depend on the size of the project and anticipated cost of the planned evaluation. The need for the assessment has to be considered, since it represents an additional cost. Evaluability assessments of large–scale projects or programs that have not previously been evaluated in depth may be both worthwhile and cost-effective, and possibly carried out by independent consultants.

An evaluability assessment uses essentially qualitative methods through interviews and observations to obtain a picture of the project and an understanding of the issues that really matter to those involved or affected. The following steps may guide the assessment:

1. Clarifying project intent

This might include a description of the project model as it is intended by its managers and stakeholders in order to assess if objectives are distinctly defined, realistic, and whether the logic between them is clear enough to be tested. The aim is to uncover any disagreement among stakeholders on project design and logic between the objectives. One may also explore the project's linkages with other activities, institutions or projects.

Reviews of documentation and interviews with project stakeholders provide the above information. Testing the cohesion between objectives and the pathway from resources to end results is discussed in chapters 1.8 and 1.9.

Two products may come out of this exercise: The first is a project design model that shows causal linkages between expected project outputs. The second is a list of indicators that project managers agree upon.

2. Exploring project reality

This is an assessment of how the project actually works compared to the intended project model. An examination of the actual flow of resources and an observation of project operations, if needed through field visits, may give some rough idea of the likelihood that project objectives will be achieved. One may compare findings with project design. In the case of an impact evaluation, one may also look into the projects' context to estimate whether anticipated effects could reasonably be attributed to project activities. See chapter 6.3 on the question of attribution.

Furthermore, the feasibility of measuring performance against the given objectives may be estimated, using an established set of indicators as starting point. For instance, is relevant data available and obtainable at reasonable cost, and is there a basis of progress reporting that may form baseline data for the evaluation?

3. Reviewing support for evaluation

The information from the previous two steps can be used to work with decision-makers on clarifying the project description and evaluation plan, a process that may take place in the form of memos and workshops. The aim would be to assert whether the project has realistic and measurable project objectives, agreed-upon indicators and if all stakeholders agree upon the agenda for the evaluation.

The evaluability assessment may conclude that all necessary conditions are in place for the evaluation, in which case managers can go ahead. On the other hand, the assessment could identify flaws in the strategic framework for the project or other obstacles to the performance of a meaningful evaluation. For instance, as is often the case, formally agreed objectives could be unrealistically ambitious. If a project is assessed against overly ambitious objectives it will most certainly be considered unsuccessful. Decision maker will then have to reconsider formally agreed objectives, or explore different options for collecting performance information. Evaluability assessments in themselves often lead to significant changes as project staff learns about the strengths and weaknesses in their project conceptualisation.

CHAPTER 3

EVALUATION STEP BY STEP

FACTS DO NOT CEASE TO EXIST BECAUSE THEY ARE IGNORED.
ALDOUS HUXLEY

Chapter 3 – Evaluation Step by Step

3.1 THE MAIN PARTIES TO AN EVALUATION

Successful evaluations are based on collaboration between key participants and due consideration to the interest of the different parties involved in or affected by the evaluation. These include the commissioning party, evaluators, users, the public and other stakeholders.

Evaluations are usually *commissioned* by the financing party or in larger publicly funded projects by the Government. In such cases the evaluation is often part of an annual evaluation programme. In some cases several stakeholders collaborate to undertake evaluations. Such joint evaluations are common in case of co-financing.

The *evaluators* are those organisations or individuals collecting and analysing data and judging the value of the evaluated subject. These are commonly selected from research institutions, consulting firms, universities, industry, etc., to ensure independence and impartiality. But evaluations may also involve internal project staff members and representatives of the stakeholder groups. Involving internal staff provides an opportunity for learning by doing and to strengthen skills and capabilities in the involved organisations.

The *users* of evaluations may be the financing party, the implementing organisation, policy makers, public authorities, auditors and all parties with a formal role in relation to the project under evaluation. In order to have an impact on decision-making, evaluations must be relevant to the users and responsive to their particular needs for information. Evaluations must also be timely in the sense that they should be available at a time that is appropriate in the decision-making process.

The *stakeholders* are those individuals or organisations that informally have an interest in the policy, programme or project being evaluated and the findings of the evaluation. In order to ensure usefulness of evaluations, the views and expertise of groups affected ought to be considered and taken into account whenever appropriate. Stakeholders can also be formally involved, for instance through steering or advisory groups. Participatory evaluation methods can be used to create consensus and ownership in relation to the project activities. Dialogue with stakeholders can help improve understanding and responsiveness to their needs and priorities. Feedback to both users and stakeholders is essential to make evaluations useful.

In regular cases, evaluation is usually commissioned as the result of decisions made already when the project was decided. Often, it will be agreed as part of the contract between the financing and the implementing parties. It could be an interim evaluation at the end of a project phase or and end evaluation before the project is terminated. The financing party usually commissions such evaluations.

In other cases, evaluations may be initiated in responses to reactions in the public, protests by affected groups in society, unforeseen consequences of the project, etc. – or in order to draw experience from an innovative project or a larger group of projects. In such cases public authorities might commission the evaluation.

The main parties to an evaluation

COMMISSIONER	❏	The financing party or other key stakeholders involved in or affected by the project.
	♦	
EVALUATORS	❏	External expertise from private or public institutions, in some cases in co-operation with internal project staff
	♦	
USERS	❏	Decision-makers with a formal role in following up the evaluation, policy-makers, auditors, etc
	♦	
OTHER STAKEHOLDERS	❏	Beneficiaries, affected institutions, individuals, etc., with an interest in the evaluation.

3.2 Carrying out the evaluation

This chapter presents recommendations for carrying out an evaluation, step by step. The description is general and will have to be adapted to the individual case, depending on the type of project in question, the scope of the study, the stage at which evaluation is to be undertaken, etc.

The presentation here covers the evaluation process from selecting the project to be evaluated and onwards to the assessment and application of results. This chapter is intended as tool for use both by the commissioning party in preparing the mandate for evaluation and by the evaluators in carrying it out.

Usually there are strict requirements when it comes to the quality of evaluation reports. Careful planning and implementation of evaluation work are essential to a good result. Especially important is the mandate: preparing a precisely specified mandate requires quite detailed knowledge of that which is to be evaluated.

We presuppose that there is some sort of co-ordination between the commissioning party and the evaluation team. The former sets the premises and must ensure that the mandate is clearly formulated and in accordance with needs. It is the responsibility of the evaluation team to operationalise the main questions expressed in the mandate and identify the most appropriate evaluation instruments. The commissioning party then needs to consider the more detailed outline provided by the evaluator, making any necessary additions or restrictions. Such a division of labour makes the best possible use of time and resources.

This chapter, therefore, deals with both roles and needs of the commissioning party and the evaluator, and principles for planning and carrying out the evaluation.

Below is a schematic presentation of the evaluation processes and the main stages involved. In the following sections of this chapter the various stages will be examined in greater detail.

Carrying out the evaluation

1. **DECISION TO EVALUATE**
   - Select projects or themes for evaluation
   - Give reasons for evaluating
   - Reach agreement between key stakeholders

   ♦

2. **PREPARE MANDATE**
   - Determine the objective of the evaluation
   - Decide scope and timing
   - Prepare the draft mandate
   - Solicit comments on draft
   - Prepare the final mandate of evaluation

   ♦

3. **SELECT AND CONTRACT EVALUATION TEAM**
   - Decide on team composition/qualifications
   - Identify appropriate candidates
   - Negotiate contracts with team members

   ♦

4. **PLANNING AND PREPARATORY WORK**
   - Prepare evaluation work plan
   - Review relevant documentation
   - Initiate pre-studies

   ♦

5. **IMPLEMENT THE EVALUATION**
   - Arrange interviews, field visits, inspections, etc
   - Collect, structure and analyse data
   - Present preliminary findings and conclusions

   ♦

6. **PREPARE THE REPORT**
   - Co-ordinate reports from team members
   - Write up and edit draft report

   ♦

7. **FINAL PHASE**
   - Distribute draft report for comments
   - Incorporate comments received
   - Prepare final version
   - Act on recommendations
   - Enter evaluation abstract into Corporate Memory systems/files, etc.

3.3 THE DECISION TO EVALUATE

The timing of an evaluation can be set when the project is still in the planning stage. Otherwise, the decision can be taken underway - for instance, on the basis of experience with the project; a need to assess the distribution of available resources among several projects, because it is pre-programmed, or perhaps because a problem has occurred which need to be explored.

It is important that the reason for having an evaluation is clearly specified when an evaluation is proposed, as this will affect the mandate, selection of evaluation team, extent of evaluation, etc. It is also important to know what type of decisions are likely to be taken on the basis of the final evaluation report.

With any evaluation there will be several interested parties among key stakeholders and other affected parties. Predominant attitudes and viewpoints should be mapped, in order to ensure that the various needs for information could be satisfied.

There is often resistance against decisions to evaluate a project since such studies often raise controversial issues. Evaluation requires considerable resources. The use of evaluation will therefore be restricted and based on considerations of costs and benefits. In setting priorities, it can be important to select projects that:

- are costly, comprehensive and involve considerable work
- run over a long period of time
- are experimenal or include new areas of activities or technology

Occasionally there may be good reasons for not evaluating, or for postponing an evaluation until a later date. This can apply to projects where everything is running according to plan and where sufficient information is already being generated to document progress, effectiveness and social impacts. There may also be factors or conditions in society that make it advisable to postpone the evaluation.

On the other hand, many people will attempt to find excuses for not to evaluate. Most projects need to be evaluated at one time or another, to enable a broad assessment of their effects and impacts. Moreover, an independent evaluation will often be an effective means of getting started an overall discussion on such aspects as management and strategy - that may be essential to get changes underway. Also for those who feel that the project is progressing in a satisfactory direction, an evaluation can prove to be of considerable value.

Deciding whether to evaluate

DECISION IN THE FRONT-END PHASE OF THE PROJECT
- In the case of pilot or experimental projects
- In large, complex or controversial projects
- In projects with considerable anticipated social or economic impact
- In projects of high political priority or prestige
- When the planning of future components depends on experience from preceding phases
- When there is a need for periodic evaluation

♦

DECISION DURING IMPLEMENTATION BASED ON EXPERIENCE WITH PROJECT
- When a project is considered especially problematic
- When a project has developed in a very positive way
- When there is a need to explore unforeseen impact
- When there is a need to decide whether the project should be changed, terminated or continued
- In order to elicit information for use in similar projects

♦

DECISION NOT TO EVALUATE
- When a project is developing as foreseen, and enough is known about its impacts
- When enough is known about the problems involved, their causes and how to solve them
- When special conditions make it advisable not to carry out or delay an evaluation

3.4 PREPARING THE MANDATE

The mandate provides the background for the evaluation, defines its objectives and the scope of work, the composition of the evaluation team and the timing.

There is usually much information available when the evaluation is planned, and it is worthwhile to do a thorough review of this information. This will provide an insight to the topic under study and make it possible to establish facts, describe processes, and establish some key hypotheses. It will also enable the evaluation team to focus more on verification and less on data collection, thereby improving the quality of the study. It may also help reduce the duration of evaluation.

Many evaluations are less than successful because the mandate has focused on details, with no overall delimitation specified in relation to the purpose underlying the evaluation.

It is thus important to take the purpose of the evaluation as the point of departure in formulating the mandate, and to concentrate on major, overall questions and issues. The detailed level should be avoided here. Rather, it should be up to the evaluation team to take care of the more detailed formulation of evaluation questions, subject to comments and approval of the commissioning party.

- It is important to state clearly what the purpose of the evaluation is, and what kind of evaluation is envisaged e.g. an interim evaluation or ex-post evaluation of a project
- Sufficient efforts should be invested in the preparatory work. This may be in the form of, e.g., a documentation phase, or an exploratory meeting of the involved parties and external expertise.
- The mandate should be built up around the major, overall evaluation questions as described in chapter 4
- The scope of evaluation and the quality standard to be applied need to be clearly spelled out.

It is important to involve all concerned parties in the preparation and final approval of the mandate. On the next page follows a summary of main points to be included in the mandate.

Evaluation mandate

1. PROJECT BACKGROUND	❑ Project context and rationale
	❑ Project description (main narrative summary of the project and its objectives)
2. PURPOSE OF EVALUATION	❑ Reasons related to formal decisions
	❑ Reasons related to project performance
	❑ Intended use of results
3. SCOPE AND METHODS	❑ Scope of work
	❑ Type of analysis, methods to be used, degree of detail
4. ISSUES TO BE COVERED	❑ Extent to which all or only selected areas of analysis and issues are to be covered (efficiency, effectiveness, impacts, relevance, sustainability)
	❑ Extent of specialisation
5. EVALUATION TEAM	❑ Number of team members and their roles
	❑ Required qualifications (professional background, experience)
6. TIMETABLE	❑ Approximate dates and allocation of time - prior to fieldwork, during and afterwards
7. CONSULTATIONS IN THE FIELD	❑ Authorities, institutions and groups to be consulted during and at the end of fieldwork
8. REPORTING	❑ Deadlines for draft version and final report
	❑ Specification of technical standard for final report

3.5 INITIATING THE EVALUATION

Contracting the evaluation team

The success of an evaluation ultimately depends on the composition of the evaluation team and the competence and personal abilities of the team members. This applies in particular to the team leader who should be the one concerned with the overall perspective, able to organise and coordinate the work of the team members, assess the quality and relevance of their contributions and act as a spokesman on the team.

The evaluation team will often be composed of consultants, experts from research institutions, universities, industry or other relevant public or private institutions. The criteria for the selection of the evaluation team are professional competence, and experience in relation to the task. Also important are personal qualities, like the ability to communicate, analytical ability, and teamwork capabilities. Their competence must be relevant for the topic under study. Breadth is important. The team should not consist entirely of persons with the same type of professional background - whether social scientists, economists or engineers.

Impartiality is a common requirement, however, individuals involved in the project may be engaged as resource persons or by actively participating in specific phases of the evaluation. This increases the relevance of the resulting report, and promotes the utilisation of findings. Project managers responsible for project co-ordination should not be member of the evaluation team. They will often have a central role to play in organisation and background work and in obtaining necessary documentation and information - but should not have any direct opportunity to influence the results of the evaluation.

Preparing the evaluation work plan

The necessary specification and preparatory work should be done by the evaluation team and be presented in an evaluation work plan. The document should give a clear description of what the evaluation team is supposed to do, as well as when, where, how and why. It represents the evaluation team's interpretation and proposed implementation of the mandate with specific questions, which the evaluation should answer. It should also describe clearly how the team intends to approach the task in terms of methods and practical approaches. In order to prepare such a document, the team will have to have familiarised with relevant documentation and consult with key stakeholders to the project. This means that planning can involve considerable work.

In the evaluation work plan, the main points in the mandate should be translated into specific problems and issues. These should be operationalised in the form of questions to be answered, indicators and methods of data collection and analysis. It should discuss how to ensure quality (validity/reliability), and the choice of method(s) should be explained on the basis of an assessment of associated costs and anticipated use of resource.

The evaluation work plan should also contain a review of available documentation and relevant literature, together with extracts from central portions of this material - such as copies of summaries, conclusions and recommendations from project reviews, previous evaluations, etc. It will often be necessary to ask the project co-ordinators to provide information in advance. In this case, the document should contain copies of such requests.

☑ Evaluation workplan

EVALUATION QUESTIONS
- Discussion of main problem-areas
- Specification of questions to be answered)

♦

METHODS
- Methodological approach, with references to main sources
- Questions of validity and reliability
- Description of indicators, including availability and overall costs/resources

♦

WORK PLAN
- Work timetable
- Team members, with qualifications
- Division of labour within team

♦

DOCUMENTATION
- Systematic review of existing information and central informants
- Project description, strategy, objectives, uncertainties affecting the project, etc
- Chronological presentation of project phases, any major changes, etc.
- Survey of budget and costs
- Copies of key project documents (etc.); summaries of any previous project assessments and evaluations
- Requests for information from key stakeholders and other relevant parties

3.6 IMPLEMENTING THE EVALUATION

An evaluation will normally follow a definite pattern of stages, as presented below.

Much of the evaluation will necessarily build on available information in the form of plans, budgets, guidelines and regulations, research reports and studies prepared by institutions, public documents, etc. All this material should have been collected before actual evaluation work is undertaken.

In some cases, pre-studies will need to be undertaken especially with complex, major projects, or where the emphasis is on studying impacts or processes. The evaluator needs to be central in planning and managing the pre-study as well. This study should be carried out either by the institution assigned to do the evaluation, or by independent researchers or consultants as appropriate. Pre-studies could include retrieval and review of existing data, interviews, surveys or special studies such as impact studies, tracer studies, etc. The results of the pre-study should be available before the evaluation takes place.

The work of the evaluation team will typically involve a review of all available information, talks with representatives of key stakeholders, affected parties and relevant authorities. The aim is to verify information and aggregate evidence that could provide the answers to the evaluation questions specified in the work plan.

In the course of the evaluation, various methods of data collection may be used. Whereas pre-studies often employ demanding methods such as measurement, questionnaires, surveys, etc., it is more common for the evaluation team to opt for simpler methods like interviews, field visits, focus group interviews and discussions, etc. This can be done, because the main bulk of the primary data should already be available. The following are important points to bear in mind:

- All concerned or involved parties should have an opportunity to express themselves, and not be excluded from formal consultations
- Inspections and field visits must cover a representative part of the project work
- Group discussions should be used in addition to individual interviews, to contribute to openness and dialogue

In many cases, the data analysis will reveal a need for additional information. That is why it is important not to postpone data analysis to the end of the evaluation work - it should be undertaken on an on-going basis as work proceeds.

The team should reach agreement on all conclusions and recommendations before disbanding. Any points of dissent must be explicitly described. Often it will be advantageous and correct to give the key stakeholders an opportunity to discuss recommendations and conclusions with the evaluation team - e.g. through a final seminar. There will usually be a need for closer discussion of controversial issues and of the practical consequences, which the recommendations should have, or may be expected to have.

Implementing the evaluation

PRE-STUDY	❑ Select who is to carry out study
	❑ Formulate study together with person responsible for carrying it out
	❑ Implement study
	❑ Report to evaluation team

♦

DATA COLLECTION	❑ Review of documents
	❑ Formal and specialist interviews on the central and local levels
	❑ Field visits, inspections
	❑ Group discussions
	❑ Testing, etc.

♦

DATA ANALYSIS	❑ Collation, analysis and control of data
	❑ Data aggregation
	❑ Formulate conclusions and recommendations before disbanding team

♦

FINAL STAGE	❑ Presentation of conclusions and recommendations, with discussion, to key stakeholders before evaluation is finalised

3.7 PREPARING THE REPORT

Writing of the report should start as early as possible in the evaluation. Team members can prepare notes and drafts within their various areas, which are then circulated and discussed in the team. It is essential for the team leader to get specific contributions from all team members, to be able to direct the work with relation to:

- progress and direction
- level of detail
- level of precision.

An evaluation report will usually contain descriptive text prepared on the basis of data and information collected, together with conclusions and recommendations, which will build largely on the team's own assessments. It can be highly useful to solicit comments from the concerned parties on as much as possible of the descriptive text, before the evaluation is concluded. This can help to clear up disagreements, misunderstandings and errors.

The team leader is responsible for the evaluation report. The individual team members will usually prepare their separate parts, which will then be edited together by the team leader. He/she is also responsible for quality assurance and that all issues in the mandate are fully covered in the report.

The team leader should have considerable freedom in editing, shortening and re-working material to make it as accessible and usable as possible for the recipients. This should be possible, precisely since the team will already have agreed the conclusions and recommendations on.

Making the report easy to read should have a high priority. Complicated technical discussions should be referred to the annexes. The main report should if possible be restricted to only 40-50 pages, with a 4-5 page summary. The text should be reviewed and edited to ensure an easily understandable language and effective communication aids. In some cases it may be useful to produce sub-reports or partial reports in the course of the evaluation work, for comment from the parties concerned.

The evaluation team should strive to describe both the positive and the negative sides of the project. To the extent possible, their conclusions should be operational, action-oriented, relevant and realistic. In addition, the evaluation team should point out specific experience and knowledge gained which may prove relevant for other projects in the future.

Below follows a standard outline for evaluation reports. In the main, this should correspond to what is set out in the mandate for the evaluation.

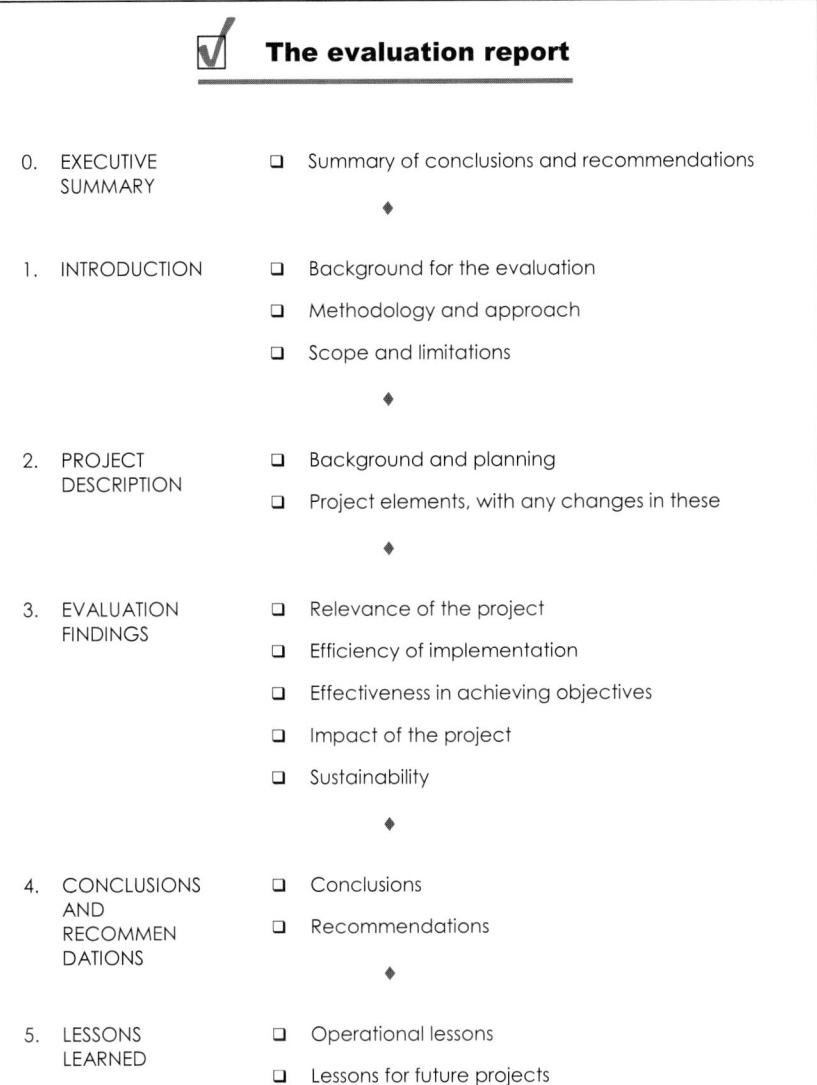

3.8 FINALISATION AND FOLLOW-UP

Finalisation represents an essential part of the overall evaluation process.

Before the final evaluation report is completed, comments are solicited from persons central to the project. This round of comments should concentrate primarily on factual information and the analysis, to ensure the quality of the report. Next, the final report is circulated to all concerned parties, with a request for formal comments within a reasonable time-limit. This round of hearings should normally concentrate on the conclusions and recommendations of the evaluation.

In many cases it can be useful to arrange a final meeting or seminar with the concerned parties, to discuss the evaluation report. This makes it possible to confront and test different standpoints up against others; dialogue can be strengthened between and among the parties, and any disagreements may also be clarified.

As a result of this round of hearings, the commissioning party will be able to prepare a written summary of conclusions and recommendations, directed to decision-makers. From this document it should be apparent what actions to be taken and lessons to be learned from the evaluation.

CHAPTER 4

THE FOCUS OF EVALUATION

*WE DO HAVE PROPER METHODS TO GET THE RIGHT ANSWER
 — BUT POOR METHODS TO ASK THE RIGHT QUESTION*

Chapter 4 – The Focus of Evaluation

4.1 MEASURES OF SUCCESS

As discussed in chapter 1.10 above, cost, time and quality are the obvious indicators used to measure project delivery. However, they are inadequate as measures of success. A meaningful comparison of success rates of different types of projects would require that not only the operational but also the tactical and strategic perspectives were taken into consideration. A comparison of the same type of projects undertaken under comparable conditions and in similar contexts could possibly be restricted to the operational perspective. However, what we then do is comparing the *efficiency* of projects by assessing the outputs that the project have produced seen in relation to the inputs consumed. This is only the operator's perspective. The financing part or the owner of the project will have to consider the project in a broader perspective to justify investments. The user will stipulate success based on an assessment of utility or needs satisfaction.

What seems to be a success in the operational perspective may be a disaster seen in a tactical perspective. The success criterion is then the *effectiveness* of the project - or whether the project has achieved its tactical objective or the goal, see figure 1.5.

As an example, consider a sub-sea road tunnel project linking an island with the mainland. The project may be a complete success in technical terms, completed ahead of time and within budgets. The tactical objective is to improve access for residents to the mainland by dramatically reducing the access time. In this particular case, the project failed entirely in this respect simply because the construction and operation costs were too high compared with the size and the financial means of the target population on the island. The user fees were correspondingly high. People therefore preferred to continue use the ferry. The tunnel project was a potential disaster in financial terms, as measured for instance in terms of its internal rate of return.

However, measuring effectiveness provides only a narrow part of the picture, namely the extent to which the *formally agreed* tactical objective has been achieved. In other words, only the anticipated positive consequences of the project. To make a fair statement of success or failure seen in the tactical perspective requires a broader assessment also of the *impact* in society: In other words – not only the positive effects but also the negative and unexpected consequences need to be considered, as illustrated in figure 4.1.

Consider the example above: the authorities now wanted to strengthen the need for the tunnel and at the same time support decentralisation, and moved part of the district's administrative headquarters to the island. This, however, caused considerable dissatisfaction with authorities and a growing conflict between the islanders and the mainlanders. At the same time, it turned out that the existence of a tunnel made the island more attractive as holiday resort for tourists. In the event of time, real estate prices increased caused more and more people on the island to sell out and move to the mainland. Seen in relation to the project's objective these were both significant negative consequences which had not been foreseen – or what is termed *impact*.

Chapter 4 – The Focus of Evaluation

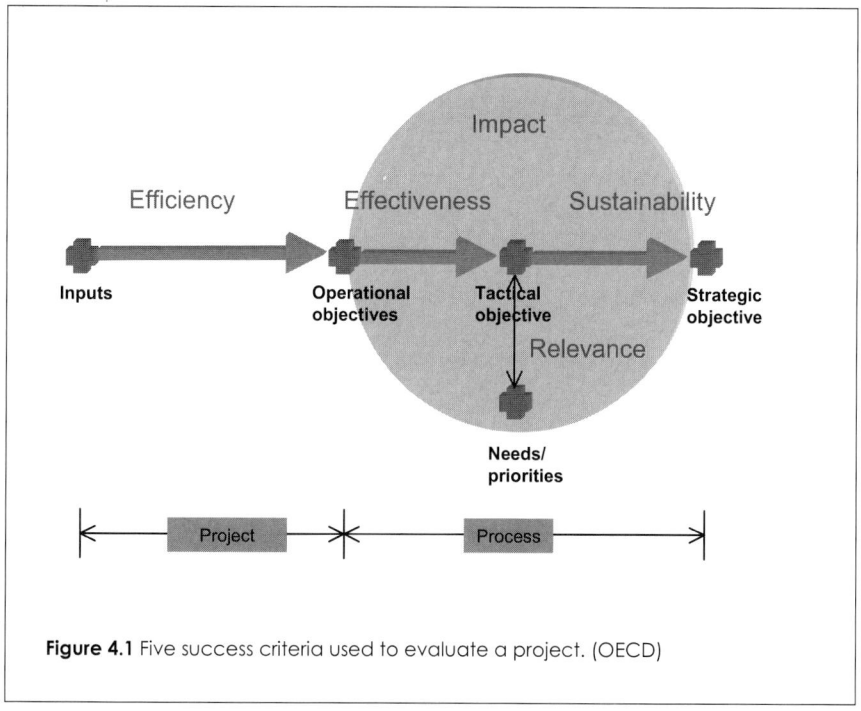

Figure 4.1 Five success criteria used to evaluate a project. (OECD)

While the three success criteria mentioned above, *efficiency, effectiveness* and *impact* certainly contribute to a fuller picture, there is also a need to look at the *relevance* of the project. In other words, to what extent the objective of the project corresponds with important priorities in society and the needs of the users. If there is a need for it – it is relevant. In a sense, it expresses the discrepancy between the formally agreed objective and society's needs. To some extent, relevance is a test of the feasibility of the initial project design, as illustrated in figure 4.1. Obviously, the project's relevance can change over time as the result of changing priorities and needs. It is therefore also an important indication of success during implementation.

Again, consider the example above: the goal in the tunnel project was to improve access to the mainland and reduce access time. The economic basis for the island's residents was basically fishing and tourism and some agriculture. Improved access would promote tourism to the island. For the resident population, however, most of the transport was by boat. Their needs in terms of infrastructure was more in terms of improved harbour facilities than an access road. It was therefore highly questionable whether the project was relevant, or whether people would have been better served by looking at their transport needs from a marine angle for fishermen and tourists alike. Rehabilitation and extensions of harbour facilities would also been far less expensive.

Chapter 4 – The Focus of Evaluation

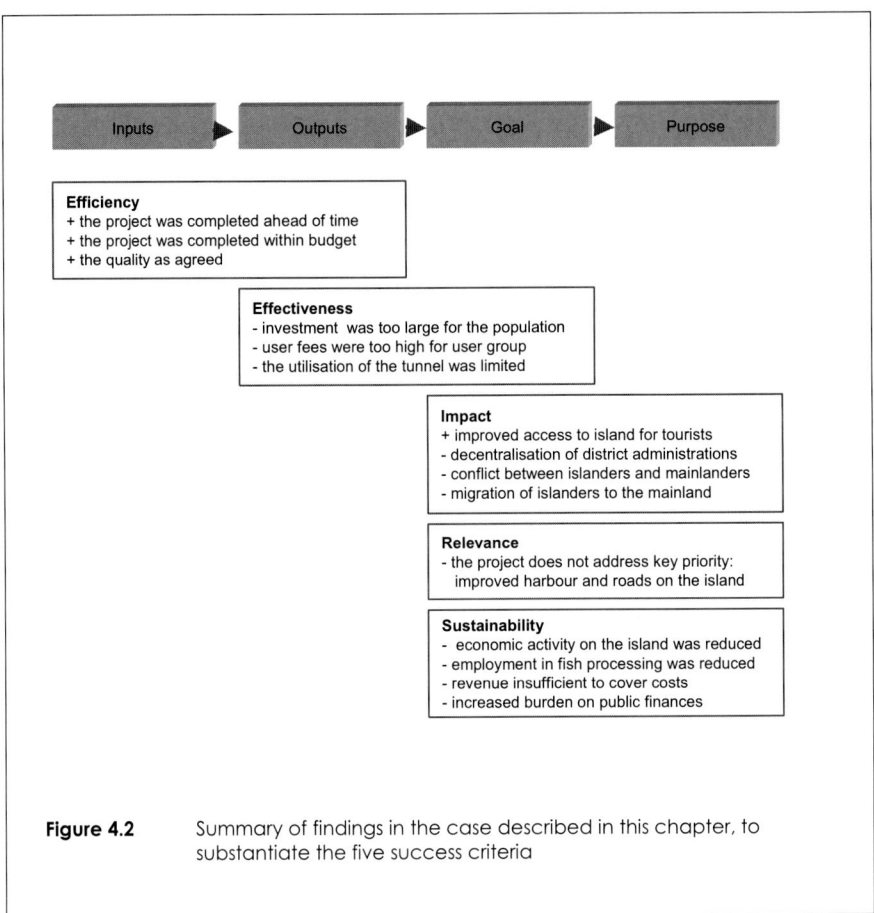

Figure 4.2 Summary of findings in the case described in this chapter, to substantiate the five success criteria

Finally, the long-term *strategic* development perspective needs to be taken into account. This is expressed in terms of *sustainability*. In other words to what extent the positive effects of the project persist in the years after the project has been completed. This is a combined measure which has to take into account all changes brought about by the project in society.

In the example of the tunnel project, the long term strategic objective was to increase economic activities and develop the economic potentials of the island. The opposite seemed to be the result. Residents moved to the mainland, employment in the fisheries went down, and their houses were taken over by tourists. The sustainability of the total project was thereby reduced. While the tourists might be more willing than the resident population to pay the high user fees, they would use the access tunnel only during the short summer months. The rest of the year their resorts would be locked up and the island more and more deserted. The economic basis for the project was therefore even worse than anticipated and a large part of the project had to be financed by the public, not by the users as planned. The conclusions of the above assessment are summarised in figure 4.2.

What is then the final verdict, is this project a success or a failure? There is not one simple answer to this question. An early evaluation of the project seen in an *operational* perspective would obviously conclude that it was a success. In a *tactical* perspective the project was not very successful, since it's formal objective was attained only for those who could accept the high user fees. Also, a number of unforeseen and negative consequences, as well as the entire aspect of *relevance* are pointing strongly in a negative direction – the project was a failure. And finally, in a *strategic* perspective, the project appear to be a disaster: the tunnel is an economic burden to society and a main cause of the death of a society of islanders.

No doubt, what perspective to use when evaluating a project is a political issue, depending on the interests of different parties: such as the contractor, the islanders, the mainlanders, the authorities, the tourists, etc. The question of how to compare success of different projects is a technical one, much related to the perspectives under which the projects have been evaluated. As the example illustrates this is a complex issue.

Most projects consider success only under the constructor's perspective. To compare success between projects would require an instrument as the one described above, which takes into consideration the effects of the project in different perspectives. In order to arrive at a valid and reliable assessment of success, a systematic analytical approach is needed. The following subchapters provide a guide to the use of the evaluation instrument described above.

4.2 EVALUATION CRITERIA

It is generally agreed that effective management will require a broad perspective on a project, taking into account not only the strategy, but also its impact and coherence with needs and priorities of target groups and affected parties. The five evaluation criteria provide a comprehensive yet simple picture of the status of a project. They constitute the key analytical elements in the definitions of the term 'evaluation' adopted by OECD and the European Commission.

Efficiency, effectiveness, impact, relevance, and sustainability are generally applicable analytical measures that can be used on all administrative or aggregation levels – whether project, programme, process, institution or sector level. Taken together, these five criteria used in combination should provide the decision-maker with the essential information and clues to make a correct diagnosis and determine what to be done next.

> An evaluation is an assessment, as systematic and objective as possible, of an ongoing or completed project, program or policy, its design, implementation and results. The aim is to determine the *relevance* and fulfilment of objectives, the *efficiency*, *effectiveness, impact* and *sustainability*. An evaluation should provide information that is credible and useful, enabling the incorporation of lessons learned into the decision making process." (OECD)

Projects can be viewed in different perspectives as discussed above. Success in the *operational* perspective is measured in terms of *efficiency*. In the *tactical* perspective it is measured in terms of *effectiveness*. And the *strategic* perspective is explored in terms of the project's *impact*, *relevance* and *sustainability*. In combination, the five evaluation criteria cover all three perspectives.

Applying these evaluation criteria presents the evaluator with several methodological challenges:

- o The first is to disaggregate these general criteria to specific evaluation questions relevant to the situation under study.
- o The second is to find the answers to these questions on the basis of reliable information.
- o The third challenge is to provide an aggregate conclusion on the basis of these answers to each of the five evaluation criteria.

Chapters 4.3 – 4.8 discuss how to apply the evaluation criteria in an evaluation.

✓ Evaluation criteria

1. EFFICIENCY ❑ The productivity of the implementation process

   ♦

2. EFFECTIVENESS ❑ The extent to which the objective has been achieved

   ♦

3. IMPACT ❑ All other positive and negative changes and effects caused by the project

   ♦

4. RELEVANCE ❑ Whether the objectives are still in keeping with valid priorities and users' needs

   ♦

5. SUSTAINABILITY ❑ Whether the positive effects of the project will be maintained after the project has been concluded

4.3 MEASURING EFFICIENCY

Efficiency is a measure of the "productivity" of the implementation process, i.e. to what degree the outputs achieved derive from efficient use of financial, human and material resources. In principle, then, it means comparing inputs against outputs.

> **Examples:**
>
> In a building construction project, the inputs are funds, labour, material, machines, etc. The main output is essentially *the building*. Efficiency is then measured in terms of the quality, costs and timeliness of constructing the building itself, as compared with budgets and plans – as well as the outputs of similar projects.
>
> In an educational project, the expected outputs may include the *training of teachers, the curriculum, teaching material and the facilities*. Efficiency is then measured in terms of cost, timeliness and quality of producing these outputs, as compared with budgets and plans – as well as the outputs of similar projects.
>
> In a road project efficiency is measured in terms of the construction of the road (the physical output); based on its quality, cost and the timeliness of construction.

The standard to adopt when measuring efficiency could be for instance:

- as against comparable projects elsewhere
- on the basis of one's own experience
- on the basis of what seems reasonable

Efficiency will be a concern from the very start when the project is planned and budgets and inputs are being decided. Data to assess efficiency will also represent a considerable part of subsequent monitoring of activities. Data will therefore usually be available. Still, in the course of a implementation it will be possible to undertake only partial efficiency assessments. A complete, overall assessment can only be done after the implementation has been completed.

Chapter 4 – The Focus of Evaluation

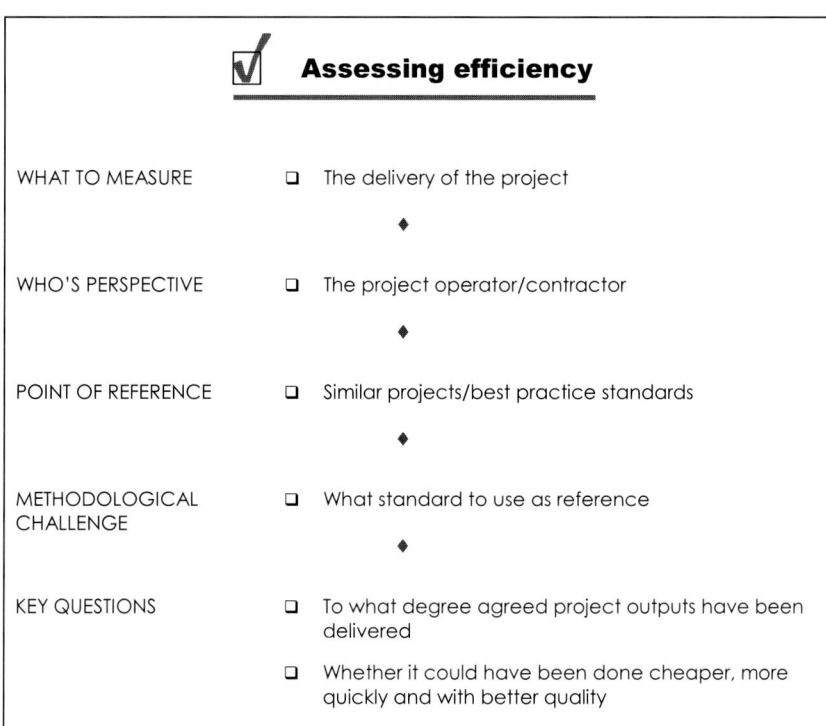

✓	**Assessing efficiency**
WHAT TO MEASURE	❏ The delivery of the project
	♦
WHO'S PERSPECTIVE	❏ The project operator/contractor
	♦
POINT OF REFERENCE	❏ Similar projects/best practice standards
	♦
METHODOLOGICAL CHALLENGE	❏ What standard to use as reference
	♦
KEY QUESTIONS	❏ To what degree agreed project outputs have been delivered
	❏ Whether it could have been done cheaper, more quickly and with better quality

4.4 MEASURING EFFECTIVENESS

Effectiveness concerns the extent to which the project's tactical objective – the goal - has been achieved, or can be expected to be achieved.

Assessing effectiveness need to be part of the on-going monitoring of the project, and the necessary information should be available when an evaluation is carried out.

> **Examples:**
>
> In a building construction project the immediate objective is to provide *the infrastructure for residents or user of the building*. Effectiveness would then be measured in terms of whether the building provide adequate shelter for the residents and is suitable for the needs of its users, seen in relation to what was planned and what can reasonably be expected.
>
> In an educational project the immediate objective is to provide *education* for the target group. Effectiveness is then measured in terms of the number of individuals trained, the quality of training, the proportion that pass examinations etc., seen in relation to what was planned and what can reasonably be expected.
>
> In a road project, effectiveness could be measured in terms of traffic flow, or transport of different commodities and the users of the road.

Assessing effectiveness presupposes that the project's goal has been unambiguously defined so as to make verification possible. Often, however, this is not the case: objectives may be unclear, highly general, or unrealistic. Some projects have complex compound statements of objectives which contains several individual, often confounding, even conflicting objectives. In such cases, the weaknesses in the design must be corrected so that the projects goal is realistic and verifiable when the evaluation is carried out. If this is not done, the evaluation team would have to stipulate what would seem to be a reasonable objective as the point of reference for the evaluation.

There are three problems in measuring effectiveness against a too ambitious objective:

- it would require unduly comprehensive and expensive investigation
- it would be difficult to isolate the effect of the project against other external factors affecting the achievement of the objective
- the assessment would be likely to be negative

Usually, the project is only one of several factors likely to contribute to achieving the tactical objective. The assessment of effectiveness should therefore also consider the causes behind effectiveness (or lack of such), especially whether expected outputs have been achieved; and whether these are sufficient to ensure effectiveness within a set time framework. Equally important is to assess the external factors - the contextual uncertainties – and whether these may have affected the process leading to the fulfilment of the tactical objective to such a degree that the question of reformulating the project should be considered.

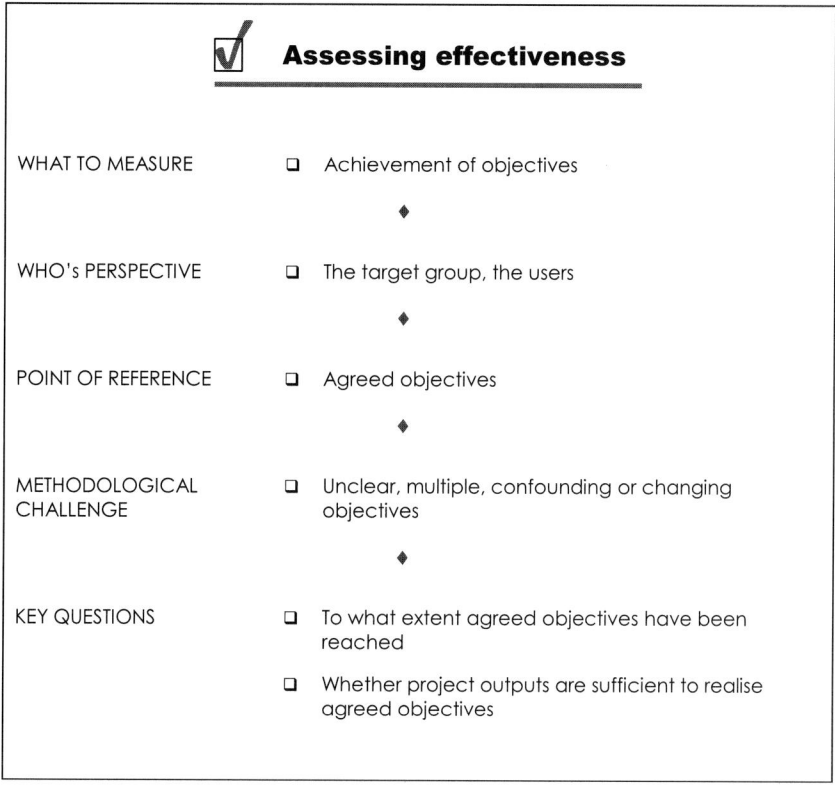

4.5 ASSESSING IMPACT

Effectiveness is a restricted evaluation criterion that focuses only on specific *positive* and *planned* effects expected to accrue to the involved parties, expressed in terms of the tactical objective. By contrast, the concept of *impact* is a far broader one, as it includes both positive and negative consequences, whether these are foreseen and expected, or not. A broad assessment of impact is essential in a comprehensive evaluation. It will often be the most difficult and demanding part of the evaluation work.

Examples:

In a building construction road project the objectives are limited to the feasibility of the building for its residents and users. Impact goes beyond that and may be measured in terms of the social or economic benefits resulting from a safe shelter for families, appropriate premises for production, etc. More specifically, this could be expressed in term of improved health and working capacity, increased productivity and production of services, etc. But it could also have negative consequences as the result of higher costs for the users, conflicts with nabours, etc.

In an educational project the immediate objective is limited to the *positive results of education*. The impact goes beyond this and includes the amount of graduated that are employed afterwards, their work performance, the number that proceeds with further education, etc. But it could also include migration effects and brain-drain resulting from the project.

In a road project, the impact may be measured in terms of economic benefits and losses that accrue to changes in traffic flow and transport capacity, through new settlement patterns, opening up new areas to agricultural production, increased pollution, etc.

In assessing impacts, the point of reference is the status of affected parties prior to the project intervention. The question to ask is: Which other effects - whether positive or negative, expected or unforeseen - have come about as a result of the project? These may be economic, technical, institutional, social, political, or environmental effects – within an organisation, locally, or even at the national level. We are now more concerned with effects for other affected parties than the target group, directly or indirectly.

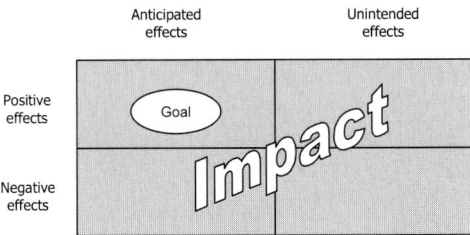

The combined impact is the result of complex causal conditions that are difficult to analyse. It may be especially problematic to prove that observable changes can be ascribed to a given project intervention. In order to understand causal connections, the evaluator may need to employ process-oriented methods that are applied over time.

Different impacts may appear at varying times, and it may be necessary to distinguish between the short-term and the long-term ones. How much time must elapse until the impacts are felt will vary with the type of project intervention. A project to improve agricultural production, for instance, may produce considerable impacts after only a few months - whereas an educational project might yield its greatest effects only several years after it has been completed.

Attempts to assess impact are often done in interim evaluations before a project is terminated. In such cases, it may be difficult to predict the long-term impacts as these can usually be evaluated only long after. Although such assessments of impact may be hinging on uncertain assumptions, they may still produce valuable insight which can be used to guide decisions.

✓ Assessing impact

WHAT TO MEASURE	❑ Intended and unintended positive and negative effects
WHO's PERSPECTIVE	❑ The society, directly and indirectly affected parties
POINT OF REFERENCE	❑ Situation of affected parties prior to the project intervention
METHODOLOGICAL CHALLENGE	❑ Lack of base-line information prior to the project ❑ Difficulties to prove if changes can be ascribed to the project
KEY QUESTIONS	❑ What are the unintended positive and negative effects? ❑ Do positive effects outweigh negative effects?

4.6 ASSESSING RELEVANCE

By relevance is meant an overall assessment of whether a project is in keeping with needs and priorities of the owners, the intended users and other affected parties. A change in policies or priorities could imply that a project is accorded lower priority, or lose some of its rationale. It becomes less relevant.

> **Examples:**
>
> In a building construction project the immediate objective is the improved infrastructure for users. Relevance could be assessed in terms of the rationale for constructing the building: was it to serve the interest of a few or in response to real needs in society or to exploit important economic potentials.
>
> In an educational project the immediate objective is to provide training. The assessment of relevance is a question of whether the trainees, the users, or the authorities give priority to the type of education provided. More specifically, this can be measured in terms of the amount of applicants, the demand for the graduates among employers, etc.
>
> In a road project relevance could be assessed in terms of the rationale for constructing the road: was it to serve a political agenda of the few or to exploit real economic potentials.

In other words, relevance is basically a question of usefulness, and in turn leads to higher-level decisions as to whether the project in question ought to be terminated or allowed to continue. And, if the latter is the case, what changes ought to be made, and in what direction? Are the agreed objectives still valid, and do they represent sufficient rationale for continuing the activities? Such questions need to be asked at various stages starting long before the project is planned. In fact, questions of relevance are particularly important in ex ante evaluations (appraisals) because its focus is on the strategy and the justification of the project. Are we doing the right thing? Within the framework of a mid-term evaluation, the questions remain the same, but in addition one might wish to look into how much the project contributes as compared to the existing needs and priorities – or in other words: are we doing things right?.

- At the highest level relevance concerns the relationship between the project and the overall policy that constitutes the framework for decision making by government.
- At the next level it is a question of how project activities fit into a larger context, e.g. in relation to other projects or activities in society.
- Then at the lower level it is a question of whether the project is directed towards areas accorded high priority by the affected parties.

Assessing relevance

WHAT TO MEASURE	❑	Appropriateness in relation to needs and priorities
WHO's PERSPECTIVE	❑	The society, the users
POINT OF REFERENCE	❑	Needs and priorities of users and other affected parties
METHODOLOGICAL CHALLENGE	❑	Conflicting views and policies regarding needs and priorities
KEY QUESTIONS	❑	Whether objectives are in keeping with needs and priorities
	❑	Whether the direction should be changed
	❑	Whether activities should be continued or terminated

4.7 Assessing Sustainability

The assessment of sustainability goes beyond the project itself and is an indication whether the positive impacts are likely to continue after the project has been completed.

The four evaluation criteria described above primarily concern the specific project, whereas assessment of sustainability is more a matter of the economic, institutional, social, etc. process itself, in a longer-term perspective. This largely depends on whether the financial viability of the process, resources made available and how users view the project.

> **Examples:**
>
> In the building construction project, sustainability can be measured in terms of whether the building is likely to be maintained, the extent to which the users will be able and willing to cover operational and capital expenses in the future, etc.
>
> In an educational project sustainability can be measured in terms of the degree to which the training institution has the resources and competence to continue the training programs in the future, whether teachers remain in their jobs, students are willing and able to pay the fees, authorities or sponsors provide financial inputs, etc.
>
> In a road construction project, sustainability can be measured in terms of whether the road is likely to be maintained, the extent to which it will be needed in the future, etc.

Thus, sustainability is in many ways a higher-level test of whether or not the project has been a success. Far too many projects prove to be a failure after the implementation phase is over. The sustainability of any project will depend to a large extent on whether the positive impact justify the investments necessary and whether, say, the local community values the project highly enough to be willing to devote resources to continuing it.

In other words, sustainability is concerned with what happens after the project is completed and should ideally be measured some years afterwards. It will be difficult to provide any sure assessment of sustainability as long as activities are still underway, or immediately afterwards. In such cases, the assessment will have to be based on projections about future developments on the basis of whatever knowledge is available about the project, the market and the users. It will require an analysis of the contextual setting – its capabilities and restraints.

Experience with projects concludes that a project's sustainability hinges mainly on six main areas, also called sustainability factors. These factors must be taken into account all along the implementation cycle, and should be used as a checklist during evaluation to identify relevant evaluation questions related to the project's sustainability. A brief description of the sustainability factors is included in chapter 5.

Assessing sustainabiliy

WHAT TO MEASURE	❏ Future viability of the process supported or initiated by the project
WHO's PERSPECTIVE	❏ The financing party, the users and society
POINT OF REFERENCE	❏ Projected, future situation
METHODOLOGICAL CHALLENGE	❏ Hypothetical answers.
	❏ Reliance on judgemental data
KEY QUESTIONS	❏ The extent to which the positive impact justifies investments
	❏ Whether future revenue exceeds cost
	❏ User's support and ability to continue the intended process
	❏ Whether authorities provide policy support and resources to continue the process, etc.

CHAPTER 5

THE CROSS-SECTORAL VIEW

EVERYTHING SHOULD BE AS SIMPLE AS POSSIBLE – BUT NOT SIMPLER.
ALBERT EINSTEIN

5.1 AN INTEGRATED EVALUATION MODEL

Projects have different types of impact in society. Some types of projects and particularly large investment projects may have large and complex effects. A comprehensive evaluation of any project will require some sort of interdisciplinary approach. The OECD evaluation model presented in chapter 4 is therefore extended to include six so-called crosscutting issues that facilitate an interdisciplinary analysis, as illustrated in figure 5.1. These are also termed sustainability factors.

The way to interpret this model is that it centres round the project strategy or the narrative summary of the project – set out in a logical sequence from inputs to purpose. A prerequisite for a viable design of a projects is that it is based on an analysis of needs and priorities of stakeholders, a realistic strategy, a logical sequencing of activities and outputs, a thorough analysis of uncertainties, etc. Such analyses automatically include different views or angles where the financial, technological, institutional, etc. perspectives are highlighted. In order to ensure quality design, most of the crosscutting issues in the model should be taken into account when these analyses are done. Phrased differently, there is a need to ensure a cross-disciplinary view of the project from the earliest start – before it is designed and most certainly before it is appraised.

The same goes when the project is evaluated. The five evaluation criteria in chapter 4 presented are chosen to ensure a broad view of the project and to include both operational, tactical and the strategic perspective. In addition, a comprehensive evaluation will require that the six crosscutting issues are considered when evaluation instruments are designed, and data are collected and analysed. Below is a brief summary of how the crosscutting issues should be interpreted. This is further discussed in chapters 5.2 – 5.7.

Policy support measures

The stakeholders' commitment is one of the most commonly identified factors affecting project success. Commitment is expressed in terms of agreement on objectives, and the strategies to get there. Commitment is a concern of evaluators and is also shaped by perceptions of mutuality of interests between involved parties as well as conformity with prevailing policy and legislation.

Economic and financial aspects

Evaluations focus essentially on three aspects of economic and financial performance. Firstly, the project's cost effectiveness. Secondly, the economic and financial benefits as compared with investments and operational costs. And finally the financial sustainability to explore whether sales or revenue will be sufficient to cover future operations, maintenance and depreciation costs.

Socio-economic aspects

Most projects affect individuals, groups, communities or larger societies in some way at some time now or in the future. They may affect people's access to means of production, products and services, their rights and benefits, employment, income, etc. Evaluators will therefore also have to look into the project's socio-economic implications.

Environmental impact

Environmental conservation is now high priority in society. Although environmental effects may be negligible seen in a narrow, short-term perspective, the broader, long-term effects may be significant. Evaluations will frequently have to look specifically at environmental policy, incentives and regulatory measures, the interests of different stakeholders, and the effects of the project.

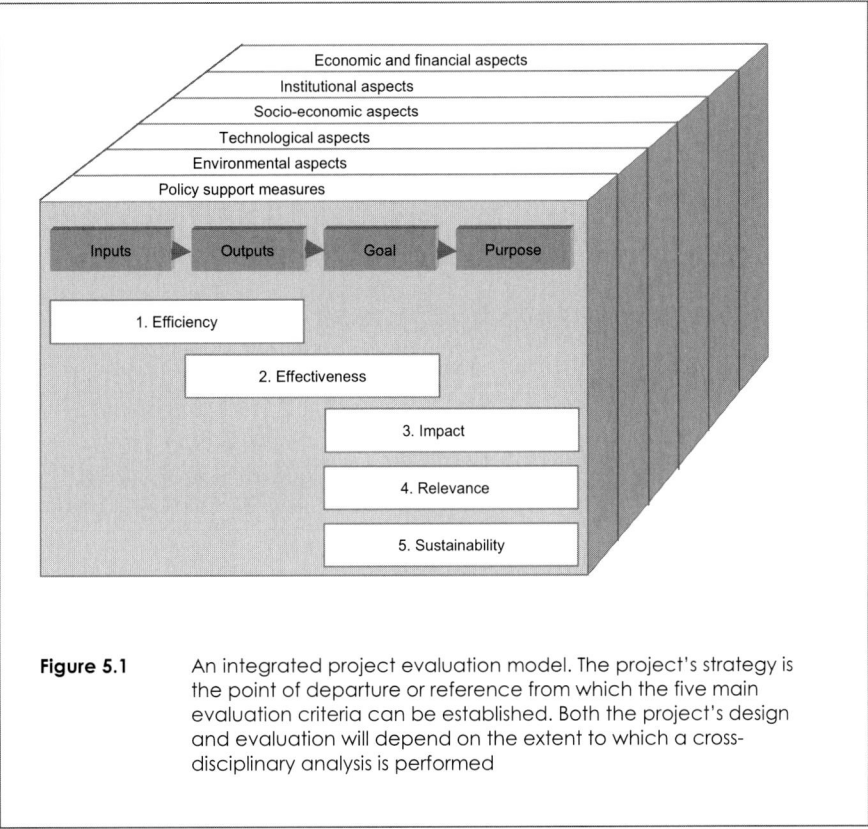

Figure 5.1 An integrated project evaluation model. The project's strategy is the point of departure or reference from which the five main evaluation criteria can be established. Both the project's design and evaluation will depend on the extent to which a cross-disciplinary analysis is performed

Institutional aspects

The role of institutions is the single most important factor determining the success of projects. Evaluators will have to look at the project in a context of supporting and interacting institutions, but also internal considerations of managerial leadership, professional competence and experience, administrative issues, etc.

Choice of technology

The choice of technology is crucial for such important aspects as the productivity, financial viability, safety, environmental hazards, etc. Evaluation teams need to consider the viability and effects of technology and the costs of providing and maintaining the technology versus the benefits generated.

Chapter 5 – The Cross-sectoral View

☑ **Evaluation criteria**

1. POLICY SUPPORT	❑	Policies, priorities, and specific commitments of owners and authorities to support the chances of success.
2. ECONOMIC AND FINANCIAL ASPECTS	❑	Economic viability and financial sustainability
3. SOCIO-ECONOMIC ASPECTS	❑	Economic and other effects on social systems, groups or individuals
4. ENVIRONMENTAL PROTECTION	❑	Exploitation, management and development of resources. Protection of the environment.
5. INSTITUTIONAL ASPECTS	❑	Institutional capacity and distribution of responsibilities between stakeholders and affected parties
6. CHOICE OF TECHNOLOGY	❑	Choice of, adaptation and use of technology under prevailing conditions

5.2 POLICY SUPPORT MEASURES

A project will need to operate within the context of current legislation, and public and institutional policy. Policy support is a major precondition for sustainability. In this connection it is important to assess how firmly embedded the project goal is within the context of public and stakeholders' priorities, as well as the degree to which stakeholders are committed to the process that will follow after the project is completed.

If from the very start there are serious discrepancies between the project goal and stakeholders' priorities, considerations as to future sustainability may make it doubtful whether the project should be implemented at all. Moreover, the policy climate and priorities may well change over time, so it is important to monitor these.

For instance, projects to construct nuclear power plants have been in discredit in Western societies for the past three decades. In countries like Sweden and Austria such projects are banned by national policy. In other countries, the resistance of certain stakeholders such as local communities and environmentalists put an effective end to all such initiatives. Also, what seems the key issue with these projects, is that experience have demonstrated that they are not economically viable, and therefore investors and other possible key stakeholders will not commit funds in such projects.

Clearly, it is therefore essential to analyse, for instance by means of evaluation, a project in light of the priorities and policies at different levels and among the main stakeholders. This applies also to prevailing political issues and ideology and how this is translated into practical policy, priorities, laws and regulations, etc. Evaluators need to investigate whether there have been changes in higher-level priorities during the course of the project.

Finally, against this background, the evaluator needs to inquire more specifically into the degree to which the various institutions actually demonstrate an involvement and commitment to the project.

On the next page is a schematic presentation of some of the points to emphasise in such analyses.

Policy support

POLICY AND LEGISLATIVE ENVIRONMENT

- Conformity with public policy and legislation
- Extent to which the project has support in
    - public funding or credit facilities
    - Price and subsidy policy
    - wage and personnel policy
    - regional/district policy
    - sector support policy, etc.
- How changes in overall policies and priorities might affect the project

♦

COMMITMENT AND INVOLVEMENT

- Degree of agreement on objectives among stakeholders
- Support from relevant institutions
    - political
    - public
    - business and industry
    - local

5.3 ECONOMIC AND FINANCIAL ISSUES

All projects use *inputs* (manpower, technology, land, electricity, water, etc.) to produce *outputs* (schools, roads, computer software, etc.). This is to fulfil the broader *goal* (education, transport, production, etc.) and subsequently the longer-term *purpose* (economic growth, etc.).

Planners compare the *value of inputs* used with the *value of outputs* produced in a project. Clearly, different sets of inputs may be used to produce the same outputs and achieve the same purpose. The set of inputs that can produce the outputs at the least cost is obviously most *cost-efficient*.

But the same inputs may also be used in a different project to produce different outputs and achieve another purpose. The alternative project may produce a higher net value when comparing the value of outputs between the projects. To determine alternative use of inputs in order to maximise the value of outputs or *benefits* from the society's national perspective, analysts apply *economic analysis*. This represents a broader perspective than just adding up what appears as costs and benefits in the project budget, since it (ideally) includes all costs and benefits of the project to the national economy.

	ECONOMIC ANALYSIS	FINANCIAL ANALYSIS
ANALYSIS	Cost-benefit	- Cost efficiency - Financial sustainability
PERSPECTIVE	Society	Project
OUTCOME	Viability	Sustainability
FLOWS STUDIED	Resources	Funds

In many projects a distinction can be made between the investment phase and the operational phase. To determine project sustainability and need for future funding, analysts apply *financial analysis*. The focus is limited to the flow of money in and out of the project as seen from the project's perspective i.e. the cash flow. The differences between the concepts are illustrated above.

In evaluations, three types of economic/financial analysis will be particularly relevant: financial sustainability, cost-effectiveness and cost-benefit assessment.

Financial sustainability is the simplest type of analysis designed to estimate the financial resources that are/will be available over time as compared with anticipated costs.

Cost-effectiveness can be estimated in most cases after some time has elapsed. Here the evaluator will ask whether similar results could have been achieved at lower cost – either if it had been designed or performed differently.

Cost-benefit analysis is used mainly where the utility of a project can be measured in monetary terms. The question to be answered is whether the utility value of the project justifies the costs involved.

In economic/financial analysis the time factor will often have to be taken into consideration, for instance by discounting the value of costs and benefits back to an equivalent "present value". This will make economic units comparable. Also, adjustments might have to be when some cost or benefits are taxed, subsidised, or otherwise do not express the 'real' value in a broad perspective. In such cases 'shadow pricing' might be used to yield a more accurate expression of the 'real' value.

Economic and financial aspects

FINANCIAL SUSTAINABILITY
- ❏ Are there sufficient funds to cover recurrent costs after external support is withdrawn.
- ❏ This presupposes comparisons of:
    - o Operating, maintenance and depreciation costs
    - o Available grants and allocations
    - o Cost-recovery; levies, etc.

(Discounting and shadow pricing will normally not be necessary)

COST-EFFECTIVENESS
- ❏ Could similar results have been achieved at lower cost? This presupposes information on:
    - o Costs of project and project components
    - o Alternative ways the same tasks could have been accomplished, and the costs involved.
    - o Costs of similar projects elsewhere

(Discounting and shadow pricing may be relevant in many cases)

COST-BENEFIT
- ❏ Can the costs of the project be justified in terms of the benefits produced?
- ❏ This presupposes information on various factors, expressed in comparable, monetary terms:
    - o Goods and services produced
    - o Work-saving
    - o Social benefits, etc.

(Discounting and shadow pricing will often be necessary)

5.4 SOCIO-ECONOMIC ASPECTS

A main acceptance criterion when projects are designed is that the financial analysis indicates acceptable economic return. Less attention is often given to socio-economic and distributional effects when the project is designed.

Projects are used increasingly in industry and society, for instance to undertake major tasks in producing infrastructure and services. Evaluation is crucial to understand the results of such projects.

The socio-economic analysis would take the results of the economic and financial analyses a step further and look at distributional effects and market effects in society. It would include impact analysis that goes beyond economic effects on individuals, groups and communities and look at effects on settlement patterns, employment, income, welfare, health, etc.

Socio-economic studies will often require extensive research design and large samples. Their cost will have to be justified against the type and size of project involved, and the potential utility of the results. Valid and reliable findings will often require that considerable time has elapsed in order for effects to become visible.

The evaluators might draw on similar studies from other projects as a supplement source of insight to reduce cost.

The distributional analysis should attempt to assess the project's impact not only on the intended users but also on other affected groups. This serves to ensure that projects are truly compatible with the needs and capabilities of those involved and affected. The analysis should clarify the groups and individuals who benefit and those who may be adversely affected by the project. In certain cases, there may be adverse social effects on some groups even when the project's objectives are fully met. The evaluation should explore such adverse effects as well as the positive ones, and consider means for alleviating them.

Socio-economic aspects

COMMITMENT AND INVOLVEMENT	❏ Degree of consent of users, customers and affected groups and individuals
	❏ Degree of interaction or conflict between groups of stakeholders
ECONOMIC IMPACT	❏ Economic impact for affected groups
	❏ Distributional effects
	❏ Market effects for consumers
	❏ Effects on ownership and financial security
	❏ Effects on material well-being, etc
OTHER IMPACT	❏ Employment effects, turnover
	❏ Effects on hazards and health
	❏ Effects on social differentiation
	❏ Effects on settlement patterns
	❏ Effects on welfare, etc.

5.5 ENVIRONMENTAL IMPACT

Today ecologically sound management of natural resources has come to be recognised as a precondition for sustainable development. This means a broadly based desire to achieve societal exploitation of resources without endangering the natural systems for maintaining life.

There is considerable awareness and a long traditional now to ensure that projects are designed with due concern of their environmental effects. A project to design computer software might not have any direct environmental effects. Other projects may represent potential environmental hazards. What characterizes our habitat or the natural environment is that even minor man-made interventions often result in a series of causes and effects that could eventually prove to be of considerable proportion. A hydropower dam project, for instance, might cause considerable changes in the local ecology, both upstreams and down-streams. It would subsequently also cause new industry and new settlements to be established, effects on agriculture, increased pollution from a new man-made environment, and could even cause local climatic changes.

A challenge in environmental studies is to trace such chains of events and explore the significance of first, second, third, etc -order effects of projects and other interventions in the environment. The assessment of environmental impact would typically address all effects on the natural environment, on human health, property, social effects, etc. It would have to explore direct and sideeffects, as well as delayed and cumulative effects. In some cases, environmental effects even cross national borders as for instance is the case with radioactive pollution from British nuclear power plants crossing the North sea and ending up in Scandinavian countries.

Evaluation of environmental effects needs to judge the scope of effects against national standards and regulations, as well as against benchmarks from similar projects. It will have to discuss the needs for mitigation measures or environmental safeguards that could be incorporated into the project to offset adverse impacts. Environmental assessment will be most useful if it is initiated at the earliest stage of the project, to ensure from the outset that the project is environmentally sound and sustainable. Evaluation of environmental effects should be conducted not only where projects may affect human health, but also in projects that might have adverse impact on the natural environment and the biological diversity. Projects undertaken in very fragile environments need special consideration.

Environmental impact

THE TERM ENVIRONMENTAL IMPACT IS UNDERSTOOD TO INCLUDE:	❑ Effects on human health and well-being, eco-systems (including flora and fauna), agriculture and buildings (classified as protected); ❑ Effects on climate and atmosphere; ❑ Use of natural resources (both regenerative resources and mineral resources); ❑ Utilisation and disposal of residues and wastes; ❑ Related aspects such as resettlement, archaeological sites, landscape, monuments and social consequences as well as relevant upstream, downstream and trans-boundary effects.
ENVIRONMENTAL IMPACT ANALYSIS INCLUDES ASSESSMENT OF THE PROJECT'S EFFECTS ON:	❑ The natural environment ❑ The natural resource base ❑ Future management of natural resources ❑ Man-made environments and related elements ❑ Health of population
PROJECTS WHERE AN ENVIRONMENTAL IMPACT ASSESSMENT MIGHT BE REQUIRED	❑ Those which cause a substantial change in renewable resource use; ❑ The exploitation of hydrological resources; ❑ Infrastructure; ❑ Industrial activities; ❑ Extractive industries; ❑ Those which substantially change farming and fishing practices; ❑ Waste management and disposal

5.6 INSTITUTIONAL ASPECTS

Institutional performance and interaction are some of the most important features that determine or explain the success or failure of projects. These would partly be factors internal to the project and partly external factors determined by supporting, co-operating and interacting institutions or projects that might affect the performance or the outcome of the project in question.

The importance of institutional interaction is not limited to the phase when the project is implemented. It goes back to the early start or phase when ideas were conceived and alliances were made. And it extends further beyond the time when the project was completed and way into the operational phase where the project will prove its worth and produce its benefits.

The evaluator will have to explore both the internal institutional matters and the external interaction between the project and its institutional environment.

Internal factors cover issues such as the competence, commitment and quality of the human resources and whether their knowledge and skills are relevant and sufficient to handle the challenges of the project. It also has to do with management and administrative issues such as the flow of information, the management structure, turnover of qualified staff, financial management etc. And finally it has to do with managerial leadership - its ability to set goals, formulate strategies, choose specific solutions, mobilise support, create conditions conducive to working collaboration with other institutions, as well as directing internal administration. The administrative system should be understood, and function in line with the tasks to be carried out. It must be able to solve problems of logistics and of maintenance, and have information and reporting routines that are both effective in application and capable of dealing with the most important aspects of what is to be administered.

A project is a temporary organisation. It can be internal to a larger organisation constituting a group of colleagues in a department, or it could be an autonomous entity outside existing institutions or a large project promoted jointly by several institutions - even by several nations. A project can be huge, like a giant international military operation, or a project to put people in outer space. In fact, in those cases where the tasks are so big that no single organisation can take it on by itself – it is usually organised as a project. If the task is to construct an airport of an offshore oil installation, then the project organisation will be sizeable. Evaluation of performance and achievements will then necessarily have to look into institutional issues, regarding the project organisation itself, but also its organisational environment. This includes the network and linkages among organisations that facilitate or constrain the achievements of the project. The involvement of local institutions and user-groups is important in ensuring sustainable development.

Institutional aspects

INSTITUTIONAL ISSUES
- Human resources: skills, experience, education, turn-over, etc
- Organisational structure, leadership
- Division of responsibilities
- Modes of co-operation
- Flow of information

♦

INSTITUTIONAL INTERACTION
- Interaction with owner/parent institutions
- Interaction with suppliers
- Interaction with user organisations/customers
- Linkage with government/public institutions
- Contact with media and the public

♦

ORGANISATIONAL ISSUES
- Networks and linkages
- Division of responsibilities
- Enabling factors in the institutional environment
- Constraining factors in the institutional environment

5.7 TECHNOLOGICAL ASPECTS

The term technology includes the systematic knowledge, techniques and tools that we apply to manufacture a product, manage a process or perform a service. Technology is a key feature of man and society, and a key agent in all our pursuits. The choice of technology is of course essential in projects.

Commonly, technology is viewed primarily as an economic factor, even though it is also a major force in social and political change. It is built into products, processes and institutions, and thus comprises one of the most important characteristics of any society. There are essentially two perspectives that need to be taken into consideration in evaluation of projects. It is the technology as a means to produce the project's agreed outputs, and the implications of the choice of technology on society.

The first perspective implies an assessment of the *technological efficiency* between different possible or comparable technologies. It requires thorough understanding of the technology itself. It is the question of whether to use concrete drilling rigs or submerged steel structures in off-shore oil exploitation, judged for instance against cost, production time and quality. It is the question of using Linux or Microsoft as the operative system in a computer network, or to use road or rail as a means of transportation in a project.

The other perspective is that which is termed *technology assessment*, and which is pre-occupied with the effects of applying a specific type of technology. It does not require deep understanding of the technology involved, but rather sees technology in a black-box perspective being concerned with what goes in and what comes out of a process. It is no longer an issue of limited adjustments or minor changes to improve performance – but more fundamental questions regarding what resources are used and what implications or effects the different choices will have on economy and society.

In terms of evaluation, this implies that the evaluation team will have to have both relevant technical expertise as well as professional that are well versed in assessing effects of technology in society. Clearly, in a routine project the choice of technology will largely be limited to the first perspective, while large and complex projects, as well as pioneering and innovative projects may to a larger extent require the second type of expertise.

Choice of technology

DEFINITION	❑ Technology includes the know-how, tools and equipment used to produce products, manage processes or perform services.
	♦
TECHNOLOGICAL EFFICIENCY	❑ Restricted assessment of efficiency of alternative tools/technologies in producing the project's outputs
	❑ Key issue particularly in routine projects
	❑ Focus on issues regarding cost, progress and quality of different technical choices, etc.
	♦
TECHNOLOGY ASSESSMENT	❑ Broader assessment of implications of different types of technology
	❑ Focus on issues pertaining to the
	o use of physical and human resources
	o economic and social impact of different technologies
	❑ Essential particularly in pioneering and innovative projects

CHAPTER 6

DESIGN AND METHODOLOGY

THEY WERE THE PERFECT MATCH. HE WAS KIND AND SHE WAS CRUEL.
NILS FREDRIK NIELSEN

6.1 DEDUCTIVE VERSUS INDUCTIVE RESEARCH

The scope of evaluation is a question of its depth and breadth. The *depth* is essentially determined by the evaluation criteria applied, as discussed in chapter 4, and the purpose of the evaluation. An evaluation to generate experience usually digs deeper than an evaluation designed to document achievements. The *breadth* of the evaluation is essentially determined by the type of project that the evaluation is intended to cover. An evaluation of a small routine project has a narrow perspective – while an evaluation of a large, innovative project or a program of several projects might have a much broader perspective, as discussed in chapter 5. A less comprehensive evaluation would be the one that focuses on a single project, for the purpose of documenting achievements. The comprehensive evaluation would be the one focusing on large and complex projects with the purpose to assess their impact and draw lessons for future projects.

In chapter 2.6, two main approaches to evaluation were discussed, the deductive and the inductive. The most common approach in project evaluation is the *deductive* approach whereby hypotheses are formulated at an early stage on the basis of common understanding and available information. These are then tested against reality when the evaluation is carried out. The advantage of this approach is that it takes as its point of departure existing experience, which makes it easier to choose indicators and interpret data. The main criticism against this approach is that it may delimit both themes and problem areas so that important aspects or conditions may be overlooked.

Both in single and in more complex types of projects, objectives will often be unclear or inadequately formulated. Also, projects may have many unforeseen impacts, both positive and negative – which may well be overlooked if the evaluation focuses only on what has been formally agreed. Overcoming such problems will depend on the experience of the evaluation team and their ability to define analytical frameworks for the investigation, which can capture the major impacts of the activities in question.

One solution to this problem is to use an *inductive* approach where the evaluation team starts with an open/questioning mind. Through observation and investigation, themes arise that in term demand new knowledge, gradually leading to new insights. The advantage is that this is often the only means available for achieving in-depth understanding. The criticism is that it is time consuming. In order to avoid subjective biases it often becomes necessary to place special emphasis on the selection of data, perspectives and methods and to explain this in detail.

Clearly, most evaluations will rely on a combination of these two approaches. The part of the evaluation that focuses on efficiency and effectiveness may benefit strongly from a deductive approach. Here the perspective is narrow. It is the implementer's and users' perspective. In measuring impact, relevance and sustainability, a more inductive approach may be more useful because the field of study is more open-ended and the perspective is the widest – it is the society's perspective.

Deductive and inductive research

DEDUCTIVE RESEARCH

- Description
  - Testing preconceived hypotheses about achievements and effects against reality during evaluation

- Advantage
  - Easier to choose indicators and interpret data using experience as a reference

- Disadvantage
  - Tends to restrict the focus so that important aspects may be overlooked

- Application
  - Evaluation of routine projects with a restricted perspective where the purpose is to document efficiency and effectiveness

♦

INDUCTIVE RESEARCH

- Description
  - Explore reality through observation and investigation without a predetermined focus

- Advantage
  - Useful both in gaining deep insight and capture a wider range of (unforeseen) impacts of a project

- Disadvantage
  - Often time-consuming and expensive, and prone to be affected by subjective biases

- Application
  - Evaluation of complex (and innovative) projects and programs where the purpose is to assess their impact and draw lessons for the future

6.2 REVIEWING THE STRATEGY

The project's strategy is the starting point for the evaluator, since it identifies the anticipated achievements against which assessments will be made. Most evaluations are primarily concerned about the broad overall assessment of the project, and less with the implementation of activities as such - in other words, the significance of the process, rather than the process itself.

The project's strategy may change during the period of implementation. The level of ambition may be increased or decreased in the course of events, as well as the direction of activities. The evaluator needs to review changes in the strategy in order to gain a full picture of what is to be evaluated.

It is a key concern of the evaluation to assess the extent to which the initial objectives are still relevant, whether a possible shift in the objectives was justified and whether other changes in the objectives are warranted.

Projects should ideally be planned within the context of a long-term strategy, where the objectives are established and formally agreed. If changes have been made in these objectives, they need to be analysed specifically. Complex projects may have several different objectives. In such cases, it may be useful to organise the objectives in a logical cause/effect sequence. This helps to provide an initial overview of the complexity of the strategy, which in many cases will reveal a picture of confounding, even conflicting, objectives. In some cases it will demonstrate that the objectives have gradually changed from what was initially intended. This could happen without it being discussed explicitly and formally approved between the involved parties.

The initial analysis of the project should consider whether objectives are realistic. Often objectives are too ambitious seen in relation to the resources available and the agreed time frame. Unrealistic objectives are a problem for two reasons. Firstly, if they are used as the formal reference for the evaluation the final assessment of the project will have to be that the project has failed. Secondly, the analysis necessary to assess the fulfilment of ambitious objectives would be unduly expensive. Also, the evaluation would not be able to demonstrate that anticipated effects could be attributed to the project and to separate them from other confounding factors that might have caused major changes.

In order to assess the realism of a project, the evaluators will need to consider the probabilities of fulfilling the various formally agreed objectives at the earliest time before the evaluation is planned. This would make it possible to identify realistic points of references when the scope of the study and the research methodology for the evaluation is decided.

Reviewing the strategy

- Consistency of strategy
- Confounding or conflicting objectives
- Realism in view of available resources
- Realism in view of agreed time-frame

♦

- Changes in strategy during implementation
- Direction
- Level of ambition
- Time perspective

♦

- Effects on realism of changes in strategy
- Attribution of anticipated effects

6.3 THE PROBLEM OF ATTRIBUTION

When a project is conceived and designed the objectives should be such that they are realistically achievable with a given time perspective. The major external risks that are likely to affect the realisation of the project strategy need to be identified and analysed. A main issue is to get the objectives right from the very start. As discussed in chapter 6.2, overly ambitious objectives are clearly a problem during implementation, since they will provide unclear guidance. Also, the chance that the objectives will be attained as prescribed will be limited. It is also a problem for evaluators, exactly for the same reason: the assessment is likely to confirm that the objectives have not been met. In addition it will cause a problem, which is commonly termed *attribution.* This means that it will be difficult to demonstrate to what extent the project under study has attributed to the objective as compared with other projects or confounding processes in society.

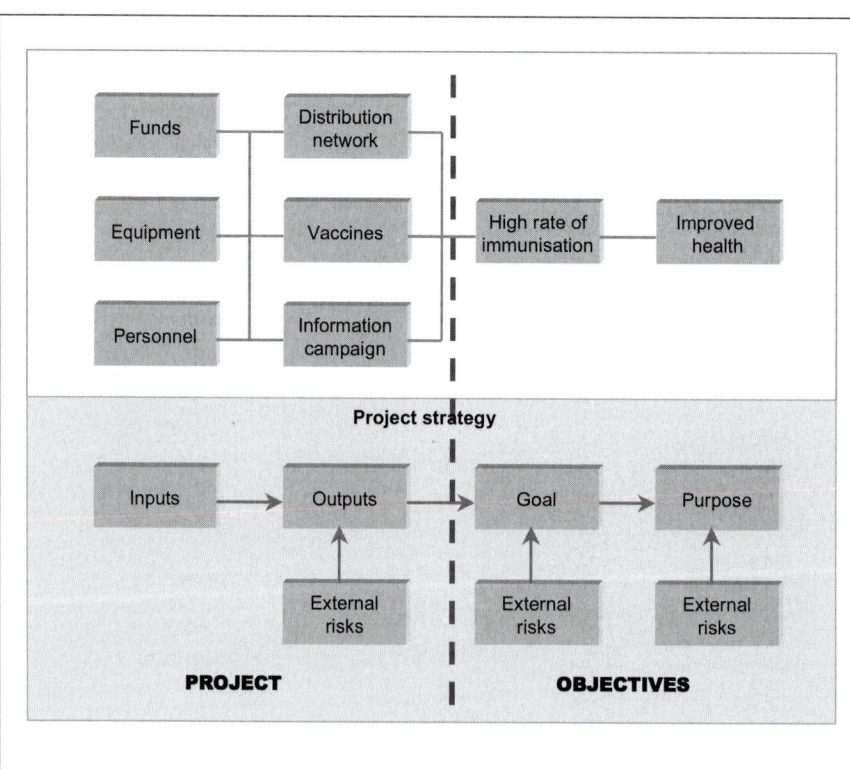

Figure 6.1 Immunisation project with formally agreed objectives at three separate ambition levels

For the evaluator, the problem of attribution becomes apparent when evaluation instruments are selected. Low attribution will typically require precise instruments and large samples. The resources available for the evaluation will therefore be a limiting factor that would force the evaluator to shift objectives, and not try to demonstrate effects that cannot be traced back to the project under study.

As an example, consider the project illustrated in figure 6.1, which is designed to administer a certain type of vaccine to a population group. The operational objectives or the outputs imply that a distribution network has to be established, for instance in co-operation with schools; information campaigns have to be carried out; and vaccination of the target group has to be undertaken. The immediate effect is expressed by its goal, i.e. a high rate of immunisation. The main long-term effect is expected to be improved health, as expressed by the project's purpose.

An educated guess would be that the projects attribution towards the goal is reasonable. However, the immunisation effect can only be ascertained after months or years, and based on a pretty large sample from the target group, possibly also with a control group. Immunisation would have to be interpreted narrowly - to the diseases affected by the vaccines in question.

The attribution as regards the project's purpose, however, is probably too low to warrant a separate investigation by an evaluation team. The vaccine affects only some types of diseases. In additions there are numerous other factors affecting health: other diseases, exposure, nutrition, preventive health measures, education, income, etc. To single out the effect of one vaccine program would be prohibitive in an evaluation of a project and it would require a health survey of huge proportions.

Evaluators might be asked to assess the degree of attribution itself, for instance in terms of the extent to which certain effects are caused by a specific project – as compared with the effects of other possible processes. This is technically difficult and would represent a considerable challenge for evaluators.

A related issue to consider when assessing attribution is the *counterfactual* question. This refers to the hypothetical question what would happen in the absence of the project. It raises the problem of measuring 'with and without' versus the traditional 'before and after' measurement. Simply comparing the situation 'before and after' leaves considerable doubt as to attribution and validity of results. Defining a counterfactual reference is a more exact way of measuring effects, but is frequently more difficult because of lack of baseline data. This is discussed further in chapter 6.5.

✓ Attribution

- Attribution is interpreted as the extent to which an observed phenomenon can be proven to be caused by another. In project evaluation the issue is related to effects that might possibly be caused by the project

    ♦

- Acceptable attribution means that it is possible with reasonable means to measure the effect caused by the project
- Limited attribution means that the effect is unclear and that large samples and precise evaluation instruments will be required to measure the effect

    ♦

- In such cases the evaluators would have to:
    - Discuss whether certain effects are caused by the project or by other possible causes
    - Focus on effects more closely related to the project
    - Discuss what would have happen in the absence of the project (the counterfactual situation)

    ♦

- Available resources will be the limiting factor in pursuing low-attribution effects in evaluation

6.4 THE INFORMATION PROCESS

The information process that takes place during an evaluation is depicted in figure 6.2. In the preparatory phase the first step is to translate *evaluation criteria* of a general nature, for instance the five criteria described in chapter 4, into specific *evaluation questions*, that relate specifically to the project under study. There is always a need to apply several evaluation questions under each evaluation criterion, in order to produce valid conclusions and provide relevant information for decision-making. The evaluation questions will constitute the main indicators used during the evaluation. The disaggregation process leading to the evaluation questions is discussed in chapters 4.3 – 4.7.

The next step is to make the evaluation questions operational by turning them into *evaluation instruments*. In this context the evaluation instrument means the evaluation question plus the information collection method applied. The evaluator must ensure that the evaluation instruments produce *valid* and *reliable* information. This is discussed in chapter 8.2.

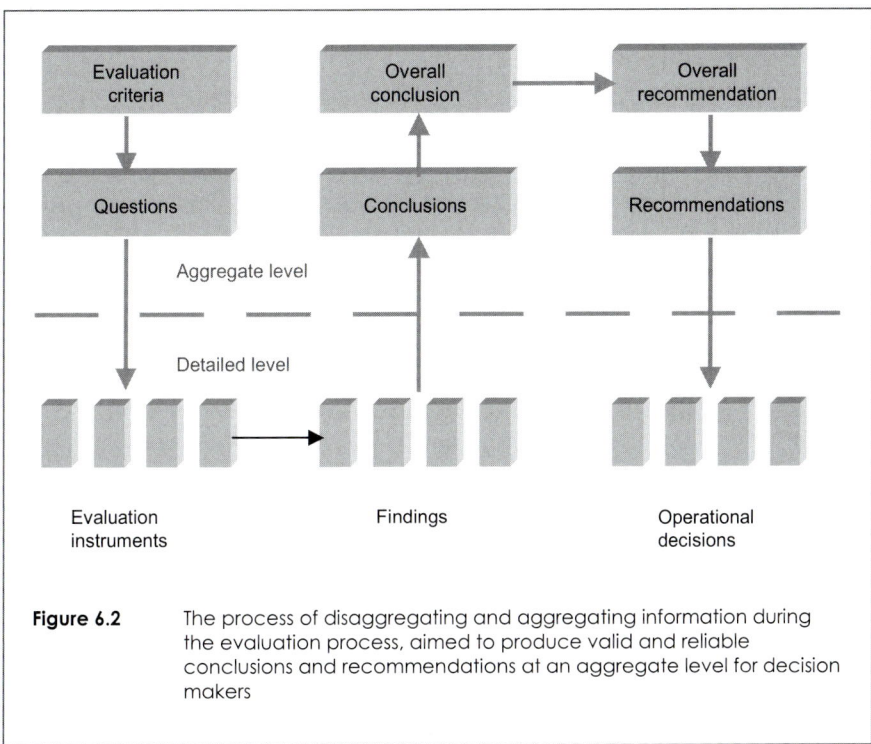

Figure 6.2 The process of disaggregating and aggregating information during the evaluation process, aimed to produce valid and reliable conclusions and recommendations at an aggregate level for decision makers

Prior to and during evaluation the instruments are used to collect data and generate findings. The information collected would be in the form of raw data, time-series, individual statements, etc. Most of this information is too detailed to be useful for decision-makers. Each piece of information provides only a small part of the combined picture. Many pieces of information may be conflicting.

The information therefore has to be analysed and aggregated to a higher, less detailed, level. This should result in a number of statements providing answers to the various evaluation questions, as illustrated in figure 6.2. These statements are the *conclusions*. Taken together, the conclusions should be comprehensive enough to accurately depict the situation. The strength of the conclusions will rely on the amount and quality of underlying information. In some cases the analysis of information will reveal conclusions that are linked to other evaluation questions, or other evaluation criteria, than the one in focus. Such conclusion will add to the picture and can provide opportunities for verifying or rejecting other conclusions.

The analytical part of the evaluation is the one that transforms the detailed pieces of information into conclusions at a more aggregate level, and finally makes use of these to draw the overall conclusion at the highest level, linked to the evaluation criterion in question.

The evaluator is then expected to translate the conclusions into main recommendations, which can be considered by management and subsequently translated into more specific and detailed decisions. The evaluator is usually not expected to provide recommendations at a detailed level. This should be the result of more comprehensive decision processes, which will involve the party that has commissioned the evaluation and the different stakeholders.

The purpose of analysis is to transform data into credible evidence about the project and its performance. Individual data are of little use unless they can be extracted or aggregated to address the questions in focus. This assumes that the evaluation design and instruments are appropriate, that the data are valid and reliable, and are analysed properly. In chapter 7, some methods to extract information are discussed briefly.

The information process

EVALUATION CRITERIA	❏ Issues at an aggregate level of relevance for decision-making or drawing lessons of a generic nature (e.g. relevance, sustainability)
EVALUATION QUESTIONS	❏ Specific issues relating to the project under study that operationalises the evaluation criteria at a dis-aggregate level
EVALUATION INSTRUMENTS	❏ Evaluation questions and the methods applied to collect the necessary information/evaluation findings

♦

EVALUATION CONCLUSIONS	❏ Answers to the evaluation questions based on an analysis of a relevant aggregate of evaluation findings
OVERALL CONCLUSIONS	❏ Answers to the evaluation criteria based on an analysis of the combined aggregate of evaluation conclusions

♦

OVERALL RECOMMENDATIONS	❏ Recommendations at the highest aggregation level (e.g. policy level), derived from the overall evaluation conclusions
EVALUATION RECOMMENDATIONS	❏ Strategic and tactical recommendations derived from the overall recommendations

6.5 STUDY DESIGN

A problem frequently encountered in evaluation is how to establish the effect of an intervention in retrospect. Five solutions to this problem are displayed in the figure 6.3 in terms of research designs. The distinction is made between cost and quality. The ultimate design is to establish the situation before and after the intervention - both in the target group (T_0, T_1), and in a control group (C_0, C_1) as well. This is a precise procedure with high validity that is used for instance in pharmaceutical testing. However, it is expensive, complicated and time consuming and rarely applied in project evaluation.

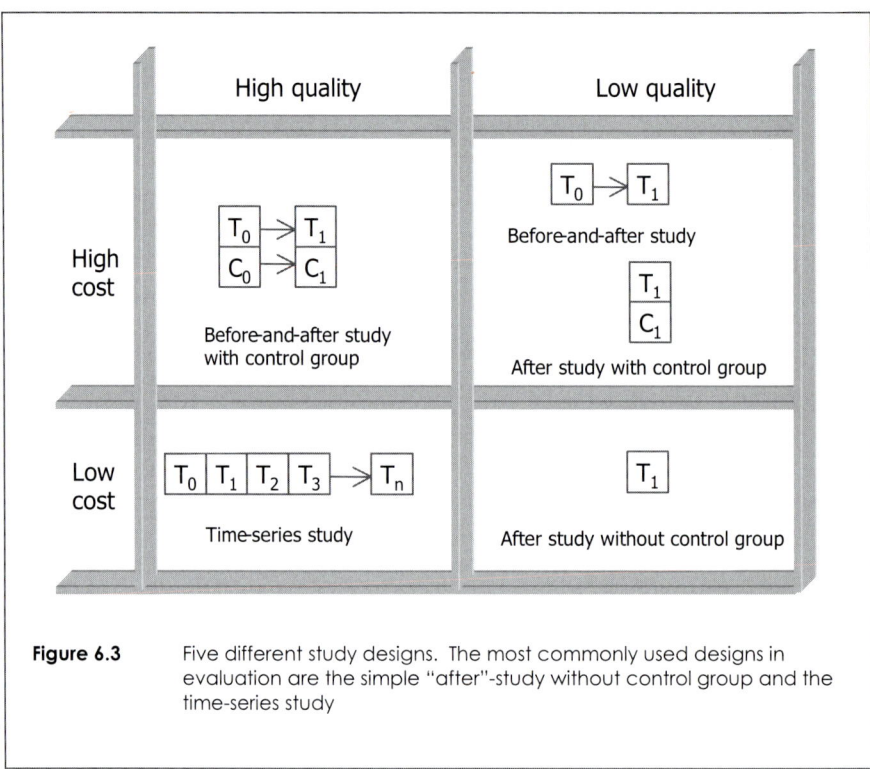

Figure 6.3 Five different study designs. The most commonly used designs in evaluation are the simple "after"-study without control group and the time-series study

Next are two types of rather high-cost methods that are seldom used in evaluation: the simple before-and-after study and the after study with control group. Few designs have as much intuitive appeal as the before-and-after study (T_0, T_1). The net effect of the intervention is estimated as the difference between measurements before and after. However, it is among the least valid of impact assessment approaches, since it is usually difficult to distinguish the effect of confounding factors from the effect of the intervention. Another complication is that it requires comparable baseline data. The simple after study with control group (T_1, C_1) may be easier to apply, but the validity will typically be low. For one thing, it assumes that the situation in both the target and control group were similar in the before-situation. Also, there is an ethical dilemma involved in studying a control group if this means that its members will not benefit from the project.

The most useful design is the time-series study (T_0, T_1, T_2, T_3, ...T_n). It may not be expensive to apply, provided data are generated as part of the project's management process. By registering data at regular intervals, it may be possible to identify changes in terms of trends before, during and after the intervention was enacted. However, also time-series studies have definite limitations, especially as regards the formation of hypotheses and understanding complex models.

The most common design in evaluation, however, is the other extreme: to study the situation only in retrospect and without a control group that could help provide evidence of changes (T_1). Such a simple design does not provide a basis for drawing firm conclusions. The evaluator will have to make judgements on the basis of general experience. Provided that this is adequate, the method may well yield useful information, but validity will remain low. Other supporting evidence must therefore be made available to verify findings.

As mentioned, the predominant study design in evaluation is the simple after-study without control group. The quality of data may be questionable and the impartiality of informants likewise. The data available will commonly be a mixture of time-series, baseline and data generated during evaluation. Much can still be done on this basis to produce quality conclusions and recommendations. The quality requirements in terms of validity and reliability are discussed in chapter 8.

✓ **Study design**

- Study with reference to base-line data or control groups are not often used in evaluation

    ♦

- The most commonly used design is the simple after study without control group, and time-series data when available

    ♦

- In order to achieve acceptable quality and be able to draw conclusions evaluators need to generate additional supporting evidence

6.6 QUANTITATIVE AND QUALITATIVE ANALYSIS

Evaluation reports aim to be read both by specialists and the public. It should be written keeping the least advanced readers in mind. The analysis behind findings may be based on sophisticated statistical analysis, but the findings need to be presented in a simple way so that all can understand it. For most users, simple tables, percentages and averages are the best way to present quantitative data, since they are not trained in quantitative research methods. For the more advanced readers, measures of spread, including percentiles and standard deviations, may add valuable information on how a variable is distributed throughout a sample population. Certainly, more sophisticated methods are needed in many evaluations where large amounts of quantitative data are analysed, for instance in order to test correlation between variables.

Nevertheless, much of the evaluation work can be done using basic methods. After all, evaluation is not scientific research and in evaluation of projects, the quality of data and the size of samples may not be such that it warrants the use of sophisticated methods. The issue is more often to what extent the evaluator should rely on *quantitative or qualitative* methods. Different parties may have differing opinions on this, but most parties, however, will agree that both types of analysis should be employed simultaneously in varying proportions.

Some aspects of qualitative and quantitative methods are discussed below.

Quantitative analysis

This involves that data are presented as numbers, and could include both objective data such as budget figures or number of individuals, and subjective attitudinal data such as expressions of opinion on a scale. Quantitative analysis lends itself to systematic manipulation of data, either to *describe* phenomena in a concise format, to *test relationships* among variables and *generalise* findings.

An appealing advantage of quantitative analysis is that it can summarise findings in an evaluation in a clear, precise and reliable way. Not all information, however, can be analysed quantitatively. For example, responses to an open-ended interview survey may provide lengthy descriptions that may be difficult to categorise and quantify, without losing subtle differences in the responses.

The validity of quantitative methods depends on initial assumptions about the data being used. Sophisticated analysis requires high quality data. Statistical packages are now easily available even in the most commonly used software such as MS Excel, and the danger is that the analysis becomes more sophisticated than the data. This weakens the credibility of conclusions, and the evaluator is therefore required to spell out the assumptions as well as the limitations of data when elaborate statistical analysis is employed. Clearly, the methods for quantitative analysis should match with the quality of data. In many evaluations this implies that simple methods should be preferred, which has the added advantage that the results will be easier to communicate to non-specialists.

Qualitative analysis

This is based on qualitative data such as detailed descriptions, statements in response to open-ended questions, the transcript of opinion of groups, and observations of different types. Qualitative analysis typically includes contents analysis, case study analysis, inductive analysis and logical and sequential analysis. All methods may produce *descriptions* (patterns, themes, tendencies, trends, etc.), and *interpretations* and *explanations* of these patterns. Using these methods makes demands on the evaluator to asses the validity and reliability of findings, for instance by means of triangulation as discussed in chapter 8.5.

Analysing qualitative data may help broaden the view of the phenomena of interest in an evaluation, but can also increase depth and detail. The process of analysing qualitative information is often inductive and without any particular guiding theory. Such inductive analysis has often contributed to major improvements in understanding of complex phenomena.

The credibility issue in qualitative analysis depends on three distinct but related elements:

- The techniques and methods used for gathering quality data that is carefully analysed, with attentions to the issues of validity and reliability.
- The credibility of the evaluator, which is dependent on training, experience, track record, etc; and
- The ideological, cultural and phenomenological paradigm subscribed to by the evaluator

Both qualitative and quantitative analysis relies on the evaluator's professional judgement concerning the relevance and validity of available data. Qualitative analysis is best done in conjunction with some sort of statistical analysis of related quantitative data. All evaluations should therefore be designed so that the two sorts of analysis, using different but related data, will be mutually reinforcing.

Quantitative and qualitative analysis

QUANTITATIVE ANALYSIS

ADVANTAGES
- Provides data in a concise format
- Tests relationship between variables
- Generalises findings to larger population

DISADVANTAGES
- Requires statistical expertise
- Much information cannot be quantified
- Data may distort as well as reveal facts

♦

QUALITATIVE ANALYSIS

ADVANTAGES
- May possess more richness of detail
- Presents more holistic viewpoints
- Provides deeper insight

DISADVANTAGES
- May be less credible that hard facts
- Dependent on evaluator's credibility and logic
- Takes more space to present evidence

CHAPTER 7
DATA COLLECTION
METHODS

THE TIME HAS COME, THE WALRUS SAID, TO TALK OF MANY THINGS.
OF SHOES AND SHIPS AND SEALING WAX, OF CABBAGES AND KINGS.
OF WHY THE OCEAN IS BURNING HOT, AND WHETHER PIGS HAVE WINGS.
LEWIS CAROL

Chapter 7 – Data Collection Methods

7.1 COLLECTING INFORMATION

Evaluations often produce controversial results. Therefore, the evaluation itself is often under criticism, and the choice of methods in data collection and analysis may be in focus.

Evaluations are frequently carried out under considerable time pressure and difficult conditions. Evaluators commonly may have to rely largely on secondary information, informal interviews and field observations. This choice is too limited. Evaluators need a wider range of data collection methods to ensure quality.

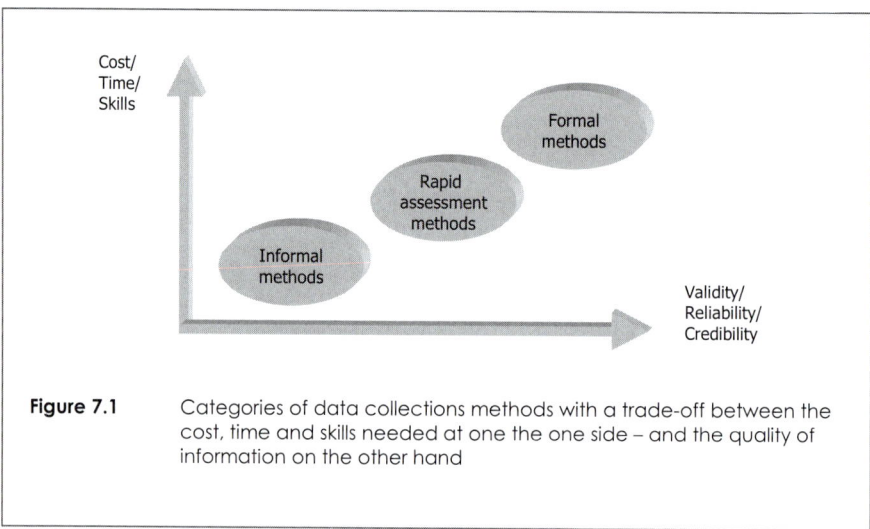

Figure 7.1 Categories of data collections methods with a trade-off between the cost, time and skills needed at one the one side – and the quality of information on the other hand

Data collection methods can be ranged according to their demand in terms of cost, time and methodological skills. On one side are the *informal* methods such as casual conversation and unstructured site visits. There are no precise procedures and the outcome relies to a larger extent on experience, intuition and subjective judgement. Such methods are not suitable for generating systematic information, since personal opinion and biases often affect validity and reliability.

Formal methods, on the other side, have clearly defined procedures from the outset, as for instance censuses or statistically representative surveys. The results will normally be qualitative or quantitative information with a high degree of validity and reliability, but typically are expensive and time consuming and require extensive technical skills.

In between the formal and the informal methods is a range of so-called *rapid assessment* methods, such as key informant interviews, focus group, group interviews, direct observation and informal surveys. These maintain a reasonable level of precision without being dependent on very time-consuming procedures to collect and analyse large amounts of data. The trade-off between these types of methods is illustrated in figure 7.1.

Which method is most appropriate in a given situation depends on the expected level of precision and credibility, versus the practical constraints of cost, time and skills available. Generally speaking, evaluation of impact will often require formal methods, while a combination of less formal methods may be more appropriate when assessing performance.

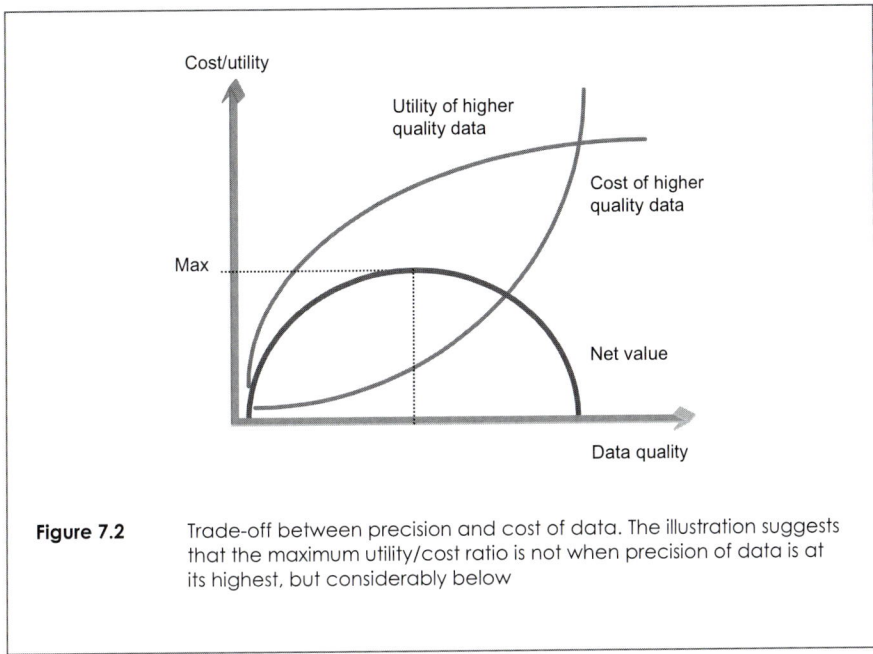

Figure 7.2 Trade-off between precision and cost of data. The illustration suggests that the maximum utility/cost ratio is not when precision of data is at its highest, but considerably below

In project evaluation, the most frequently used data collection method is interviews with key informants. This will inevitably produce subjectively biased information that will have to be verified. The evaluator therefore has a need for supplementary methods that maintain a reasonable level of precision without being time-consuming and expensive. The quality of information, especially in terms of validity and reliability, should be a main concern for the evaluator. If the expected degree of precision is low, the evaluator may simultaneously employ various methods and sources of information in order to cross-validate data (triangulation). In the report, particular mention needs to be made of the choice of instruments and any limitations due to the quality of data and the analysis.

Evaluators will have to decide on a trade-off between precision and cost of information. As a rule we assume that the cost increases sharply when precision increases, as illustrated in figure 7.2. The utility of information, however, does not increase correspondingly with precision but is expected only to increase marginally as precision becomes high. The maximum utility/cost ratio will therefore most likely be when precision is still quite limited.

Below is a list of commonly used data collection methods, ranged from informal, inexpensive methods to precise, formal but expensive methods, with a notion of some of their key features. In chapters 7.2 – 7.10 the methods are discussed in more detail.

Chapter 7 – Data Collection Methods

 Data collection methods

1. EXISTING DATA — Examination of documents both of a general nature and related to the specific case under study. Economic and efficient way of obtaining information. Difficult to assess validity and reliability on secondary data

2. KEY INFORMANT INTERVIEWS — Flexible, in-depth approach. Easy to implement. Useful for idea-generation and verification. Risk of biased presentation and interpretation from informants/interviewer.

3. DIRECT MEASUREMENT — Registration of quantifiable or classifiable data by means of analytical instrument. Precise, reliable and often requiring few resources. Registers only facts, not explanations.

4. DIRECT OBSERVATION — Involves inspection, field visits, and observation to understand processes, infrastructure/services and their utilisation. Suited for providing insight and context. Dependent on observer's understanding and interpretation.

5. FOCUS GROUP — For analysis of specific, complex problems, to identify attitudes and priorities in smaller groups. Reasonable in terms of cost, and efficient. Stimulates the generation of new ideas. Risk of one-sidedness on the part of participants and the moderator.

6. INFORMAL SURVEY — Involves quantitative surveys of small samples. Extensive use of non-probability sampling procedures. Reasonable and rapid. Risk of sampling errors/biases. Less suited for generalisation.

7. CASE STUDIES — In-depth review of one or a small number of selected cases. Well-suited for understanding processes and for formulating hypotheses to be tested later. Can yield comprehensive, highly detailed information but with limited potential for generalisation.

8. EXTENSIVE OBSERVATION — In-depth observations over an extended period of time. Participatory or non-participatory. Well-suited for understanding processes but with limited potential for generalisation

9. FORMAL SURVEY — Oral interviews or written questionnaires in a statistically representative sample of respondents. Data collection is demanding but often produces reliable information

7.2 USING EXISTING INFORMATION

The evaluator needs to make the best use of previous work in the field being studied, and hence to learn from the experiences, findings and mistakes of those who have carried out similar or related work in the past.

The first source of information would be general research reports, databases, and relevant papers and books. By reviewing these documents, models, hypotheses and issues related to the project can be explored, and generalizations that might apply to the issues under consideration can be examined. Such a search may identify other evaluation questions and relevant methodological issues, and lead to new approaches that might make the study more effective or suggest potential methodological problems to be avoided. As an example, a past research project studying industrial efficiency suggests that there are major differences based on the size of firm. This would imply that any sampling procedure used in the evaluation should include representation from all sizes of firms (via stratified sampling), in order to be better able to generalize the evaluation results.

A second source of information would be specific studies pertaining to the project under study, as well as past evaluations. This information can provide input and valid data into various components of the evaluation study.

The third source of information would be a file review aimed at discovering what secondary data exist that could be used in the evaluation. A file review focuses on the specific project being evaluated. Data already collected about the project and its results can be selected and used directly in the evaluation. Gaps in available data can be identified and primary collection methods used to complete the picture. As with any secondary data collection method, the aim is to reduce the need for new primary data.

There are usually two types of files: general project files and files on individual project components or activities, clients and other stakeholders. File reviews typically cover the following types of program documents:

- Planning documents, agreements and Memorandum of Understanding between main stakeholders, multi-annual operational plans, auditor's reports, and minutes of executive meetings
- Administrative records, budgetary and cost data, progress reports, market information, personnel data, risk assessments, data from monitoring systems, information on project impact, etc.

File data may commonly be retained form the project's management information system or be collected specifically by management for the purpose of the evaluation according to an agreed evaluation framework.

Existing data

THE METHOD IS MOST SUITABLE

- To provide quick and cost-effective input of information during the early design and assessment phase of an evaluation
- As a source for hypotheses and preliminary conclusions to be tasted during evaluation
- To identify methodological difficulties at an early stage
- To provide essential background data and information of project performance and achievements and to put project results in context

♦

IMPORTANT TO BEAR IN MIND

- Sources of secondary data may be uncovered which lessen the need to collect more expensive primary data.
- Even when secondary data cannot directly provide the answer to the evaluation question, they might be used with primary data as input to the evaluation strategy, or as benchmark data for a validity check.
- The weaknesses of the data from a literature search are those associated with the inherent nature of secondary data; the data are generated for a purpose other than the specific evaluation issues at hand.
- More often than not, a central filing system is relegated to a secondary position, containing brief memos from meetings, agendas of final decisions, etc., which, in retrospect, tell an incomplete story.
- The accuracy of secondary data is often difficult to determine

7.3 KEY INFORMANT INTERVIEWS

This is the method used extensively in evaluation work. The main advantage is that it provides an inexpensive quick and efficient means of gaining deeper insights into concrete questions and issues. Moreover it is flexible: the interviewer may take up a variety of issues through the choice of informants and through questions that can yield insight on matters outside the planning framework as such - e.g. concerning unforeseen impacts of a project.

The selection of key informants is important. They should be individuals who, through their position or role, know a lot about the subject under study. To avoid bias it is important to include informants representing the interests of various stakeholders. It is essential to also include those directly affected by the project. This can be done by listing all affected groups and select a certain number of informants from each group.

Interviews with key informants require thorough preparation. An interview schedule should be prepared in advance, and the same questions put to representatives of different interest-groups. Interviews should as much as possible refer to specific, existing information, which the informant can then add to, explain or comment on.

The main limitations of this method lie in the danger of a biased selection of informants, which will impair the validity of the results. A further danger is that the data obtained may be of low reliability as a result of biased interpretation on the part of the interviewer. It is also obvious that the method cannot be used in cases where there is a need to generate quantitative data.

Key informant interview

THE METHOD IS MOST SUITABLE	❑ For producing general, descriptive information
	❑ For yielding insight into motives and attitudes of different parties
	❑ For interpreting available quantitative data
	❑ For eliciting suggestions and recommendations
	❑ For developing questions, hypotheses and proposals for later testing and elaboration
IMPORTANT TO BEAR IN MIND	❑ Informants should be selected on the basis of role, function or special insights
	❑ Major interest groups should be represented
	❑ Interviews need to be prepared so as to confront informants with actual substantive knowledge and practical experience
	❑ Interviews should be conducted in an open, informal atmosphere
	❑ As new information is gained, it can be useful to confront informants again during the course of the evaluation work
	❑ The interviewer should take detailed notes from the interviews
	❑ The criteria used in selecting informants should be specified in the report

7.4 DIRECT MEASUREMENTS

Direct measurement is an important way to obtain exact information which can be placed within a larger context and contribute to overall verification.

Direct measurement will often be linked to physical phenomena or processes, involving specific instruments to measure weight, temperature, volume, speed, density, etc. In other cases the measuring device may be conceptual e.g. in the form of well-defined categories. Frequently measurement will be connected to an indicator, which provides information on something else than the focus of the measurement as such - for instance, education as a measure of skills or expenditure as a measure of progress.

It is usual to distinguish four levels of measurement:

- The nominal level - units are grouped into mutually exclusive categories (e.g. gender, nationality)
- The ordinal level - units are grouped into mutually exclusive categories ranked according to certain criteria (e.g. varying degrees of attitude held)
- The interval level - rank-ordered units with a given yardstick that enables measurement of the distance between the various units (e.g. economic costs)
- The ratio level - as with the interval level, but with the addition of a zero point in the quantification e.g. age, temperature).

Well-calibrated direct measurement methods will usually yield highly accurate data, free from personal bias or errors of interpretation. Such data can help the evaluator in assessing the quality of information gathered by other methods. If new measurement techniques or instruments are to be used, it is important to pre-test them first, to determine their validity and reliability.

Evaluators often tend to select instruments more advanced than is strictly necessary. The results are then out of proportion to the cost of the instrument and the affiliated costs - for instance, the cost of training personnel to use them. It is often possible to use less advanced measuring devices with a lower degree of precision and considerably lower costs, and still achieve acceptable results.

In making broad, overall assessments, for instance, it is often more important to define central main categories (nominal level) than to quantify these (ratio level).

Direct measurement

THE METHOD IS MOST SUITABLE	❑ For obtaining quantitative data on physical phenomena or processes
	❑ For controlling direct or indirect indicators which are measurable
	❑ In cases where results can be systematically graded or classified
	♦
IMPORTANT TO BEAR IN MIND	❑ Cost and complexity of measurement must be weighed against probable returns, before measurement is started
	❑ New measuring techniques must be pre-tested to determine validity and reliability
	❑ Most measurement techniques require trained personnel to employ them
	❑ The purpose of undertaking measurement, and the use of the instrument, should be explained to those affected
	❑ The methods employed, as well as probable margins of error, must be specified in the report

7.5 DIRECT OBSERVATION

Direct observation is a systematic informal method. It presupposes the use of an instrument - e.g. in the form of checklists or observation record forms. In many cases, interviews will also be conducted. Whatever the instrument, the number of observations required should be specified; likewise the procedures followed for obtaining information free of bias which would mean low validity and reliability. When possible, observation should yield quantitative data.

Direct observation should not be confused with participant observation. The latter is frequently employed in ethnographic and anthropological studies; it is characterised by the investigator being present for a longer period in the setting under study, for instance in order to understand social and cultural phenomena, see chapter 7.10.

Direct observation is fundamental to all types of investigations. Study of phenomena in their natural surroundings makes it possible for the researcher to gain a more comprehensive understanding of conditions, as well as enabling the verification of other data. Direct observation can often reveal conditions or patterns of behaviour which key informants may be unaware of, or incapable of describing adequately.

One problem in using this method is that the analysis hinges on the observer's ability to understand what is observed, so-called "observer bias". Such bias can be minimised by using several independent observers, all with enough background knowledge and experience to employ this method.

Furthermore, the units under observation have to be representative of the wider population under study; moreover, it must be borne in mind that the very act of observation can affect the behaviour of the people and organisations being studied, resulting in incorrect information.

Direct observation

THE METHOD IS MOST SUITABLE	❏ For providing information on physical phenomena
	❏ For collecting information on the suitability and use of public and private services, infra-structure, etc.
	❏ For eliciting preliminary, descriptive information
	❏ For understanding phenomena, processes and how things are organised and carried out

IMPORTANT TO BEAR IN MIND	❏ Whatever is to be observed (a sample, a phenomenon or a process) should be representative of the whole population or subject in question
	❏ Observation should be systematic, with check-lists, observation record forms, etc.
	❏ Systematic errors can be avoided by using several independent observers
	❏ Observers should have a thorough grounding in the subject under study
	❏ Possible "observation bias" should be taken into consideration: i.e. that observation can in itself influence what is being observed"

7.6 FOCUS GROUP INTERVIEW

With smaller groups of resource persons - up to 8-12 participants - focus group interviewing can be an efficient method for generating information. In such a group setting, participants provide mutual stimulation, so more can be achieved in the course of a few hours than by conducting far more lengthy individual interviews.

In focus group interviews, discussion centres on specific topics. In evaluation work, it may be fruitful to use focus group interviews to discuss matters relating to the design and implementation of projects. The method is also well suited for eliciting information on the impacts - both foreseen and unforeseen - of a project.

To enable an open exchange of views, the group should not be composed of individuals with too highly diverging interests in the topic under discussion. Any bias should be compensated by checking, verification or using this method with participants from other interest groups as well.

Focus group interviews is a demanding method that requires a moderator experienced in conducting group discussions, using visualisation techniques, managing group dynamics, etc. The moderator needs to remain strictly neutral, but should also have a thorough understanding of the subject to be discussed.

Participants in such group discussions cannot be expected to reveal information on attitudes and behaviour they would not wish to discuss openly. A further problem that may affect the validity of results is that the discussion may reflect social norms rather than actual behaviour, precisely because the participants are responding "in public". This underscores the need to obtain supplementary information, e.g. through individual interviews.

As with individual interviews, there is also the danger that the moderator may misinterpret the information (investigator bias), which will mean uncertain reliability. A further problem is that the discussion may be dominated by one or a few especially articulate participants with a non-typical perspective. And like in-depth interviews, focus group interviews cannot provide quantifiable data.

Focus group interview

THE METHOD IS MOST SUITABLE

- For generating ideas and hypotheses for later analysis
- For eliciting reactions to various suggestions and recommendations
- For getting explanations of the group's choices and priorities
- For the analysis of complex, composite problem-areas
- For achieving agreement on conclusions and recommendations

IMPORTANT TO BEAR IN MIND

- Group should be homogeneous in terms of interests, and limited to 8-12 participants
- Group discussions should be conducted by an experienced moderator who is responsible for keeping the discussion focused
- Visualisation techniques may be used to advantage
- The moderator needs to remain neutral, but should be knowledgeable on the topic under discussion
- The focus should be on one topic at a time. It is desirable to try for consensus before going on to the next topic
- Detailed notes should be taken

7.7 INFORMAL SURVEY

Formal surveys based on probability sampling are often comprehensive and time-consuming. Less formal surveys can also be employed to yield quantitative data, on a smaller scale and based on only a few variables to save time and resources.

Instead of a large, representative probability sample, this method often uses quota sampling: the population is classified into categories - on the basis of characteristics, attitudes, roles, etc. - and respondents are selected from each category

This method will often place greater demands on the interviewer; on the other hand, it also permits greater flexibility, as the interviewer can ask questions not pre-specified in the questionnaire, as well as making observations.

A main advantage of informal surveys is that the method can generate quantitative information in cases where it may be difficult or inadvisable to undertake comprehensive probability sampling. Moreover, informal surveys can be conducted in a short-time, using limited personnel and economic resources. If the interviewers are few in number and work well together, using relatively few questions, the result will normally be fewer errors in data collection and qualitatively better data than in large sample surveys.

On the other hand, because probability sampling is not used, informal surveys are susceptible to sampling biases. The results will not be suitable for complex statistical analysis. The number of questions is kept to a minimum to shed light on a specific pre-determined problem-area; this method is not appropriate for providing in-depth insights and information. Other methods would have to be used in conjunction if a more intensive understanding is required.

As noted in chapter 7.1, formal surveys should be the final resort in data collection, as they demand greater resources than other, less formal techniques, as well as being more rigid by testing pre-determined problems and questions only. A natural approach would be to use focus group interviews and other interviews as well as observation at an earlier stage in order to generate hypotheses, to ensure that the questions posed in a more formal survey are meaningful and central to the subject under study.

Informal survey

THE METHOD IS MOST SUITABLE

- For generating quantitative information on a relatively homogeneous group - e.g. on attitudes, opinions and reactions
- In cases when it would be too time-consuming and expensive to use a representative probability sample
- For supplementing existing quantitative information

♦

IMPORTANT TO BEAR IN MIND

- The survey should build on pre-studies and existing knowledge of the subject in question
- The number of questions should be limited to 10-20
- The number of respondents should also be limited, usually to 30-50
- Before undertaking the actual survey, the questionnaire should be pre-tested on a smaller sample
- Interviewers should be well-versed in the subject under study as well as being experienced in using this method
- Sampling criteria and any limitations resulting from the selection must be specified in the report

7.8 CASE STUDY

When a project is made up of a series of components or cases, it might be useful to undertake special case studies. Also, when there are special topics that should be given special attention, or if one needs an example to illustrate a certain phenomenon it might be useful to do case studies.

The purpose of case studies is to explore something through in-depth, rather than broad, coverage. Unlike the data collection techniques discussed so far, a case study usually involves a combination of the various data collection methods discussed in this chapter. Case studies are usually chosen when it is impossible, for budgetary or practical reasons, to choose a sample large enough to be statistically representative to the population as a whole, or when in-depth data are required.

A case study commonly examines a number of specific cases, which the evaluator anticipates will be revealing about the project as a whole. Thus, selecting appropriate cases becomes a crucial step. The evaluator might choose to take a small sample of those cases that are felt to be *representative* of the population as a whole. Generalization of the results to the entire population based on a sample of cases would then be only as valid as the validity of the assumption that the results of one case will hold for a number of other similar cases. This is a strong assumption, and one that is very susceptible to questioning and doubts. Thus the credibility of any conclusions reached may be affected. In most case studies, however, the sample is chosen in a non-systematic manner (or too few are selected) for statistical generalizations to be made.

Alternatively, a case may be chosen because it is considered a *critical* example, perhaps the purported best case. If a critical case turned out badly, the effectiveness of the whole project might be seriously questioned, regardless of the performance of other cases. The critical case may be more defensible than the case study with a representative sample. It can illustrate a valid and important phenomenon that is essential to understand a project but does not purport to be representative.

Case studies are usually used in evaluation less for specific measurement than for insight into how the project operated, and why things happened as they did. The in-depth analysis possible with case studies usually requires significant resources and time, limiting the number that can be carried out. It is usually recommended that case studies be carried out before (or at least parallel with) other, more generalizable, data collection procedures.

Case studies

THE METHOD IS MOST SUITABLE	❑ To explore the multiple consequences of a project
	❑ To add sensitivity to the context in which the project actions are taken
	❑ To identify relevant "intervening variables"
	❑ To estimate project consequences over the long term
	❑ To generate explanatory hypotheses for further analysis
	♦
IMPORTANT TO BEAR IN MIND	❑ They are not normally expected to provide results that are statistically generalizable.
	❑ Case studies often allow the evaluator to go into a depth of analysis beyond what would be possible with other approaches
	❑ Case studies could be expensive and time-consuming
	❑ Case studies should usually be carried out before applying other more formal data collection methods

7.9 EXTENSIVE OBSERVATION

Observation is an essential aspect of all methods of data collection. Also in using more formal methods, we will always receive additional information on the surroundings, people's reactions, etc.

Observation is the least structured of the methods described here. A basic distinction is made between participant observation - a method much used by anthropologists - and non-participant observation, which is much used e.g. in medicine and the educational sector.

Participant observation means that the observer takes part as a member of the institutional or social system to be studied. Since this type of study is conducted over a longer period of time, it is possible to lower the risk of the observation as such becoming a source of error in relation to what is being registered.

The advantage of this approach is first and foremost that it can provide in-depth information of high quality. Factual conditions are registered, but in addition there is a wealth of background information, which can help to explain what is observed. For this reason, it is often held that this method should be employed at an early stage, when evaluations projects are being planned.

In evaluation work, this method will be particularly valuable for mapping any unforeseen impacts at the level of the individual or the local community, and for expanding the perspectives drawn up in formulating a project.

On the negative side, the method is very time-consuming. In connection with evaluation, it therefore seems most natural to use it in pre-studies, to explore any unexpected impacts and uncertainties that might influence the outcome of a project. Participant observation can prove relatively costly in the short term. Seen in a longer-term perspective, however, it may build up is a reservoir of experience that can be drawn on later, and thus the use of resources may be justified.

This is a demanding method, where the quality of the results will depend on the observer's experience, skill and objectivity. Personal opinions and the inability to understand what is happening can be major sources of error. Personal characteristics of the observer will frequently influence what information is made assessable.

In order to reduce such possible sources of error, several observers can be used, and information can be collected from various informants in the same position and with similar roles. It is also important to use resources on the interpretation of information, and to compare with information obtained through other methods. Frequently it will be appropriate to discuss the results with representatives of the stakeholders under study - for instance, by means of focus-group interviews, see chapter 7.6.

Extensive observation

THE METHOD IS MOST SUITABLE

- To gain deeper insight into socio-economic conditions, processes and patterns of behaviour
- When there is a need for background knowledge to enable interpretation of existing data gathered by other methods
- To study unforeseen effects and processes not taken into consideration when the project was formulated
- To avoid that the actual collection of data influence on the quality of the data

IMPORTANT TO BEAR IN MIND

- Observation is a time-consuming method; work must be started early so that results will be available when they are needed
- At an early stage, consideration must be given to whether the observer's presence represents an important source of error
- The use of several independent informants and observers can help to correct possible mis-information
- Ample time should be set aside for discussing and interpreting the results
- Further error-correction can be achieved by discussing the results with those who have been under study, e.g. through focus-group interviews

7.10 FORMAL SURVEY

Formal surveys are used to produce precise, quantitative information (at the individual level) on the basis of standardised questionnaires. This method places considerable demands as to resources, so with a large population it is common to limit the survey to a sample that is, e.g., statistically representative of the entire population, in order to keep costs down. As a general rule, comprehensive surveys ought to be one of the last data-collection methods to be employed, after more reasonable and flexible approaches have been used to identify major issue-areas, establish hypotheses, etc.

It has been usual to employ this method with "baseline" studies in mapping out conditions in a population before a project is started. Formal surveys are also used in connection with retrospective studies of a control group, or with time-series studies.

The main advantage lies in the possibility of obtaining precise data that can be used as a basis for generalisations.

On the other hand, this is a highly demanding approach - in terms of preparations, training of interviewers, fieldwork and data analysis. If several interviewers are used, this will increase the possibility of errors; thus, it is essential that all interviewers receive thorough training, and that the questions to be asked are clear and unambiguous.

Furthermore, the quality of the information obtained also is highly dependent on the composition of the sample. Special attention must be paid to including all relevant groups - and not excluding those that may be geographically or socially less easily accessible.

Formal survey

THE METHOD IS MOST SUITABLE
- When there is a need for precise, generalizable, quantitative information
- When it is not possible or appropriate to include the entire population
- When the aim is to map the extent of variation or deviation in a population
- When there is a need to test hypotheses or stereotyped opinions in a quantitative manner

IMPORTANT TO BEAR IN MIND
- Formulating a meaningful survey presupposes a solid foundation of knowledge about local socio-cultural conditions
- Thorough training of interviewers is important, to reduce the number of errors in registration and interpretation
- Questionnaires must be pre-tested, to control for possible ambiguity, whether questions are understood in the same way, and whether they cover all aspects of what is to be studied
- In sampling, care must be taken to ensure that all relevant groups are included, also those that are less easily accessible
- In the report, sampling criteria and methods must be explained, and mention made of any statistical limitations that apply to the sample

CHAPTER 8

ENSURING QUALITY

IN THE ROOM PEOPLE COME AND GO, TALKING OF MICHELANGELO.
T.S.ELIOT

8.1 KNOWLEDGE AND EVIDENCE

The lowest level of understanding is based on conviction. This is interpreted as an understanding based on belief, authority or common opinion that is maintained in the absence of evidence to alter the point of view. This type of knowledge is not necessarily false but we don't know whether it is or not.

A higher level of knowledge is based on intuition. Here, reason in terms of logic or common sense is the criterion of truth. The problem arises when different persons arrive at different conclusions on the basis of the same evidence.

The highest level of knowledge is based on science. It is based on systematic inquiry where self-correction is applied to improve the body of knowledge in face of new evidence, as a cumulative process.

Evaluation is not scientific research, nor is it hearsay. But it is systematic inquiry in combination with logic aimed to raise awareness of the project or process in question to a higher level of knowledge and understanding. However, available time and resources are usually severely restricted. Both researchers and evaluators strive to maximise the use of factual information to the extent possible and generate statistical evidence when feasible. However, also where formal data collection methods are applied, the quality of information may vary, as described in chapter 7.

A weakness in evaluation is that it in varying degree has to rely on judgemental "evidence" that commonly is derived from three different sources:

1. **Experts' assessments,** where experts with particular insight in the topic under study are employed to render a judgement. These may be aided by the use of generic controls in terms of existing estimates, or be based on more or less educated guesses of what would be normal progress, or benchmarks.

2. **Managers' assessment,** where managers responsible for implementation are asked to estimate impact. Because of their obvious interest in making their efforts appear successful, such judgements are far from impartial and could overestimate impact as compared with empirical evidence.

3. **Users' assessment,** where the target group is asked to judge the effect of an intervention. Such judgements may have some validity, but is frequently confounded by the respondents' lack of knowledge for making such judgements.

The problem described in chapter 6.5 was that of low validity and reliability of information, as the result of a quite primitive research design. Reliance on judgemental information will clearly add to this problem. The remedy or the preferred approach used in evaluation to secure the quality of information is *triangulation.* This means to compensate the use of simple data collection methods and a simple study design with the use of several information sources and different methods simultaneously to generate information about the same topics, see chapter 8.5.

Evaluation is a type of 'research light' that takes an interdisciplinary approach to generate an overall understanding of a complex phenomenon. It combines quantitative and qualitative analysis and strive to uncover reliable and valid evidence when confronted with conflicting or inaccurate information, subjective bias and prejudice, likes and dislikes, rules of thumb, analogy and deceit.

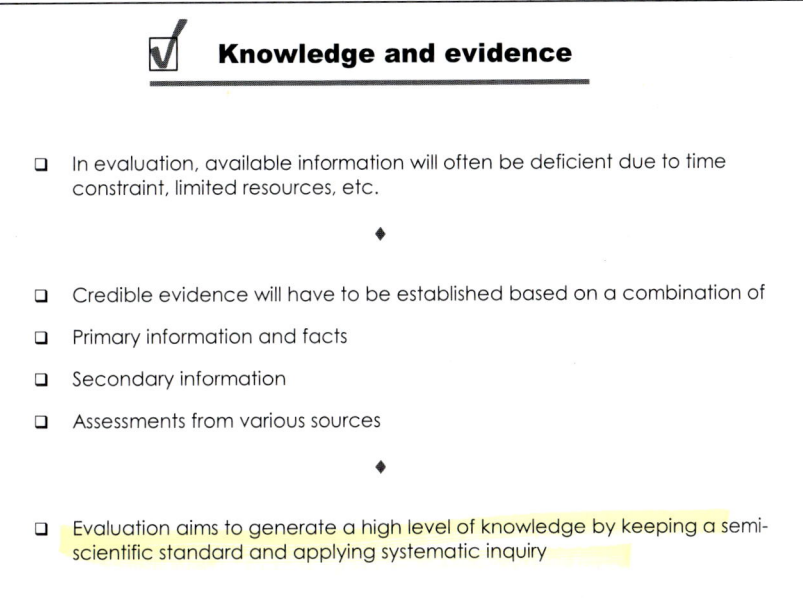

8.2 QUALITY OF INFORMATION

The international community of evaluators have over several years developed what is now regarded as a common standard of what constitutes quality in evaluations. There is no system of professional certification of evaluation or evaluators, anywhere in the world, which institutionalises rules and quality criteria. This book attempts to provide elements of an operational standard that can be applied in practice. It takes as its point of departure what is now regarded the four commonly agreed quality criteria in evaluations: *utility, feasibility, propriety* and *accuracy*. However, these are described only in qualitative terms, and there are no quantifiable norms attached to them. The aim is to encourage useful, feasible, ethical and sound evaluation based on what can be considered best practise among evaluators. Below is an interpretation of these terms.

Utility

This is the issue of serving the users' information needs. It should guide evaluations so that they will be informative, timely and influential. Evaluations must be useful. If they are not, they are a waste of money. It is those who have commissioned the evaluation, who have the main responsibility to make sure that the exercise is useful. But utility also requires that evaluators acquaint themselves with their audiences, define the respondents and users clearly, ascertain their information needs, plan the evaluation to respond to these needs, and report relevant information clearly and timely. This is discussed in chapter 2 in more detail.

Feasibility

This is the issue of being realistic, practical, cost-effective and diplomatic. It recognises that evaluations are conducted in a natural setting and not under laboratory conditions. A main concern in evaluation is to learn about the factors causing success or failure of particular project. Feasibility requires that evaluators focus both on what can be learned from successes and failures, and present both types of findings in a manner that reflects the situation under study. Evaluations should be critical, but criticism should be constructive. The purpose is not to attribute praise and blame to individuals. Also, evaluations require valuable resources. Therefore the evaluation design must be operable in field settings. Evaluations should not consume more resources, material, personnel or time than necessary to adequately address the evaluation questions. This is discussed in more detail in chapter 4.

Propriety

This is the issue of legal and ethical conduct, with regard to those involved and affected. It reflects the fact that evaluations affect many people in a variety of ways. It concerns the protection of the rights of individuals affected by an evaluation, and warns against unlawful, unethical and incompetent action by those.

Accuracy

This is the issue of producing trustworthy, valid and reliable information. An evaluation is a selective investigation aimed at collecting and analysing data, formulating observations and making recommendations of practical relevance to the stakeholders. The evaluation team has the primary responsibility to make sure that the evaluation confirms with high accuracy standards. The accuracy standard determines whether the evaluation has produced sound information. It suggests that the evaluation should be comprehensive; that is, evaluators should consider as many features as is practical in a given case and should gather data on those features that are considered important for assessing the worth and merit of the project under study.

These four attributes are regarded necessary and sufficient for sound and fair evaluation. The attributes relate to each other. An evaluation that is not feasible is not likely to yield accurate conclusions, and conclusions that are not accurate are not likely to be used. Similarly, an evaluation that is conducted according to high standards of propriety will generally have higher utility than one with shortcomings in these respects.

Evaluation is supposed to be a practical tool – and not scientific research. However, the quality standard for evaluations is based on standards for research. It is the evaluator's responsibility to strike a balance between precision and available resources – so that the result is quality for the users.

✓ Evaluation standard

1. **UTILITY** — To ensure that an evaluation will serve the information needs of intended users.

2. **FEASIBILITY** — To ensure that an evaluation will be realistic, prudent, diplomatic, and frugal.

3. **PROPRIETY** — To ensure that an evaluation will be conducted legally, ethically, and with due regard for the welfare of those involved in the evaluation, as well as those affected by its results

4. **ACCURACY** — To ensure that an evaluation will reveal and convey technically adequate information about the features that determine worth or merit of the program being evaluated

(American Evaluation Association)

8.3 SECURING VALIDITY AND RELIABILITY

Any evaluation report should describe the methods and sources of data used. Similarly, the limits of the methods and data should also be clearly described, for the report to be accepted. One should make sure that the methods are described in enough detail to assess *reliability* of data, and that *validity* of data and the tools used are clearly indicated and discussed.

Because causal analysis of effects is essential in evaluations, the methods used to analyse such relationships is a priority. *Reliability* is essentially a question of whether or not the instruments used to measure are accurate. *Validity* is a question of whether we measure what we intend to measure. Consider a thermometer placed in pure boiling water at 1 atmosphere pressure. If it repeatedly reads 90 ºC, the data are reliable – but not valid. If the readings differ, say between 98 ºC and 102 ºC, the data are valid - but not reliable.

Reliability

The quality of information is poor if relationships and conditions it represents are subject to variations that it does not capture. Information is *reliable* if the measurement procedure yields the same results if applied repeatedly. In other words, that the evaluation instrument with a degree of confidence can ensure that the measurement results correctly represent empirical relationships. This means that the simple process of repeating measurement under the same or similar conditions can be used to test reliability.

Making sure that the evaluation instrument is unambiguous, so that different persons interpret and use the instrument in the same way ensures reliability. Clearly, to ensure reliability is important for instance in surveys where different persons are involved as enumerators, or in a monitoring where the same type of information will be registered by different persons over a period of years.

> An IQ-test administered in English to a group of French students would probably give reliable results when repeated. But the validity would be uncertain – it would probably be a test of language proficiency rather that their IQ.

Validity

A fundamental aspect of information quality is the extent to which it corresponds to what we want to measure. Validity is the closeness or fit between an intellectual construct and the things we measure empirically.

Ensuring *validity* in evaluation is not easy, since social concepts are often multi-dimensional. One specific measure might emphasise one dimension at the expense of another: for instance per capita net income as a measure of economic welfare as opposed to family or gross income.

Validity cannot be verified or tested directly, but will have to be based on the evaluator's judgement. However, validity can often be improved by using several different measures, information sources of methods for the same phenomenon. This is discussed in chapter 8.5. Ensuring validity also requires that the evaluation instruments are checked as to whether the evaluation questions correspond to the evaluation criterion being focused.

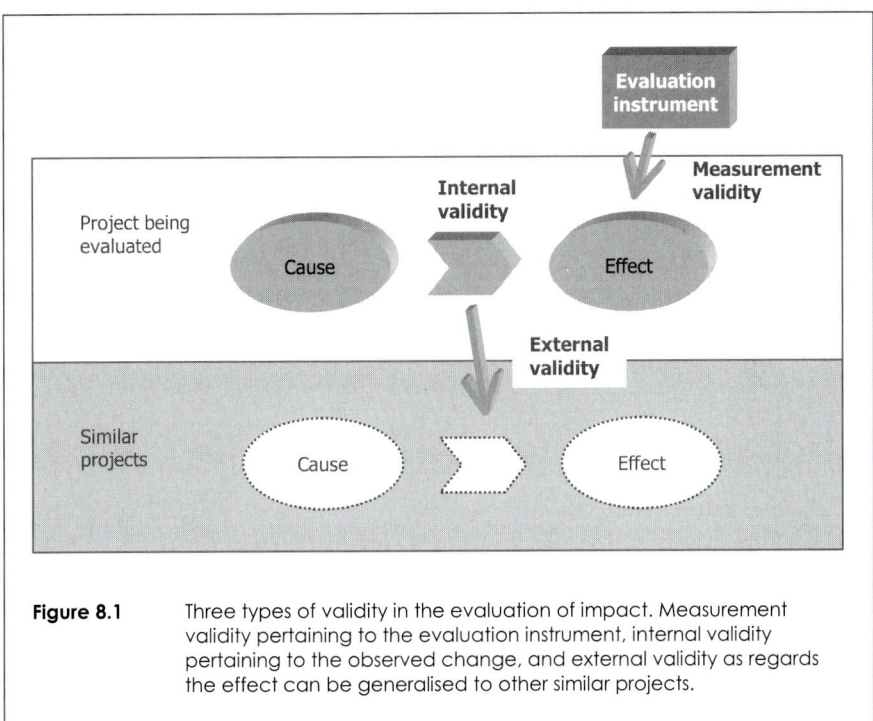

Figure 8.1   Three types of validity in the evaluation of impact. Measurement validity pertaining to the evaluation instrument, internal validity pertaining to the observed change, and external validity as regards the effect can be generalised to other similar projects.

In impact assessments it is common to distinguish between measurement validity, internal validity and external validity as illustrated above.

Measurement validity means that the evaluation instrument is capable of measuring the observed changes. In a project to develop computer software, for instance, that the indicators to measure customers' satisfaction actually focus on effects related to the use of the program and not on effects that might have other causes. This requires that the impact be expressed in sufficiently precise terms, and that observations in the field are strictly coherent with what has to be measured.

Internal validity is established when the evaluation team reaches an indisputable conclusion as to the effect that is caused by the project. In the project to develop computer software, for instance that certain operations are performed more accurately with the new software. This type of conclusion requires that collection and analysis of data have taken into account all key characteristics of the improvement.

External validity is established when it can be concluded with confidence that conclusions regarding impact in one particular case can be generalised to other projects. In the software project, for instance that improvements are attributable to the software and not to particularly favourable conditions in the case studied, such as motivation or training. External validity is difficult to assert and will need to be based on evidence from several cases. To establish external validity is clearly of great value in a context where several projects apply similar methods.

✓ Validity and reliability

VALIDITY	❏ The extent to which the information measures what it is intended to measure.
	❏ Validity is ensured:
	❏ By choice of types of indicators
	❏ By providing the most direct possible measure
	❏ By using several indicators which combine to give a good indication of what is to be measured
RELIABILITY	❏ Consistency or dependability of data, with reference to the quality of the instrument or procedure used to collect data.
	❏ Information is reliable when repeated observations using the same instrument under identical conditions produce similar results.
	❏ Reliability is ensured:
	❏ By the indicator being unambiguous
	❏ By testing that repeated use of the same instrument will yield identical results

8.4 SECURING CREDIBILITY

Credibility is a prerequisite for evaluation findings to be used. Hence the requirements that evaluation to the extent possible should be objective and impartial.

Securing *objectivity* is to a large extent a question of the quality of what is presented as factual information. This depends on the resources available, how the evaluation research is designed, and the methods used to collect and analyse data. This is discussed in some detail in chapter 6 and 7. In addition, objectivity requires that facts are not confused with judgement. The purpose of evaluation is exactly to make value judgement based on facts, and the two must be clearly separated, as discussed in chapter 6.4.

> - By objectivity is meant making a clear distinction between value judgement and statements of fact, and ensuring that the statements of fact are based on reliable methods of observation and interference.
> - Impartiality is observed by making sure that differences in perspectives between stakeholders in the activities under review are promptly taken into account in the planning, implementation and reporting of an evaluation. Impartiality also requires the evaluation to give a fair and balanced view of the strengths and weaknesses of the activities evaluated.

Securing *impartiality* is to a large extent a question of allowing different stakeholders to be equally heard in the evaluation. With multiple stakeholders conflicts of interests are common. All projects have their supporters and critics. It is not possible for the evaluator to please everyone. Whatever the findings of an evaluation, they will be welcomed by some groups and rejected by others. The situation can be particularly difficult when the results do not confirm the expectations of those who commissioned the evaluation and have vested interests in the outcome.

The immediate answers to these problems is firstly to make sure that conflicts between the different stakeholder perspectives are openly acknowledged and not ignored, because there is a danger of evaluation findings being discounted if there is any misunderstanding among the participating groups. Second, the various stakeholders should be allowed to make some input into the evaluation design process. Third, there is the importance of maintaining contact with the participating groups throughout the course of the evaluation.

There is no doubt that all evaluations are a potential arena for conflict. Therefore, persons who prefer to avoid controversy or have difficulty facing criticism should not be used as evaluators. Also, the entire setting suggests that evaluators should be external to the project and the stakeholders involved. This would help ensure impartiality and objectivity, and illustrated in the table below.

This type of objectivity has a cost. As discussed earlier, the evaluation also represents a unique learning arena for project managers and others in involved organisations. Involving internal staff would also make it more likely that the evaluation is internalised and used.

Internal and external evaluators

INTERNAL EVALUATORS

ADVANTAGES
- Familiar with the project, its history, setting, etc.
- Committed to use results
- Focus on key management concerns

DISADVANTAGES
- Over-influenced by history
- May be biased
- Less committed to the evaluation

◆

EXTERNAL EVALUATORS

ADVANTAGES
- Impartial, independent, fresh view
- Unbiased, critical approach
- Experience with similar cases

DISADVANTAGES
- Insensitive to internal matters
- Can be mislead by key stakeholders
- Responsible to external organisation

8.5 TRIANGULATION TO ESTABLISH FACTS

Evaluations frequently probe into a setting where there are many stakeholders with different interests and different access to information. Data may be uncertain because of conflicting interests, extensive use of secondary data, etc., and therefore need to be verified and validated. This is why evaluators increasingly adopt diverse methods in tackling evaluation problems. This is called *triangulation*. By combining several analysts, theories, methods and data sources, evaluators hope to overcome the bias that comes from single-methods, single-observer, and single-theory studies.

Types of triangulation

- **Methods**: using multiple methods to study a single problem
- **Data**: using a variety of data sources in a study
- **Analyst**: using several different evaluators to review findings
- **Theory**: using multiple perspectives or theories to interpret the data

---

For instance, in a situation that affects several parties with different interests, the evaluators will interview representatives of all parties as well as some neutral parties. This provides a triangulation effect, which largely helps to verify information, cut through conflicting evidence and acquire insight in a cost-effective way.

The term 'triangulation' is borrowed from surveying or navigation, where it refers to the practice of establishing the exact position of a given object by taking readings or measurements from multiple viewpoints. Using more than one reference point enables greater accuracy of measurement. In evaluation, the distinction is between four different types of triangulation: *methods, data, analyst, and theory*.

Triangulation of methods

Triangulation of *methods* will most often revolve around comparing data collected through some kind of qualitative and quantitative methods. This gives different viewpoints a chance to arise, and postpone immediate rejection of information or hypotheses that seem out of joint with the majority viewpoint. It is useful to bring different data and methods to bear on the same problem. For instance, explanations derived by observation are particularly vulnerable to dismissal, and may be supplemented with general experience data and interviews with key informants to provide contextual information. Using different methods is seldom a straightforward process because it is likely that quantitative methods and qualitative methods will eventually answer different questions that do not easily come together, to provide a single, integrated picture of the situation.

Triangulation of data

This means comparing and crosschecking the consistency of information derived at different times and by different means. For instance, to compare observational data with interview data; to compare what people say in public with what they say in private; to check for the consistency of what people say about the same thing over time; and to compare the perspectives of people from different points of view: project staff, suppliers, users, government staff, etc. It means validating information obtained through interviews by checking project documents and other written evidence that can corroborate what interview respondents report. Triangulation of data generated by qualitative methods will seldom lead to a single, totally consistent picture. The point is to study and understand when and why there are differences. If observational data produce different results than interview data, it does not necessarily mean that either or both kinds of data are invalid, although that may be the case. More likely, it means that different kinds of data have captured different things and so the evaluator attempts to understand the reasons for the differences.

Analyst triangulation

This involves using several observers or analysts. Triangulating analysts, or using several interviewers, helps reduce the potential bias that comes from one single person. Frequently, evaluators may require specialist knowledge in substantive areas in addition to their technical expertise in evaluation methodology. Where this is the case there are advantages to be gained from working together in multi-disciplinary evaluation teams.

Theory triangulation

This involves using different theoretical perspectives to look at the same data. There are always multiple theoretical perspectives that can be brought to bear on substantive issues. For instance, economic processes can be assessed in a private sector or a public sector perspective. The benefit of theory triangulation is to understand how different assumptions and fundamental premises affect findings.

Triangulation is a process by which the evaluator can guard against the accusation that a study's findings are simply an artefact of a single method, a single source, or a single investigator's biases. It allows the evaluator to have greater confidence in the findings.

There is no doubt that evaluation offers ample opportunities for mixing methods. However, there are no fixed rules for multi-method evaluation design. Obviously, triangulation is applied in all evaluations by the team member's different professional background, experience, and perspectives – and by the vast amount of information that the team is presented with, which have been produced by different methods. What is called for here is therefore to consciously and systematically take triangulation a step further as a tool to improve quality in evaluation.

☑ Triangulation

TRIANGULATION	❏	Overcome biases, inaccuracy and erratic information by combining related data from several sources or analysts, using different methods and theories
	♦	
APPLICABLE WHEN	❏	Information is uncertain or conflicting
	❏	The issue under study is controversial
	❏	Secondary data are used extensively
	❏	There are many respondents with different interests
	♦	
APPLICATION	❏	To be considered from the outset when preliminary information is reviewed and evaluation instruments are selected
	❏	In some cases require repeated confrontations with respondents in order to verify information

8.6 SECURING RESOURCES FOR EVALUATION

The resources needed to conduct evaluation could be considerable. When evaluations are planned it is important to break down the tasks with schedules so that a detailed estimate can be made of the necessary personnel and expenses. The sum total of resources required must of course fit with what is available - or some changes in either the plan or the resources must be made.

Available funding is only one of the critical resources needed. Also the right technical *expertise* must be available to do a quality job. Sufficient funding does not guarantee that the necessary expertise is available. Considerable resources are also used by those commissioning evaluations to plan, manage and follow up on studies. And finally, the evaluation requires critical resources in terms of support from involved parties, stakeholders, and other people interviewed by the evaluation team. The degree of cooperation from these can have considerable influence on how much an evaluation can accomplish. Barriers to access and lack of cooperation or worse, active resistance, can be very expensive to the evaluation effort.

The crucial point here is that the evaluator must view cooperation from different stakeholders and the nature, quality, and availability of data as major resource issues when planning an evaluation. The potential for misunderstanding and resistance can be lowered considerably if the evaluators meet with project personnel and other relevant stakeholders and discuss their role in the evaluation and issues of access to staff, records, clients, and other pertinent information sources.

Alongside adequate funding and cooperation from project personnel, *time* is one of the most precious resources. Evaluation results are frequently inputs to decision-making that is already scheduled, with correspondingly tight deadlines for the evaluation. The trade-offs here are quite significant. An evaluation can have breadth, depth, and rigor but will require proportionate funding and time. Or it can be cheap and quick but will, of necessity, either deal with a very narrow issue or be relatively superficial, or both.

> It is generally better to answer a limited number of important questions well - than a larger number poorly.

With few exceptions, the higher the scientific standard to be met, the greater the time, expertise, effort, and amount of cooperation is required. Evaluations with limited resources must either focus on a circumscribed issue or rely on relatively informal procedures for obtaining information.

It takes careful planning to get the scope of work in balance with the funding and available resources, and there will always be a potential conflict between the two. The best way to prevent this is to negotiate very explicitly about the resources to be made available and the tradeoffs associated with the inevitable constraints on resources.

There is no standard formula to guide the amount of resources needed in an evaluation. The principle, however, should be that utility should guide *cost*. For instance, a routine evaluation of a single project could be quite limited, if the purpose essentially is to ascertain accountability, since the utility will largely be limited to that single project. On the other hand, a thematic evaluation designed to draw lessons from a number of projects could warrant large resources because the potential for application of lessons would be a considerable.

As discussed, the cost of evaluation increases with the degree of accuracy required. Accuracy is to a large extent a question of the quality of data and analysis. This in turn is to a large extent a question of the study design, whether primary or secondary data, the size of samples, the way data is generated, etc.

In general terms, the cost of data usually increases progressively as the precision increases, as illustrated in figure 7.2. This is because secondary data is usually much cheaper than primary data. Or because the sample in a sample survey needs to increase dramatically in order to raise the confidence level somewhat. The utility, however, increases more rapidly initially when the quality of data is improved from poor to good than when it is raised from good to excellent. The cost-effective choice is therefore some acceptable level of accuracy – a compromise between low and high quality information. This will be acceptable in most evaluations, primarily because of restrained resources, but also because the evaluator has means to validate information, as discussed in chapter 8.5.

☑ **Securing resources**

SUFFICIENT FUNDING	❑	In relation to what should be done
	❑	In relation to the size and complexity of the project
	❑	In relation to the possible economic benefits or cost savings that could result from the evaluation
		◆
QUALIFIED EXPERTISE	❑	With the necessary professional qualifications and relevant experience
		◆
ADEQUATE INFORMATION	❑	By securing cooperation from stakeholders and respondents
		◆
ENOUGH TIME	❑	To accomplish what is planned and still meet required deadlines for decision-making

8.7 EVALUATION ETHICS

Evaluation is a profession of persons with varying interests and differences in training, experience and work setting. Despite the diversity, the common ground is that evaluators aspire to provide quality information and assessment. Also that the evaluator has a responsibility versus the commissioning organisation, and the institutions, groups and individuals involved or affected by the evaluation.

As mentioned in chapter 8.1, organisations of professionals such as the American Evaluation Association or Canadian Evaluation Society have developed ethical standards for evaluators. The full text of AEA's ethical standard is included below.

Utility Standards

The utility standards are intended to ensure that an evaluation will serve the information needs of intended users.

1. Stakeholder Identification—Persons involved in or affected by the evaluation should be identified, so that their needs can be addressed.
2. Evaluator Credibility—The persons conducting the evaluation should be both trustworthy and competent to perform the evaluation, so that the evaluation findings achieve maximum credibility and acceptance.
3. Information Scope and Selection—Information collected should be broadly selected to address pertinent questions about the program and be responsive to the needs and interests of clients and other specified stakeholders.
4. Values Identification—The perspectives, procedures, and rationale used to interpret the findings should be carefully described, so that the bases for value judgments are clear.
5. Report Clarity—Evaluation reports should clearly describe the program being evaluated, including its context, and the purposes, procedures, and findings of the evaluation, so that essential information is provided and easily understood.
6. Report Timeliness and Dissemination—Significant interim findings and evaluation reports should be disseminated to intended users, so that they can be used in a timely fashion.
7. Evaluation Impact—Evaluations should be planned, conducted, and reported in ways that encourage follow-through by stakeholders, so that the likelihood that the evaluation will be used is increased.

Feasibility Standards

The feasibility standards are intended to ensure that an evaluation will be realistic, prudent, diplomatic, and frugal.

1. Practical Procedures—The evaluation procedures should be practical, to keep disruption to a minimum while needed information is obtained.
2. Political Viability—The evaluation should be planned and conducted with anticipation of the different positions of various interest groups, so that their cooperation may be obtained, and so that possible attempts by any of these groups to curtail evaluation operations or to bias or misapply the results can be averted or counteracted.
3. Cost Effectiveness—The evaluation should be efficient and produce information of sufficient value, so that the resources expended can be justified.

Propriety Standards

The propriety standards are intended to ensure that an evaluation will be conducted legally, ethically, and with due regard for the welfare of those involved in the evaluation, as well as those affected by its results.

1. Service Orientation—Evaluations should be designed to assist organizations to address and effectively serve the needs of the full range of targeted participants.
2. Formal Agreements—Obligations of the formal parties to an evaluation (what is to be done, how, by whom, when) should be agreed to in writing, so that these parties are obligated to adhere to all conditions of the agreement or formally to renegotiate it.
3. Rights of Human Subjects—Evaluations should be designed and conducted to respect and protect the rights and welfare of human subjects.
4. Human Interactions—Evaluators should respect human dignity and worth in their interactions with other persons associated with an evaluation, so that participants are not threatened or harmed.
5. Complete and Fair Assessment—The evaluation should be complete and fair in its examination and recording of strengths and weaknesses of the program being evaluated, so that strengths can be built upon and problem areas addressed.
6. Disclosure of Findings—The formal parties to an evaluation should ensure that the full set of evaluation findings along with pertinent limitations are made accessible to the persons affected by the evaluation, and any others with expressed legal rights to receive the results.
7. Conflict of Interest—Conflict of interest should be dealt with openly and honestly, so that it does not compromise the evaluation processes and results.
8. Fiscal Responsibility—The evaluator's allocation and expenditure of resources should reflect sound accountability procedures and otherwise be prudent and ethically responsible, so that expenditures are accounted for and appropriate.

Accuracy Standards

The accuracy standards are intended to ensure that an evaluation will reveal and convey technically adequate information about the features that determine worth or merit of the program being evaluated.

1. Program Documentation—The program being evaluated should be described and documented clearly and accurately, so that the program is clearly identified.
2. Context Analysis—The context in which the program exists should be examined in enough detail, so that its likely influences on the program can be identified.
3. Described Purposes and Procedures—The purposes and procedures of the evaluation should be monitored and described in enough detail, so that they can be identified and assessed.
4. Defensible Information Sources—The sources of information used in a program evaluation should be described in enough detail, so that the adequacy of the information can be assessed.
5. Valid Information—The information gathering procedures should be chosen or developed and then implemented so that they will assure that the interpretation arrived at is valid for the intended use.
6. Reliable Information—The information gathering procedures should be chosen or developed and then implemented so that they will assure that the information obtained is sufficiently reliable for the intended use.
7. Systematic Information—The information collected, processed, and reported in an evaluation should be systematically reviewed and any errors found should be corrected.

8. Analysis of Quantitative Information—Quantitative information in an evaluation should be appropriately and systematically analysed so that evaluation questions are effectively answered.

9. Analysis of Qualitative Information—Qualitative information in an evaluation should be appropriately and systematically analysed so that evaluation questions are effectively answered.

10. Justified Conclusions—The conclusions reached in an evaluation should be explicitly justified, so that stakeholders can assess them.

11. Impartial Reporting—Reporting procedures should guard against distortion caused by personal feelings and biases of any party to the evaluation, so that evaluation reports fairly reflect the evaluation findings.

12. Metaevaluation—The evaluation itself should be formatively and summatively evaluated against these and other pertinent standards, so that its conduct is appropriately guided and, on completion, stakeholders can closely examine its strengths and weaknesses.

CHAPTER 9

REPORTING AND USING RESULTS

*IF YOU DON'T GIVE PEOPLE INFORMATION,
THEY WILL FIND SOMETHING TO FILL UP THE GAP.
CARLA O'DELL*

Chapter 9 – Reporting and using Results

9.1 MAKING REPORTS THAT ARE USED

The focus of evaluation may vary from a single project, to a project portfolio or a program, to a theme, etc. There is no standard format for reporting to match all types of evaluations. What is essential is that the format should be simple, the report well structured with an easily understandable language. The report should be written keeping target groups with the least advanced readers in mind.

The evaluators are collecting and processing information at different aggregation levels, as illustrated in figure 6.2. One common mistake in reporting is to indiscriminately present all possible detailed pieces of information alongside the aggregate conclusions, item by item. The result is a bulky document that is difficult to access. Another mistake is to present evidence in a logical sequence and eventually end up with an aggregate conclusion, instead of, like journalists, present the conclusion up-front and subsequently substantiate it with relevant evidence. A third common mistake is not to use a common reporting format. This helps making the report easier accessible and also in drawing lessons on specific issues from several reports.

Below is some general advice to make reports easier to read:

Structure of the report

- The report should have an executive summary, written as a self-contained paper providing the bare essentials for decision-makers regarding the background, major conclusions, recommendations and lessons learned.

- The main report should be relatively short. A substantial part should be the main conclusions and recommendations. These should be substantiated with more detailed information only to the extent necessary.

- Detailed findings should be referred to the annexes. Conclusions and recommendations in the main report should have references to the relevant findings in the annexes. The Terms of Reference, the team's itinerary, list of persons met, and list of documents used should be annexed.

Editorial guidance

- The main point should be presented early in the paragraphs while the remainder is used to substantiate and discuss the main point.

- Main points should as far as possible be supported by illustrations, graphs, tables, etc. with subtexts that focus the reader's attention on the important points that are derived.

- Jargon and difficult words should be avoided. Essential technical terms that may be new to the reader should be defined in the text, and in a glossary at the end.

- Long and complicated sentences should be broken down in shorter sentences. Active sentences should be preferred. Passive sentences should be used essentially to focus attention on specific topics.

- Ideas should not be crammed together in complex sentences with commas and brackets. Separate main ideas should be presented in separate sentences.

- The meaning of abbreviations and colloquial words should be explained. Abbreviations should be used as little as possible.

- Numbers should be presented in data tables or diagrams. The written text should highlight only the most important numbers and explain their implications. Percentages should in most cases be rounded up to the nearest whole number.

- It should be possible for the reader to get the main message from a table without consulting the text. Every table must therefore have a title, table number, reference to the source of information, sample size, and full description of what each figure refers to.

✓ Reporting format

1. **BACKGROUND** — Introduction, explaining why and how the evaluation was undertaken, as well as a discussion of the methodology used

2. **SETTING** — The setting of the project under study in terms of location, institutional setting, policy framework, etc.

3. **PROJECT** — A brief account why and how the project was undertaken, emphasising objectives, stakeholders, components, financing, management, etc.

4. **MAIN CONCLUSIONS** — The main conclusions based on overall assessments, including efficiency, effectiveness, impact, relevance, and sustainability – substantiated on the basis of main findings

5. **MAIN RECOMMENDATIONS** — The main recommendations with an assessment of implications for the key stakeholders

6. **LESSONS LEARNED** — An account of lessons that could be generally useful for other projects, policy, management procedures etc.

ANNEXES — All evidence that may be useful in substantiating the reports findings and conclusions

9.2 THE USE OF EVALUATION

The purpose of evaluation is to provide relevant and timely input to decision makers, and useful lessons in learning processes. This requires modes of communication and channels for feedback and learning, for instance through publications, seminars, workshops, training, library services, advisory services, and databases. Many evaluation reports are made for internal use only and are not open to a larger audience. In the public sector, there has been a steady increase in the use of evaluation, and an increasing and substantial part of these reports are open to the public. There is a trend to make such material available through the Web.

The responsibility for the contents of evaluation reports rests with their authors. The users of evaluations are the commissioning party, project managers, other stakeholders, authorities, the media, politicians, the public, and external resources such as researchers and consultants.

Systematic *dissemination* is essential for ensuring improved planning and implementation of project activities. Evaluation results may be disseminated in several ways apart from the evaluation report itself e.g. annual reports providing a synthesis of findings; abstracts/ summaries providing a synopsis of findings.

Feedback is an essential part of the evaluation process as it provides the link between past and future activities. To ensure that the results of evaluations are utilised in future policy and project development it is necessary to establish feedback mechanisms involving all parties concerned. These would include such measures as evaluation committees, seminars and workshops, automated systems, reporting and follow-up procedures. Informal means such as networking and internal communications would also allow for the dissemination of ideas and information. In order to be effective, the feedback process requires staff and budget resources as well as support by senior management and the other actors involved.

(OECD)

Making information available is essential to generate a general awareness, interest and support for projects. The evaluation report provides a status of strength and weaknesses and suggests solutions to major problems.

After the final report has been received, the commissioning party decides what actions to be taken in the light of conclusions and recommendations presented. Salient issues are brought to the attention of senior level management. Conclusions and recommendations may eventually be used to further develop and improve overall policies and methods of work. It is a challenge therefore to systematise experience and formulate practical proposals on that basis.

The significance of an evaluation report is different for different users. It is essential that the final users of the information are able to utilise the evaluation for their own needs. This implies that ==for the evaluation to have maximum effect, the different parties' need for information have to be carefully analysed.== The commissioning party has a role in assessing the needs of users and develop the mandate for the evaluation to respond to these needs. Also, it is vital to assess continuously the quality of evaluation activities and explore mechanisms for feedback and improved learning.

The main feedback linkages are to make use of evaluation findings to manage the existing project, in planning new projects, to develop policy and strategies, to train staff members and to inform the public.

Apart from the evaluation report itself, feedback is provided through documents to summarise evaluation findings, specific studies and reports produced on the basis of the evaluation, seminars and workshops, informal discussion and learning processes, etc. Accumulation of evaluation findings in databases has proved useful as a basis for drawing general conclusions, establishing benchmarks, etc.

 **Using evaluation**

THE USERS OF EVALUATION	❑ The commissioning party ❑ Project managers ❑ Stakeholders related to the project ❑ Authorities ❑ The media and the public ❑ Other resources such as researchers and consultants
DISSEMINATION OF FINDINGS AIMED TO IMPROVE PROJECT ACTIVITIES	❑ Evaluation reports ❑ Abstracts ❑ Workshops and seminars ❑ Formulation of practical proposals
FEEDBACK AIMED TO IMPROVE POLICY AND FUTURE PROJECTS	❑ Systematised experience based on evaluation reports ❑ Formulation of policy and strategies ❑ Training staff ❑ Adequate and up-dated databases ❑ Benchmarks

9.3 USING EVALUATION AS A LEARNING ARENA

Learning from experience means to extract lessons that may be applicable to a generic situation rather than to a specific circumstance. The lessons learned should be structured along the same lines as the findings, conclusions and recommendations, i.e., with a focus on relevance, performance and success. They should include both positive and negative lessons - the best and worst practices - that have a bearing beyond the project or program at hand. Cluster evaluations including more than individual projects offer the advantage of providing a broader basis for generic lessons.

Evaluations represent a huge potential for institutional learning. Learning in an organization means the continuous testing of experience, and the transformation of that experience into knowledge - accessible to the whole organization, and relevant to its core purpose. The main factor that must be considered when drawing positive lessons from experience is their applicability.

Studies of institutional learning indicate that the most important learning areas for the staff and the decision makers are to be present in the field themselves, participating in internal reviews, drawing on experience from organisations, and discussing with colleagues. Evaluation reports represent a comprehensive and reliable source of substantive information about projects.

What this suggests is that apart from using evaluation reports as decision-making tools, there is much to gain from using evaluations more pro-actively, for instance as follows:

- Allow project staff to participate in evaluation teams. The advantages in terms of learning would in many cases outweigh the problem of making the team less impartial.

- Encourage more active use of evaluation reports from similar projects produced by others. Databases of evaluation results, some of which are available online on the web are useful resources.

- Use evaluation studies as a basis for broader or in-depth thematic studies. Such studies may cut across different projects, sectors, institutional and geographic settings, and may benefit from using evaluation studies because of their high score on reliability and validity.

General experience suggests that there is a need for a certain minimum of common understanding and knowledge in an organisation before institutional learning will gain momentum. Initiatives by some organisations to organise internal learning have proved successful in this respect. More so when evaluation reports have been used systematically to develop training material, and when evaluators have been involved as trainers and resource persons.

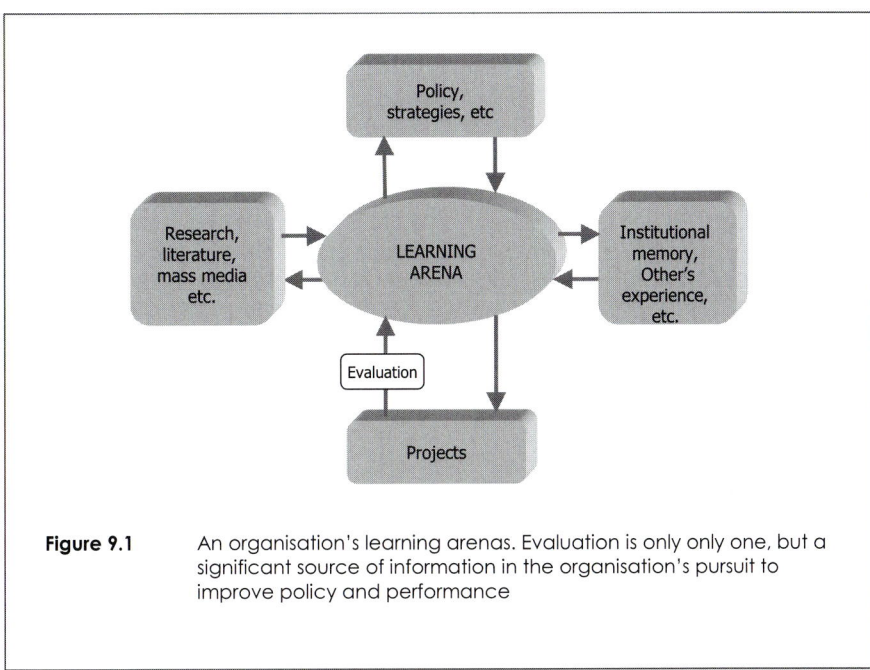

Figure 9.1   An organisation's learning arenas. Evaluation is only only one, but a significant source of information in the organisation's pursuit to improve policy and performance

Whether evaluation reports should be made public has been a matter of debate. Evaluation activities are seldom meant to be a means of strengthening public debate. A large share of evaluation activities results in reports that is confidential. However, an increasing part is made openly available. Experience shows that initiatives to make evaluation reports available to the public have been generally positive. Access to reliable information tends to lift the professional debate regarding projects and their impact. Researchers, students, companies and individuals have benefited. Initiatives to make evaluation reports available via the web have opened up an entirely new dissemination channel.

Evaluation findings are increasingly finding their way to the public directly or indirectly. It is done voluntarily to give the public correct information in a controversial case, and it is increasingly used up-front to forego controversial discussions that might otherwise develop. Whichever channel is preferred, the best way to ensure that it is used successfully is to improve both the quality and content of reports and the way material is presented. The main purpose of evaluations is still to improve the quality of projects. The extent to which they will also improve transparency and public insight will be a welcome, but secondary benefit.

CHAPTER 10

PROJECT CASES

EXAMPLE MOVES THE WORLD MORE THAN DOCTRINE.
HENRY MILLER

10.1 Evaluating a project

This chapter discusses a case that illustrates the step-by-step approach to evaluation described in this book. To make it simple, we will focus on a single project aimed to raise an airline's safety and service level. What is presented in this chapter is essentially a qualitative analytical process. In reality, when a wealth of quantitative data is available, the entire process would automatically be more quantitative.

Raising an airline's service level

An airline is licensed to operate a major part of a national network. The company handles about 80 per cent of passenger transport in the network, while the rest is handled by three small airlines. During the last ten years, incidents and accidents have increased significantly. This causes delay and inconvenience for passengers. In some cases serious accidents have occurred, resulting in growing distrust. The media have repeatedly highlighted the problem, and criticised the main airline in particular. It is now loosing passengers to other operators. The risk is that these as the result would be licensed to take over some of its routes.

The company initiated a project to address the problem. The strategy was to reduce the frequency of incidents and accidents (*goal*) and improve the service level of the company in general (*purpose*). This was to be achieved basically through: upgrading and replacing some aircrafts, train the pilots; introduce safety measures, and improve maintenance.

After two years a second phase was initiated with the increased ambition to make the company financially viable (*goal*) through: improved management, human resources development, as well as investments in additional new aircrafts (*outputs*). Evaluation took place at the end of the project's second phase.

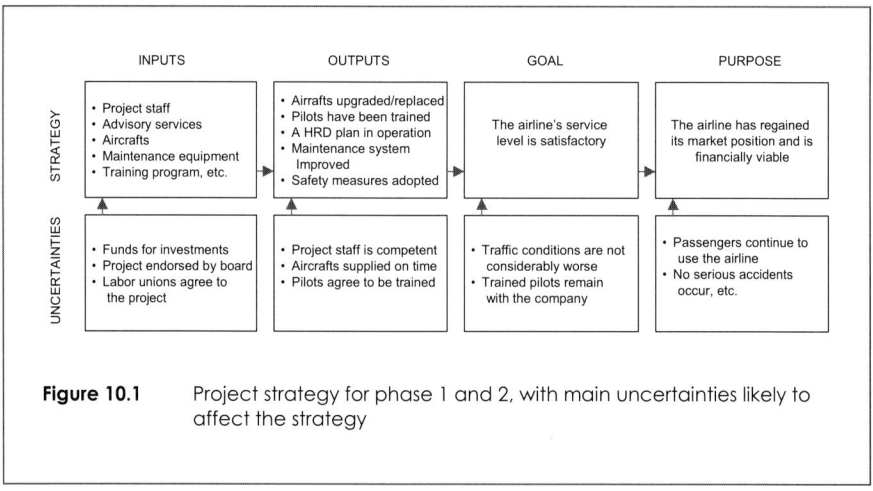

Figure 10.1 Project strategy for phase 1 and 2, with main uncertainties likely to affect the strategy

Step 1: Establish the project strategy

Evaluations commonly focus on projects' achievements and not their activities. Project strategies are therefore expressed in terms of the *inputs* and objectives at different levels, i.e. the *outputs, goal* and *purpose*. The strategy may change during a project's lifetime. Many projects are implemented in phases where inputs and outputs may be entirely different from one phase to another, and where even the goal and purpose may be altered. In this case, the project was extended in a second phase and expanded. The evaluator will take the latest strategy as the point of departure for the evaluation. Figure 10.1 summarises the strategy, with some main uncertainties that might influence the project. See also chapter 1.9.

Step 2: Review the project strategy

In many projects agreed objectives are unrealistic, and the probability to achieve the objectives correspondingly limited, in some cases negligible. See chapters 6.2-6.3. Clearly, to evaluate against unrealistic objectives makes little sense, since the project would certainly fail to meet such objectives. The evaluator therefore needs to make a preliminary review of the project's attribution in relation to agreed objectives. If objectives are too ambitious, the evaluator needs to point it out and suggest more realistic objectives for the evaluation. In this case this is not necessary since the probability to attain the goal (adequate service level) and purpose (financial viability) is considered realistic.

Step 3: Identify evaluation questions

The evaluation focuses on five main *evaluation criteria*. Together, they represent the key issues that the evaluation will address in order to provide a solid basis for decisions to improve a project's performance and utility, see chapter 4.

1. *Efficiency* relates to the delivery of the project and covers all major issues related to the production of outputs in quantity, quality and time.
2. *Effectiveness* concerns the extent to which the project goal has been or can be expected to be achieved.
3. *Impact* refers to all effects of the project other than the achievement of the goal, positive or negative; expected or unforeseen
4. *Relevance* concerns whether the rationale behind a project (the purpose) is in keeping with the priorities of the users and society
5. *Sustainability* indicates whether the positive impacts are likely to continue in the future after the project has come to an end

These evaluation criteria build directly on the elements in the project strategy, as shown in figure 4.2. The evaluator needs to operationalise these criteria in terms of disaggregate *evaluation questions* that relate to the project under review. A few such main evaluation questions have been identified for each evaluation criterion, and the result is summarised in figure 10.2.

Chapter 10 – Project cases

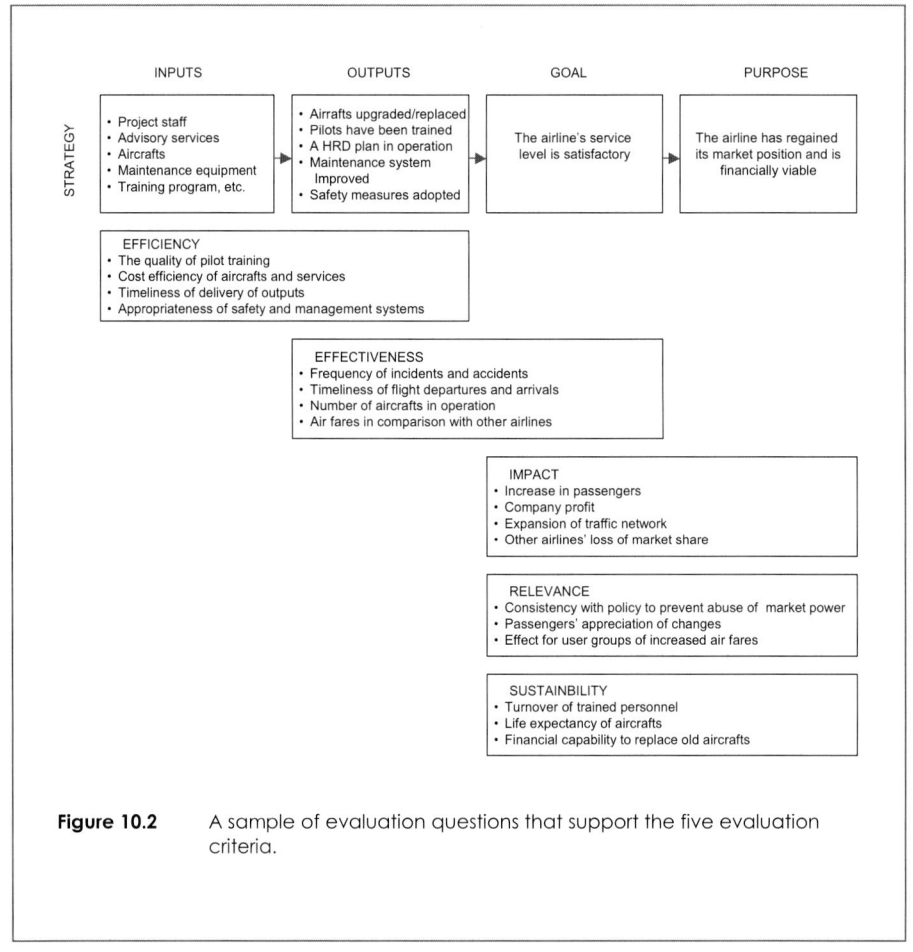

Figure 10.2 A sample of evaluation questions that support the five evaluation criteria.

Step 4: Ensure adequacy of evaluation instruments

The evaluation instrument[7] is used to collect the right information in an appropriate way. The evaluation question specifies what information is needed, and the data collection method how to get the information. What is required is that the evaluation instrument provides information that is valid, reliable and accessible, in a cost effective way

Ensure valid information

It is critical to the evaluator that information helps understand relevant problems and make sound decisions. The most essential aspect of information quality is its validity, or the extent to which it corresponds to what we want to measure. Validity cannot be verified or tested directly; but will have to be based on the judgement of the evaluator.

---

[7] The evaluation instrument is a term used for the evaluation question and the data collection method in combination

> **Testing validity**
> 1. Check that the evaluation questions are closely attributed to the evaluation criteria
> 2. Check that the evaluation questions in combination are sufficient provide a valid answer to the evaluation criterion
> 3. Add/subtract evaluation questions as appropriate

Take effectiveness as an example: the service level of the airline is in focus (goal). Several evaluation questions have been identified (frequency of accidents, timeliness, number of aircrafts in operation). All these are directly associated with the goal. Other questions that reflect the passengers' view could be added to complete the picture (queuing, costs, complaints against flight attendants, etc.). In combination, the questions will increase validity, and also provide opportunities to crosscheck information.

Ensure reliable information

In order to ensure reliable information, evaluation instruments need to be accurate. The problem is: what methods can be applied to obtain sufficiently reliable answers to the different evaluation questions? In other words, we focus on the evaluation questions, and explore what methods can be used to collect the information. See chapter 7.

> **Checking reliability**
> 1. Consider each evaluation question
> 2. Identify alternative data collection methods that may be used
> 3. Consider the reliability of each instrument (question plus method)

Some examples are given in table 10.1, below: for instance, we assume that the frequency of incidents and accidents can be established with a high degree of reliability based on official records of incidents and accidents; while interviews with passengers would reflect subjective opinions and their lack of information, and therefore would not be very reliable.

Chapter 10 – Project cases

	Evaluation instrument				
Question	Method	Reliability	Access	Cost	Conclusion
Quality of pilot training	• Interviews with pilots	Medium	+	+	
	• Interviews with trainers	Low	+	+	
	• Group focus interviews	Medium	+	++	OK
Frequency of incidents and accidents	• Airline records	Medium	-	++	OK
	• Official records	High	+	++	OK
	• Passenger interviews	Low	-	-	-
	• Passenger survey	Low	+	-	-
Changes in passenger groups	• Survey among passengers	High	--	--	
	• Interview with flight attendants	Medium	+	+	OK
	• Observation	Medium	+	-	
Airlines' market share	• Company records	High	+	+	OK
	• Interviews with directors	High	+	+	OK

Table 10.1   A review of a sample of evaluation instruments

Ensure accessibility

With the time and budget constraints in evaluation, it is useful to consider at an early stage to what extent the desired information is accessible when using different evaluation instruments. Clearly, findings from existing studies may be easily accessible; while information on sensitive issues generated through formal surveys and case studies need special efforts and resources on behalf of the evaluator.

Checking accessibility

1. Consider each evaluation instrument
2. Does it make use of information that is already avialable
3. Would informants be willing/able to produce the information
4. Does it require comprehensive and time consuming studies

In this particular case, individual and group focus interviews would provide relatively easy access to information. However, to interview passengers in order to establish the frequency of incidents and accidents is not feasible, it would require a large number of respondents. It could be done with a survey, but the information would not be reliable. A user survey to determine whether the passenger groups have changed is fairly reliable, but a rather complex way to obtain information.

Assess costs

The cost of information varies with the quality of data. Precision is expensive. When we want very precise answers, study costs may be high. Costs go up as we increase the number of study questions. But when those questions are used to cross-validate information, our confidence in the answer also goes up.

> **Assessing costs**
> 1. Consider each evaluation instrument
> 2. Does the instrument require expensive studies
> 3. Would the information return be considerable in relation to costs
> 4. Is the precision level higher than necessary
> 5. Is the balance between sample size and reliability appropriate

It is usually possible without much effort to give a rough opinion of costs associated with the different evaluation instruments under consideration. In this particular case, when considering how to obtain information on the "quality of training", we would assume that a group focus exercise is less expensive than individual interviews since a number of persons needs to be present at the same time. The next question is the "frequency of incidents and accidents". To extract information from airline records is inexpensive. Interviews with a large number of passengers, or a user survey are relatively expensive. Regarding the third question, observation in order to determine changes in user groups will be more expensive than to interview flight attendants, because a relatively large number of observations will have to be made.

Based on the previous considerations the final selection of evaluation instruments can be made. The selection will be a trade-off between reliability, accessibility and costs. In the present example the selection is fairly obvious. Conclusions regarding quality of training should primarily be based on focus group interviews, frequency of incidents and accidents on the airline's own as well as official records, and changes in user groups on interviews with flight attendants. Finally, the question of market shares should be explored through interviews with directors as well as airline records, which could be used to help cross-validate information.

Step 5: Collect and analyse information

Information is collected using both informal and formal data collection techniques from simple and inexpensive approaches, like the use of existing information and interviews, to accurate and resource demanding methods such as formal surveys, measurement and testing. A few selected examples of findings are described in table 10.2 below.

Chapter 10 – Project cases

Evaluation question	Findings
1. Quality of training	• The standard of training is very high. • Not all training elements are relevant for the airline's operations
2. Frequency of incidents and accidents	Year 0 1 2 3 Accidents 20 5 2 5 Incidents 60 30 45 60
3. Changes in passenger groups	• Because of increased fares, the business class segment has increased • Low-fare passengers tend to shift to other airlines
4. Other companies' market share	• Their combined market share has increased by 10 per cent after three years • This is caused by an increase in low-fare passengers

Table 10.2 Examples of evaluation findings at a disaggregate level

Much of the information collected is in the form of raw data, time-series, individual statements, etc. that has to be analysed and aggregated so that conclusions can be extracted. In the end, the analysis should result in a number of single statements that provide answers to the different evaluation questions.

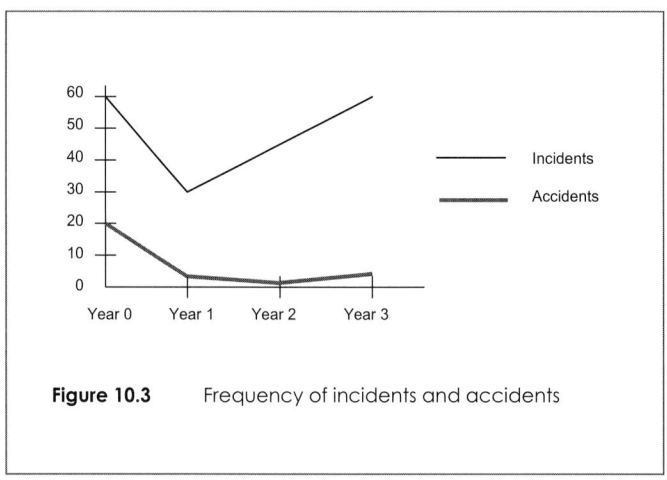

Figure 10.3   Frequency of incidents and accidents

Findings in table 10.2 regarding the frequency of incidents and accidents provide two time-series of data. Each figure provides little insight into the situation if seen in isolation. Together they can give clear indications about the effect of the project, when the data are plotted in the graph in figure 10.3.

The data suggest that the project has been only temporarily successful in reducing incidents, while its effect on accidents seems to be more permanent. One suggestion could be that the reduction of minor incidents is primarily the result of the training of pilots, and that training needs to be continued in order to maintain the positive results. Further, that the reduction of more serious accidents may rather be ascribed to the upgrading and maintenance of aircrafts. Such hypotheses need to be tested against other data before they are accepted and used as conclusions.

Often analysis will reveal conclusions that are linked to other evaluation questions or evaluation criteria than the one in focus. Such conclusions will add to the picture and provide opportunities for cross-verification. The conclusions need to be linked to the appropriate evaluation questions before a final overall assessment or evaluation of the project can be made.

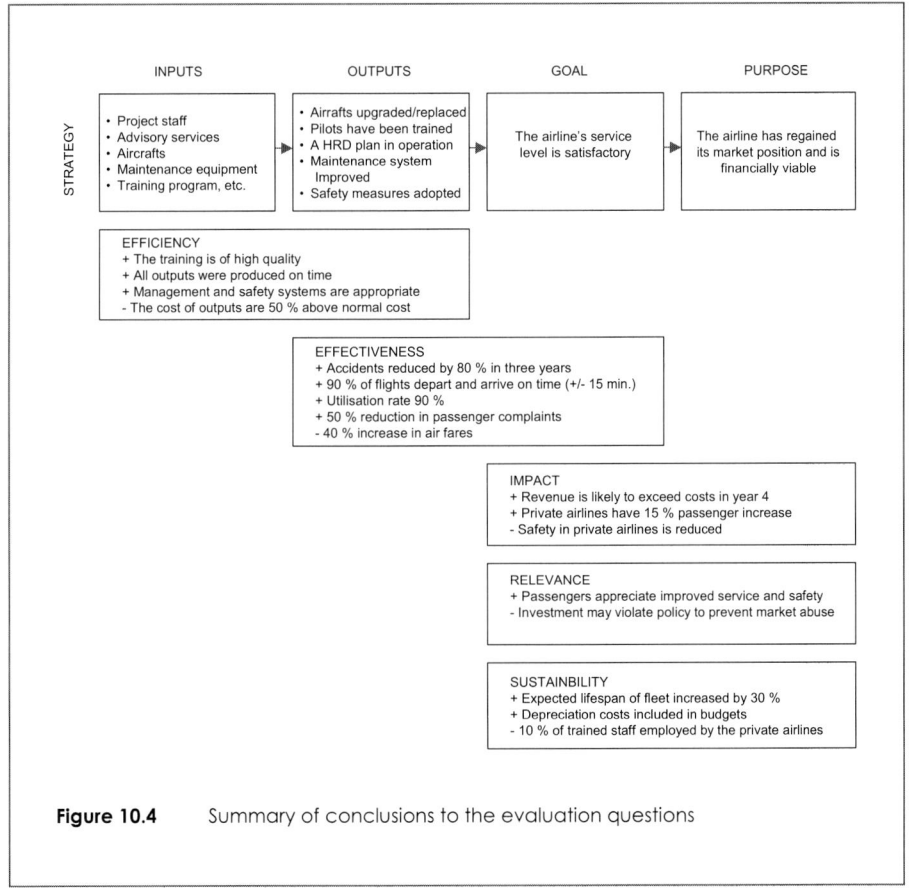

Figure 10.4   Summary of conclusions to the evaluation questions

Step 6.   Make the overall evaluation

At this stage, a number of answers to the evaluation questions have been generated and further aggregated in the form of a series of specific conclusions. This is summarised in figure 10.4.

In order to make the final, overall evaluation of the project, one needs to assign value and weight to each of the conclusions. The normal procedure would be to judge the totality and value each element in the total picture. For illustration purposes it can also be done formally for instance by assigning values, positive or negative, to each conclusion, or each conclusion could simply be assigned a plus or minus to help provide a broad overview. It should be noted that assigning values and weight could be highly controversial, because different parties may have entirely different opinions on the same conclusion according to their values and preferences.

After values and weights have been assigned, more aggregate conclusions can be drawn, which provide answers to the overall evaluation criteria. In figure 10.4 values have been added to the different conclusions simply by using pluses and minuses. At the more aggregate level, these conclusions suggest that the project by and large has been successful in terms of *efficiency:* the outputs have been delivered as intended (although at a high cost); and *effectiveness:* the goal has by and large been achieved (also at a high cost). The conclusions regarding the project's *relevance*, however, are mixed. Improvements in terms of safety and timeliness are appreciated by passengers. Increased costs as a result of the project has caused a flow of low-fare passengers to the smaller airlines while business class passengers remain and enjoy improved service at a higher cost. The project aims to strengthen the dominant operator in the market, and this may be in conflict with the Government policy to prevent market power abuse. On the other hand, the effect seems to go in the opposite direction, increasing the market for the smaller airlines. The problem may be that with their existing capacity and limited fleet of aircrafts the service and safety level is going down (*impact*). The smaller airlines also benefit from a recruitment of trained personnel from the major airline, which adversely affects the project's *sustainability*.

The evaluation provides a basis for overall conclusions and for drawing up a strategy for the future. In this particular case a change of strategy which stimulates a healthy competition between the major and the smaller companies may be called for.

10.2 THREE STRATEGIES ASSESSED

The project case described in this chapter is used to illustrate how the evaluation methodology can be used at the earliest stage before funds are committed. The aim is to make a rough assessment of a project's feasibility seen in different perspectives. The evaluation is made essentially as a qualitative assessment based on information from the media debate, whatever little factual information was available in the public debate as well as estimates. No attempt was made to verify information or ensure precision.

The opera house project

After years of debate, the Norwegian Parliament decided year 2000 to finance a new opera house in the capital. An architectural competition was carried out. The winning team came up with a low-rise monumental building to be placed at the waterfront in an undeveloped part of the harbour area, presently dominated by a complex highway system.

The public debate has since circled around the project's price tag. The initial estimate was the equivalent of 0.2 billion USD. After two years and various analyses the realistic budget was set at about 0.5 billion USD. However, that was only for the Opera house itself. If necessary infrastructural development were included, the price tag would be much higher, possibly as high as 3 billion USD.

The project was controversial, and there were strong forces for and against it. Still, the debate was largely concerned with the size of the budget, and possible alternative use of the funds. More fundamental questions regarding the purpose and the project's overall objective was not raised formally. Apparently, the purpose of an opera house seemed so obvious that there was no need to discuss it.

Three alternative project strategies

The project strategy with three alternative objectives is illustrated in figure 10.5. In terms of *inputs*, the assumption is that the estimated 0.5 billion USD will be the total cost for the new opera house. If the scope of the project should go beyond this, the cost would clearly increase, as indicated.

The *project* output would be the opera house completed as designed, and fully equipped for its purpose. Again, if the scope of the project increased, it could also include infrastructural development as well as other outputs.

However, as discussed above, the official documents did not provide a clear statement of the project's *objectives*. From the public debate, one could implicitly discern the following three suggested objectives that could be used to guide and justify the project:

1. Increased tourism to Oslo, from inside the country and abroad, either to see the building or the opera performances, or both.

2. A general increase and improvement of cultural activities in the country, the idea being that the opera would be a locomotive for cultural development and art

3. Urban development of a neglected part of the harbour area in Oslo, the idea being that the existence of an opera would attract investors to modernise and reconstruct the area.

These objectives differ significantly. To fulfil them would require additional projects. In this context we shall no go into a debate of alternative concepts, but rather look at the extent to which the opera project would help realize each of these objectives.

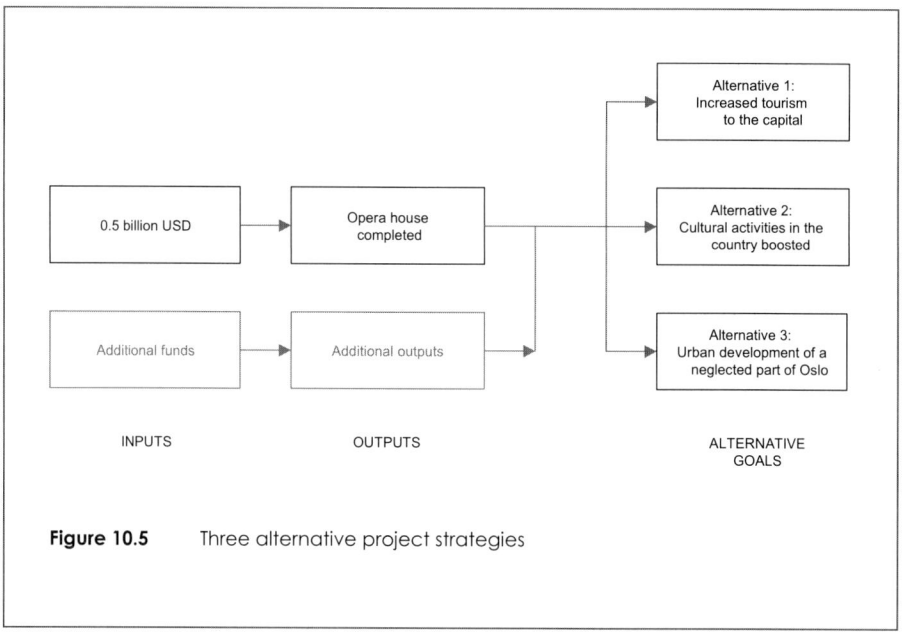

Figure 10.5 Three alternative project strategies

Identifying evaluation criteria

In order to establish a basis for comparison, we have applied the five evaluation criteria in chapter 4 on each of the three project strategies. Each evaluation criterion has been operationalised in one or more evaluation issues that are essential to assess the strategy involved. The results are displayed in figure 10.6.

Strategy 1: Increased tourism

The project's *efficiency* can be established in terms of the cost efficiency; seen in relation to similar projects elsewhere, as well as the project's compliance with budget, time schedule and quality requirements. Efficiency would be measured in the same way in the three cases discussed.

Effectiveness expresses the achievements of the project's goal. In this case it would depend on the building's attraction for the public, and the extent to which the building and the opera performances would attract people from inside and outside the country.

There could be many *impacts* from the project, foreseen and unforeseen, positive and negative. A positive impact would be the share of tourism that could be attributed to the existence of the new opera house. A negative impact could be the adverse effect it could have in terms of reduced visits to other tourist attractions.

The project's *relevance* is measures in terms of its political and public support, for instance expressed in terms the Government's willingness to invest in tourism, and the share of the public supporting the project.

The project's *sustainability* would be the test of whether the opera can operate in the future without external financial support. In this case, it would be the project's long-term financial viability, taking into account the full capital and operational expenditures.

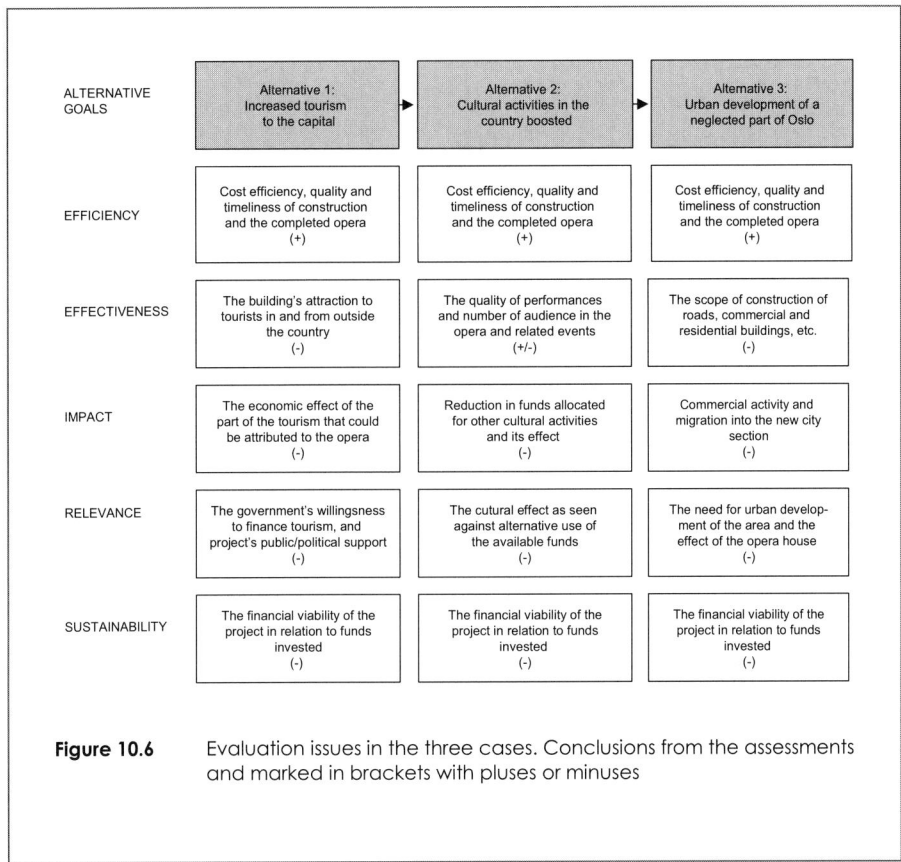

Figure 10.6 Evaluation issues in the three cases. Conclusions from the assessments and marked in brackets with pluses or minuses

Strategy 2.: Increased cultural activities

As mentioned, our concern is to assess the opera house project in a wider perspective where it is thought to help boost cultural activities in the country. The *efficiency* of the project is the same as in strategy 1, and restricted to the construction and completion of the opera house itself.

Effectiveness in this case is associated with a broader objective of the quality of performances and the number of audience, not only restricted to the opera but also including cultural activities and events that could be attributed directly or indirectly the opera.

A positive *impact* could be the opera's economic effect on tourism and on other cultural activities.

The *relevance* of the project would primarily be measured in terms of the cultural effect of the project as compared with the possible effect of alternative use of the funds to support other cultural activities, institutions, groups, events etc. in the country.

Again the *sustainability* would be measured in terms of the long-term financial viability of the opera in its new location.

Strategy 3.: Urban development

In this case, *effectiveness* would have to be measured in a wider and more long-term perspective of urban development in terms of the construction of infrastructure, roads, new commercial and residential buildings, etc.

The main *impact* would be assessed in terms of the scope of commercial activities, permanent population, etc in the new township.

The project would be *relevant* to the extent that it succeeds as a locomotive for urban development. But one would also have to consider the need for the development of this particular area as compared with its present use, as well as possible alternative projects in other more suited locations of the city.

Sustainability would again be restricted to the opera project in terms of its long-term financial viability. In a wider perspective, sustainability would be the financial viability of the township when taking into account the total investments.

Evaluation of the project as strategic element

Evaluation is based on what little factual information that exists in the projects preliminary phase, as well as estimates and educated guesswork. The assessments will be either negative or positive in varying degrees. For simplicity, the conclusions have only been marked with (+) or (-), as indicated in figure 10.6

Strategy 1.: Increased tourism

With the amount of planning laid down in this project and the professional quality and competence of the contractors involved, we could assume that the project will be *efficient* both in terms of cost, quality and progress.

In terms of *effectiveness*, it is not likely that the low-rise building will become a major architectural attraction, but rather dominated by existing high-rise buildings behind. Also, since operas appeal only to a limited audience and the city in this case has less than 0.5 million inhabitants, it is not likely that there will be a major sustained increase in the audience even when there is a new opera house.

It follows from the above that the economic *impact* on tourism will be limited. In terms of the project's *relevance* the majority of people are against the expensive opera project, and suggestions for alternative use of the funds are numerous. Its effect on tourism will probably be very limited as compared with the effect of existing attractions.

In terms of financial *sustainability* the project is a disaster, and will probably have a cost recovery of less that 10 per cent. Even if the investment is fully covered and written off by the Government, the project will operate with more than 50 per cent deficit annually in the years to come.

Strategy 2.: Increased cultural activities

Again, we assume that *efficiency* is acceptable. In terms of *effectiveness*, however, it will most probably be low, assuming that the long-term *impact* of the opera on cultural activities in general will be limited. Its short-term impact might rather be negative, since the huge investment for the opera house is likely to have adverse effect on funding to other cultural activities and institutions. We will also assume that the *relevance* of the project is negative if we consider the counterfactual situation: that the same funds be used in a decentralised manner to support local institutions, event and various groups in different parts of the country.

In terms of financial *sustainability*, the opera as already mentioned will be a disaster, and will also probably have an adverse effect on the financial sustainability of other cultural activities.

Strategy 3.: Urban development

Also in this case, *efficiency* will be the positive. The *effectiveness* of the project is uncertain and difficult to associate with the opera house. Reconstruction and erection of an entirely new township in the city will surely rest on more than a single opera project. If successful, an indirect impact of the project could be the successful completion of this wider project of urban development. However, the extent to which it could be attributed to the opera project would be uncertain. The *relevance* of such a project would depend on the financial viability of the urban development project, but also judged against a possible similar project in another location where development costs would be much less.

Conclusions

The conclusions from the assessments above are marked in figure 10.6 with pluses and minuses. As can be seen, the opera project seems to fail to support all three strategies. The main problems are that the project is:

1. not relevant as a significant strategic element in fulfilling the overall goals. In all cases, there are examples of alternative use of funds that would be more effective

2. not likely to become financially sustainable. In financial terms it is probably a disaster.

The findings are quite obvious and hardly news to decision makers and the public. It illustrates a common phenomenon that funds are committed for projects even when objectives have not been agreed and made explicit. This results in conflicting views and a confused debate. Agreeing on the overall purpose and goal that the project should support will always make it easier to reach consensus regarding the selection of the project. Supporters of the opera house project would have been well advised to be explicit about this.

Consensus regarding objectives should definitively be reached before an architectural competition is carried out. In this case, like in many other projects, the architectural competition was used to distract the debate from essential and problematic issues and to force decision-making, without solving the controversy that existed.

The opera project serves the purpose of satisfying the demand for opera performances in a small minority in society, as well as being a conducive factor in refining musical and performing art in general. This endeavour requires pubic funding and the opera will probably never be financially sustainable. A huge investment for a new and monumental opera house will have to paid with public funds and written off by the government. This is the issue that should have been on the political agenda, to be accorded political priority in competition with other tasks.

This project, like other major projects such as the pyramids or the Eiffel tower was not based on rational thought and politically expressed needs. It remains to be seen if it will also become a success in the perspective of decades and centuries.

10.3 FOUR PROJECT CASES REVIEWED

INTRODUCTION

Projects are managed within a context of uncertainty about the future. Two key questions in project management are how to plan and how to handle the elements of chance, or in other words *strategy* versus *tactics*. In a situation with much uncertainty that is difficult to predict, the chance that a predetermined strategy will be realised may be small. Plans are overtaken by events, and it would therefore make little sense to use many resources on laying a detailed strategy.

In a situation where the uncertainty is more limited and predictable, it makes more sense to invest in strategy making. The chance of realising the strategy may be higher. But only to a certain extent. Because even events that may appear insignificant could have major effects on the way the project develops. And experience shows that project management frequently fails to comply with the requirements of the strategy in the course of events. It is common experience that detailed plans are not used to the extent that was intended. The concept of strategy is rooted in stability, not in change. According to *Pinto and Slevin (1988)*, success is very much related to adaptation to external conditions and identification of external determinants. Failure is much related to internal aspects.

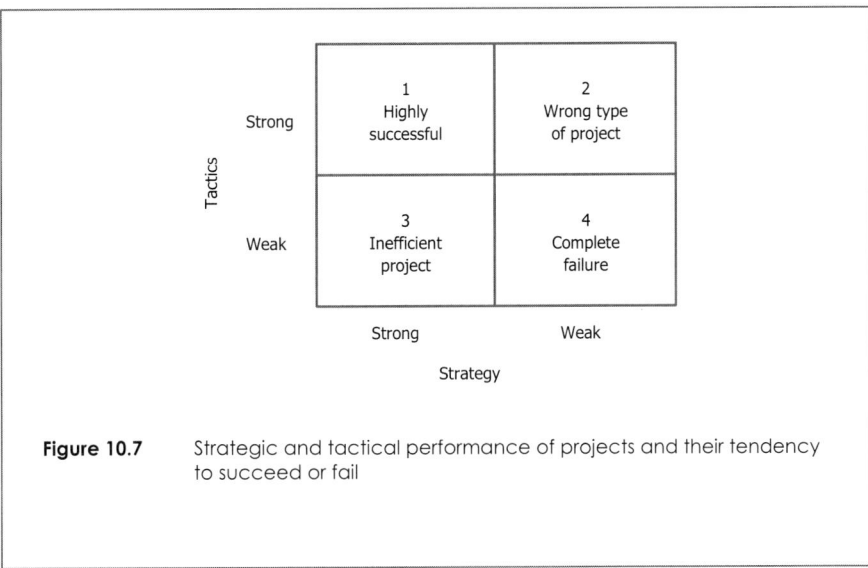

Figure 10.7   Strategic and tactical performance of projects and their tendency to succeed or fail

Most authors emphasise the importance of balancing strategy and tactics. *Pinto and Slevin, (1989)* use the concepts of tactical and strategic performance to distinguish between four types of projects, as illustrated in figure 10.7.

Projects that score high on strategic and tactical performance (1) tend to turn out successful. However, if the tactical performance fails (2), they have a tendency to err because of inaction and low acceptance/involvement. If the situation is the opposite, i.e. a weak strategy but high score on tactical performance (3), then the projects may be successfully implemented but fail to address actual needs. Finally, with a low score on

Chapter 10 – Project cases

both strategic and tactical performance (4), the potential for implementation failure is high.

The four project cases described below are international development projects and illustrate the projects' performance in a strategic and tactical perspective. The cases illustrate that a favourable environment is not enough if a project's design and management is inferior. On the other hand, a favourable environment seems to be a prerequisite for success. In these cases a few major uncertainties are critical in determining success or failure. They demonstrate the importance of strategic planning to guide the project in the right direction and avoid some main stumbling stones - and at the same time be able to respond tactically to unforeseen events in order to coach the project towards a successful conclusion. The evaluation criteria described in chapters 4 and 5 are applied to the project cases to illustrate their use in evaluation, but also to show that they can be used pro-actively to establish design and performance standards and ensure quality-at-entry.

PROJECT	STRATEGY	TACTICS	PERFORMANCE
1. Earthquake disaster centre	+	+	Highly successful
2. Entrepreneurial training	-	+	Wrong type of project
3. Industrial quality assurance	+	-	Inefficient project
4. Rural water supplies	-	-	Complete failure

Table 10.3 The four project cases and their strategic and tactical performance

The projects are characterised in terms of the strategy and tactics applied, and the uncertainties and the risks encountered when they were implemented. On the basis of this information the evaluation criteria described in chapter 4 are applied to do a qualitative assessment and determine the degree of success.

The projects differ in their score on tactical and strategic performance. The first project established an earthquake disaster centre and scored high on both variables. The next aimed to train refugees to become entrepreneurs, and made some achievements despite a faulty strategy. The third project was a quality assurance programme for industry in a number of countries, which started out with good intentions but failed in the way it was conducted. Finally, the last project should construct water supply facilities in a large rural area. It failed both in the way it was conceived and implemented.

CASE NO. 1: THE EARTHQUAKE DISASTER PREVENTION CENTRE (SUCCESSFUL STRATEGY AND TACTICS)

The project was designed to establish a national centre for disaster prevention in a Latin American country. The initiative came from the government two years after a major earthquake with devastating effects hit the capital. The government sought support from an industrial country with some of the world's best expertise in earthquake engineering and prevention of earthquake disasters.

A thorough pre-study and appraisal process was initiated, to come up with the best concept. It lasted for two years, and was concluded with an agreement that spelled out clearly the objectives, expected outputs and inputs, and the division of responsibilities between the two countries. The industrial country was supposed to finance construction of all facilities, provide all equipment, and supply long-term and short-term technical expertise for the project period. The developing country should create the legal framework for the institution, provide the land, recruit qualified management and staff, and cover the expenses of future operation and maintenance.

The facilities were constructed by local contractors under local supervision and with advisors from the industrial country. Local companies installed the equipment with advice from resident and visiting specialists from the industrial country. The local staff was trained, and an information programme was developed with advice from these advisors. The project accomplished its operational objectives (to establish the centre) and was completed on target, within budget, and with acceptable quality of outputs. It was also well on its way to meet its tactical objectives. The progress was remarkable: the centre was able without delay to operate a seismic early warning system designed to detect seismic waves on their way from off-shore epicentres to the capital. On its own initiative the centre also designed a computer-based system to identify the high-risk micro-zones where earthquakes would make most damage, based on accumulated seismic data. A research programme to test and design low cost reinforced building structures was in operation, and a comprehensive information programme had been initiated to educate and train contractors in the building industry, civil defence, researchers, and the public.

Furthermore, the canter rapidly became a national coordinator of all seismic research, and expanded its activities also into other areas such as chemical hazards and surveillance of volcanoes. It established training programmes for Masters and Doctoral levels students and became increasingly involved in international projects in the region. It also maintained contacts with several of the involved institutions in the industrial country.

The strategy

In a strategic perspective, the strength of this highly successful project was that there was a strongly felt need by the country's government and a commitment to recruit qualified staff and use sufficient resources to develop and maintain the centre. The project was carefully planned, based on information from a very thorough initial investigation with ample communication between the main parties. Many aspects, which would otherwise be uncertain, were thereby discussed and sorted out in advance.

Its strategy was well balanced in terms of probabilities of realisation at different levels in the project design. The *operational* objectives or the outputs were essentially to deliver the basis for an effective institution, i.e. well designed facilities, competent and well-trained staff, appropriate equipment and sufficient funds to operate. The highly experienced and specialised foreign expertise that was used in the early phases of the project would be the best guarantee for a realistic design. The *tactical* objective or the project's goal was simply to establish an efficient and reliable early warning system for disaster prevention in the case of earthquakes. This is a technical objective, which is not very ambitious in the sense that the probability of its fulfilment is rather high once the centre has been established and is in operation. The chance of success was therefore good. The *strategic* objective or the purpose was to reduce the disastrous effect of earthquakes in society. This is also essentially a technical objective with a reasonable chance of realisation, although it depends on the active involvement of a number of other external institutions such as civil defence, building industry, law enforcement, fire departments, mass media, etc., in order to succeed. The role of the centre would be to disseminate information and advisory services to these institutions.

Project evaluation – assessing the degree of success

The success criteria described in chapter 4 have been applied on the four project cases to illustrate their significance in providing a well founded conclusion regarding the project's success:

EFFICIENCY	The achievement of operational objectives in terms of cost, timing and quality of outputs
EFFECTIVENESS	The achievement of the tactical objective
IMPACT	All other effects of the project, positive of negative, foreseen or unforeseen
RELEVANCE	The significance of the tactical objective seen in relation to needs and priorities
SUSTAINABILITY	The extent to which the positive achievements of the project will be continued in the future

---

Tactics

In *tactical* terms the strength of the project was that it was implemented by highly qualified people both locally and from abroad. Resources were sufficient. The purpose of the project was clearly understood by decision-makers and the public, exactly because of its down-to-earth, realistic design, and there was ample political support for the project. The centre had no competitors in its field and did not have to compete for public funds. A clear but not too detailed agreement which spelled out the obligations of both parties, and careful monitoring of the project helped ensuring that the strategy was followed quite meticulously when the project was implemented. This was possible also because the project did not encounter any major contextual problems or risks during implementation.

Uncertainties and risks

The uncertainties in this case were correspondingly limited. A main uncertainty was whether the government would provide sufficient operational funds in the future. After the project was completed, it turned out that the operational funds provided by government did not compensate for inflation. However, the management responded to this problem with a constructive, down-to-earth approach: to cut down on some of its theoretical research and focus more on activities that were more immediately useful to society, in the fields of developing surveillance and early warning-systems, analysis and management of data, and information activities. Some of the most sophisticated equipment was transferred to research institutions and replaced with simpler equipment, which was less expensive to maintain. This was an effective way to avoid not only a future budgetary problem but also possible conflicts with counterpart institutions in the future. It was definitely an unexpected manoeuvre, most institutions would probably prefer to keep their sophisticated equipment and wish to develop their own capacity to operate it.

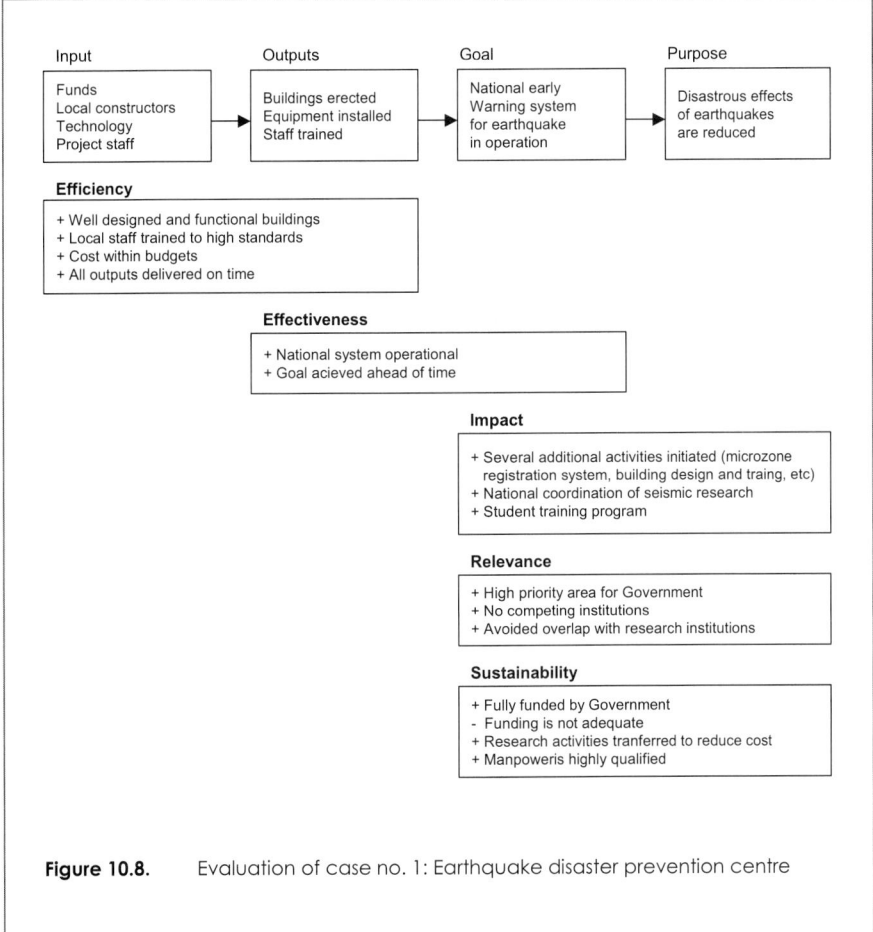

Figure 10.8. Evaluation of case no. 1: Earthquake disaster prevention centre

Evaluation

As can be seen from figure 10.8, the project scores high on all variables. In terms of *efficiency* it was completed on date, within budget and with the planned quality. In terms of *effectiveness* it significantly contributed to an improved disaster prevention capability in the country through its early warning systems, its research and information activities. The *impact* of the project was positive. The centre rapidly expanded into new areas such as volcano surveillance and chemical hazards. It became a national coordinator in its field and carefully avoided duplicating the work of other institutions involved in more theoretical research. The *relevance* of the project was unquestionable because of frequent earthquakes and volcanic eruptions in the country, some with devastating effects, and particularly since this was the first centre of its kind. Finally, the project was *sustainable* in the sense that all commitments were taken over by the government, which provided funds and qualified manpower for future operations. The project was therefore considered highly successful.

CASE NO. 2: ESTABLISHING ENTERPRISES FOR REFUGEES (UNSUCCESSFUL STRATEGY, SUCCESSFUL TACTICS)

This project was designed to assist a group of refugees from one country to become self-employed in their new country of residence. The programme was initiated by a UN agency with the consent of the government in the host country. The motivation was simply to cut down on the agency's emoluments to permanently settled refugees. The project was implemented by another UN agency with particular expertise in the field of setting up small-scale industries. The project used the agency's standard design for such projects without a prior appraisal or pre-study, and without any involvement by the host country's government.

The implementing agency employed an international specialist and local staff to coordinate the project. The project recruited the refugees. Training was done through existing institutions in the country. Fees were paid by the agency. The project staff was then involved in following up the candidates, providing advice and support in setting up their small-scale industries. Loans were provided through local banks, while collateral for the loans was provided by the agency.

Strategy

The main problems in this project were related to its strategy and design. It turned out when the project was set in motion that the number of resident refugees was much too small to provide a recruitment basis for the planned number of candidates. Certain minimum qualifications and abilities were required. In order to fulfil the stipulated quota, the project therefore also admitted unqualified resident refugees and younger temporary refugees in transit to other countries. As the result, a sizeable proportion of the candidates either failed to establish businesses or had already left the country before this could happen. Consequently, when evaluated, the cost efficiency of the project was very low, with overhead costs four times the amount of loans disbursed.

The remaining part of candidates succeeded in setting up small-scale businesses, some succeeded very well. These were people with high qualifications seen in relation to the situation in the host country. Their businesses created employment for local people. Some businesses expanded rapidly. The group of refugees started to earn money and it soon became an issue of concern that they were exploiting local manpower and paying low salaries after having been set up on very favourable terms by a UN agency. The project generated an ethnic conflict of some dimension. In a small country this became an issue, which added to the general hostility towards a large group of refugees and caused considerable concern for the host government.

The design of this project was inadequate. The project was a straightforward initiative to train a group of people during a relatively short period of time and provide them with financial means and advice to set up their businesses. The tactical objective was simply that these businesses would be established. This is a simple technical objective with a fairly high chance of realisation once the operational objectives have been produced. The strategic objective, however, was very restricted. It was just to cut down emoluments to the refugees involved from the UN agency. The potential benefit for the target group was substantial. By restricting the project only to a small group of resourceful foreigners, the chance of realisation was high. In a small, transparent society with less than one million inhabitants, the chance of causing internal conflicts was correspondingly high. Had the project been slightly more ambitious in the sense that it also included people from the host country in the target group this problem could have been avoided. Had the host government been consulted before the project was planned, this would have been the likely result. The strategic objective as it was formulated did not give sufficient justification for the project and misguided the use of resources.

Tactics

In *tactical* terms, the strength of the project was that it had a competent staff, a resourceful target group, and that the necessary services were provided by using existing institutions in the country. The project achieved it operational objectives and was implemented as planned, within schedule and budget.

The two major problems in this project were the limited recruitment base and the potential ethnic conflict that the project could cause. Both were identified as key problems by the project management at an early stage. However, the project had been designed and approved by people from the agency Headquarters in Europe. The project manager operated under a very centralised bureaucratic regime, reporting to the Headquarters according to pre-determined, detailed performance indicators. He did not challenge the Headquarters' strategy but did his best to comply when the project was implemented. Under a more flexible regime he could probably have made the necessary corrections to the strategy in the course of events as the project developed.

Uncertainties

A main uncertainty in this case was the size of the target group. This could obviously have been foreseen if an appraisal had been made initially. With this simple piece of information available, a reasonable solution would have been to admit the refugees in existing programmes on the same footing as locals, without creating a special, expensive project that gave the refugees preferential treatment also in setting up their businesses and securing their financial situation. This would have reduced overhead costs significantly and the competition would be fairer for the two ethnic groups.

Another main uncertainty was the socio-cultural effect of providing assistance to a foreign ethnic group of resourceful individuals. In a small, transparent society the problems that might result were also largely predictable. In this particular case the financing UN agency had initiated a project based on its own agenda to reduce recurrent expenses. An obvious solution would have been to leave the initiative with the government. The responsibility to think through the ethnic issue would then be in their hands, as well as the responsibility to lie down and enforce the rules for refugee entrepreneurs. A major conflict could have been avoided.

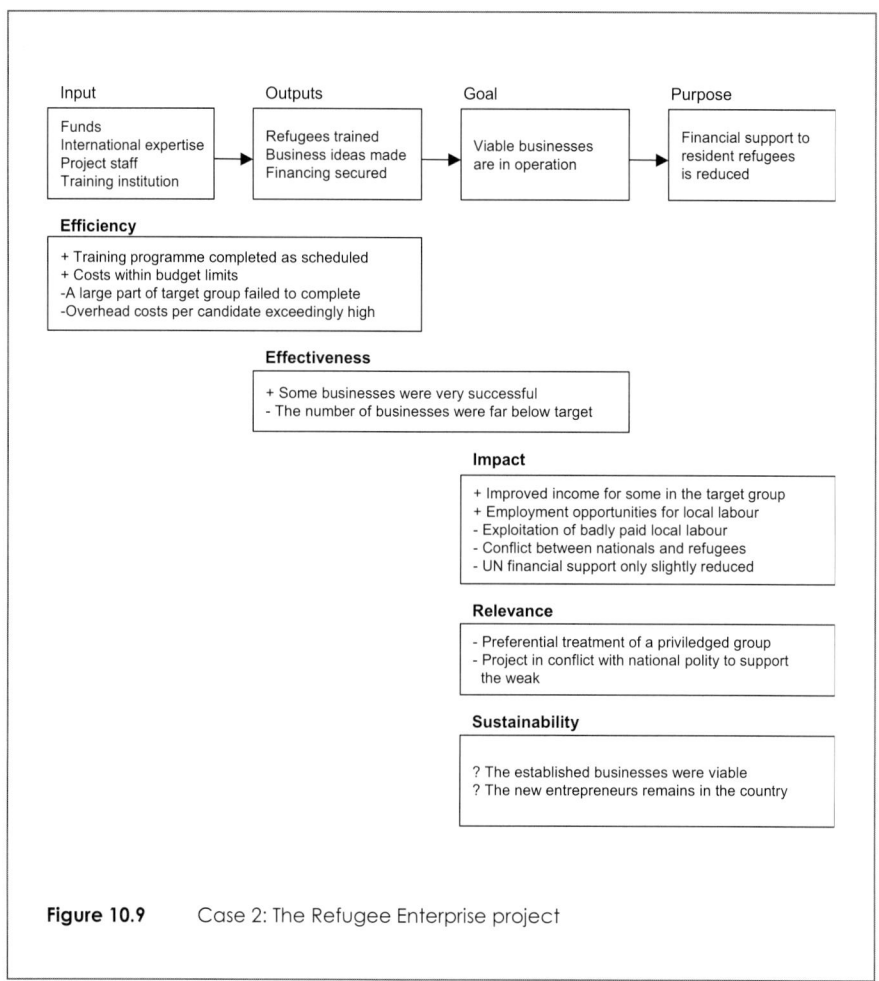

Figure 10.9   Case 2: The Refugee Enterprise project

Evaluation

The project was successfully implemented, but it was the wrong type of project in its societal setting. In terms of *efficiency* it was conducted on time, within budget and with acceptable quality. However, without an internationally recruited coordinator it could have been considerably cheaper. In terms of *effectiveness* it was successful in setting up enterprises for the qualified part of the refugees that had settled permanently in the country, but it failed with the larger parts of the target group. The positive *impact* of the project was in terms of improved income for part of the target group and employment opportunities for local people. The negative impact was in terms of exploitation of local labour and an emerging ethnic conflict. In total, the project may have been successful in reducing the UN agency's payment of emoluments to resident refugees, but the combined effects were predominantly negative. The project was designed primarily in response to the needs of the agency itself. It did not focus specifically on the needs and priorities of the target group of permanently settled refugees. It was not in tune with the needs of the larger group of temporarily settled younger refugees or the unqualified refugees, and it also may have been in conflict with the priorities of the government in the host country. In total therefore, the project was not *relevant*. Finally, the project was *sustainable* only to the extent that the small number of businesses that was established would actually survive.

CASE NO. 3: PROMOTING QUALITY ASSURANCE IN INDUSTRY (SUCCESSFUL STRATEGY, UNSUCCESSFUL TACTICS)

This project was designed to introduce quality assurance and raise the quality in production in 100 industrial companies in ten developing countries. The initiative came from an international organisation with representatives from individual governments. This organisation was the commissioning party. The project was implemented by a multinational company accredited to the highest level in field of quality assurance. The tactical objective was to develop capability in the countries to encourage and assist industry in implementing quality assurance and quality management.

The implementing company chose a centralised approach in its implementation of the project. It was coordinated from the company's Headquarters in the industrial country, with resident project offices in two of the participating countries. The international experts in these offices and a number of short-term experts from Headquarters conducted all training courses and serviced local industry directly in all the ten countries. This resulted in very high travel costs and manpower fees, and also a type of training, which was more adapted to the conditions in industrial countries than in developing countries.

As the result, in-plant services were provided only in four of the ten countries. The project staff did not have the time, capacity, or funds to cover all intended countries. The response in those companies that had been serviced, however, was good, and in some cases remarkable results were achieved in terms of improvement of products, working conditions, reduced pollution, improved market responses, etc.

Strategy

In *strategic* terms, the strength of the project was a strongly felt need for quality assurance activities, both by governments and by the industry. With quality being a general problem, small investments in quality awareness and improved procedures in industry would be a win/win suggestion for all parties.

The project was designed as a two-step strategy where the first step was to develop capability in local institutions to introduce quality assurance in industry and assist companies in improving quality. The second step would be for these bodies to make contact and provide services to industry. The operational objectives of the projects were associated with the first step in the process. The tactical objective was that industry improved quality and the strategic objective was that the target industry should be strengthened. Both these objectives are technical objectives, which would be realistically achievable with the resources available for the project.

Tactics

In terms of *tactics* it turned out that in the course of events, the implementing company had focused its attention on two levels primarily: the national standardisation organisations, which had received some general training, and industrial companies directly, which had received training and in-plant support. However, nothing had been done to build the capacity to service industries in the countries, as was the original intention. The project should have trained and coached quality inspectors in the national standard organisations, other technical institutions, the consulting industry, etc. That would have been a more cost-effective use of the highly qualified and expensive expertise from the multinational company.

In this project, the implementing company had not complied with the original strategy but taken a short cut to service industry directly. In the short term this would no doubt produce more tangible results. However, it was an expensive approach, and the long-term effect would probably be more limited than the effect of the intended strategy.

Uncertainties and risks

A main weakness of this project was that the commissioning international organisation did not have the qualifications, capacity or national backing to manage the contract properly with the implementing company.

A main uncertainty in this case seems to lie in the motives of the implementing company itself. Despite being financed entirely by a client organisation to provide a professional service, the company apparently had its agenda to create a market for its own services in the region, rather than creating a network of potential competitors as it was asked to do. An obvious solution in this case would have been to focus the attention on institution building in each country and to train trainers or instructors, who would then be the ones to service industry. Instead the organisation failed to honour its agreement with the commissioning organisation. From the point of view of the latter, the incident was probably not predictable from the outset. However, proper follow-up of the contract should have corrected the company's performance. This is therefore a tactical issue, not a strategic one.

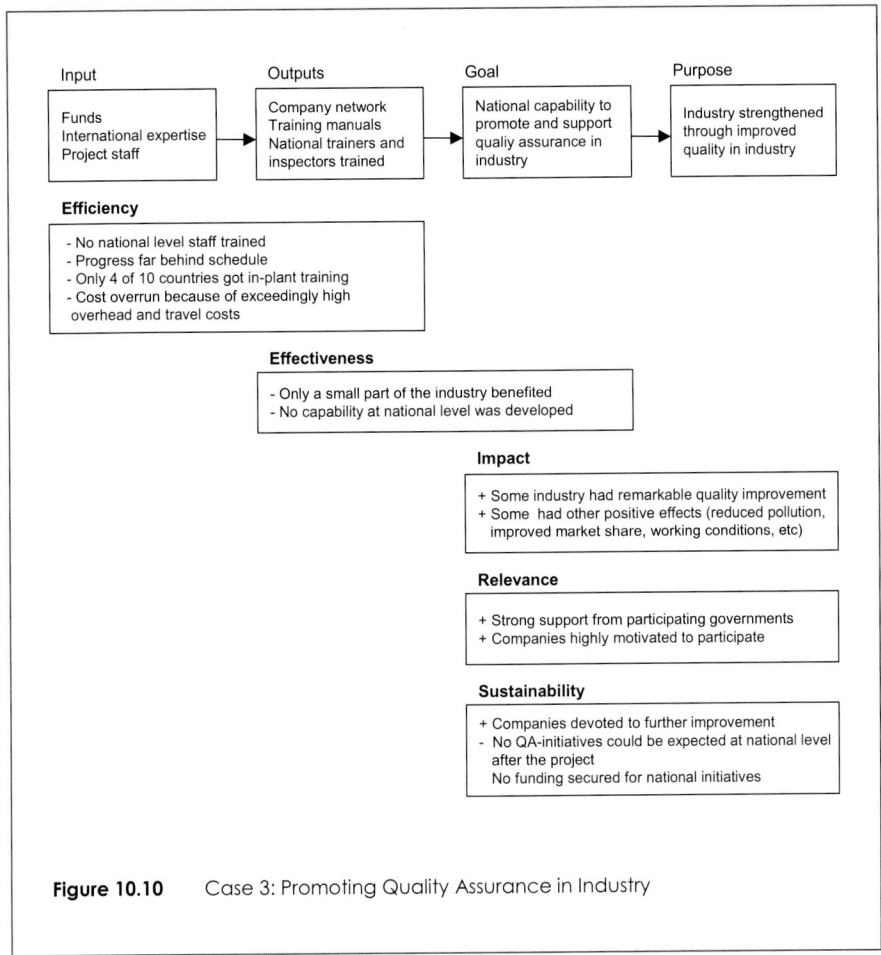

Figure 10.10   Case 3: Promoting Quality Assurance in Industry

Evaluation

This was the right type of project, but implemented inappropriately. In terms of *efficiency*, it wasted considerable resources by servicing industry directly, instead of transferring the necessary expertise to existing institutions in the countries involved so that they could perform the services at lower costs. As the result, the project was not *effective* since it was only able to service a part of the target industries. The *impact* however, was predominantly positive with no obvious negative effects. There were signs of quality improvement of products, increased productivity, better working conditions, reduced pollution, recycling of waste, etc. in some of the companies. In terms of *relevance* all parties seemed to agree that there was a strong need for the project in order to develop a competitive industry. Finally, the project was *sustainable* in the sense that most companies were sufficiently motivated to pay for quality assurance services in the future and apply quality assurance measures in their activities.

CASE NO. 4: BUILDING WATER SUPPLY IN RURAL AREAS (UNSUCCESSFUL STRATEGY AND TACTICS)

The project was designed to construct simple wells and boreholes to provide domestic water in rural areas in an African country. The project came out of a global initiative to promote this type of projects for the poor. The formal request came from the local government in response to a situation where an industrial country already had committed funds for projects in this sector. It was initiated with a very brief appraisal mission, which basically discussed the technical and economic aspect of a possible project, but not the contextual issues. The project agreement specified a number of water supplies to be constructed but gave no guidelines on which target groups should be served by the project.

The project was implemented through the local water authority. This institution was strengthened with a number of international experts and local staff, and considerable investments in buildings, equipment, vehicles, etc., to make it capable of constructing and maintaining the facilities. In terms of its operational objectives, it exceeded its time schedule by 300 per cent, and the budget over-run was some 2000 per cent. After construction was completed there were no more funds forthcoming from government for further construction, the institution that had been built up disintegrated, and people were laid off. Large investments in institutional development and equipment had been wasted.

Furthermore, it turned out that availability of water was not a major problem in the area and not a priority issue for the target population. As the result, it was difficult to make people pay water fees or maintain the facilities, which then frequently broke down. Also, it was found that the target population consisted of two distinct ethnic groups. One group lived in more marginal areas while the other group had the legal rights to most of the natural resources. They lived in the most fertile areas with the easiest access to water; they were in control of all political, administrative and legal institutions in the area, etc. As it were, it turned out that most of the boreholes and wells had been constructed in these areas where it hardly was a need for improved water supplies.

Strategy

In strategic terms this project was designed according to general experience from a large number of similar projects in the field. The operational objectives were a specified number of simple manually driven water supplies and certain initiatives to improve the awareness of water-related health and hygiene among the beneficiaries. The tactical objective was to achieve increased consumption of safe water in the target population. This is a technical objective, which would appear to be realistically achievable. The strategic objective was reduced incidents of water-related diseases in the target population. This is also a technical objective, which appear achievable provided that other conditions such as hygiene is improved simultaneously. The problem was therefore not the strategy per se but the mismatch between the strategy and the needs and priorities of the beneficiaries. This problem was aggravated further since the project failed to specify target group. The ruling ethnic group therefore automatically became beneficiaries.

Tactics

In tactical terms the main weakness of the project was that it was implemented by a government institution. For all practical purposes it was an initiative, which did not originate in genuine local priorities. It was rather obvious that an already bankrupt government would not be in the position to continue investing in water supplies for the rural population after external funds had been exhausted. The project set out to strengthen a public institution to construct facilities. This was a slow and expensive process, which in the end was doomed to be wasted.

Uncertainties and risks

A main uncertainty in this project is related to the users' need for the project. In reality, this type of projects were initiated as the result of a policy decision by the United Nations and not based on an assessment in rural areas of the users' need and priorities. With basic knowledge of the geographic (and hydro-geological) characteristics of the area, the problems could have been foreseen, although it was complicated in this particular case by the existence of two distinct ethnic groups. This added a political uncertainty of whether or not the disadvantaged group would be left out of the project. In a society where the favoured group was in control of all political and administrative bodies - this was exactly what happened.

A second main uncertainty was institutional in terms of whether or not the project would be continued. Would it be worthwhile building up institutional capacity for this purpose? Based on general experience in this particular country and the resources available from government, this was also largely predictable. The answer would be negative and an obvious alternative would therefore be to commission all construction work to private contractors and let the water authorities coordinate their work, which would have been radically less expensive.

A third type of uncertainty was related to the personnel situation in the international funding agency. Because of the extended implementation period and the high turnover of staff in the organisation where desk officers and decision-makers were changed every second year on average, decisions were very much left with the foreign project staff, the water authorities, and a third party consultant assigned to monitor the project on behalf of the water authorities. They all had vested interests in continuing the project. All funding from the international agency was provided on the basis of budgetary commitments. The agency was therefore hostage to it's own personnel policy. With it's high turnover of desk officers and decision-makers it was not able to raise or respond to major questions like those described above. This type of uncertainty is also highly predictable.

The final major uncertainty is related to the selection of technology. The lack of experience in this particular field among the international experts resulted in a trial and error process with regard to technology, which resulted in high failure rates and increased expenses. Because of the tremendous overhead costs in the project, the total investment cost per water supply was exorbitant and far beyond the users' financial abilities.

In summary, this project failed both strategically and tactically. There was no genuine need for the project in the target group. Also, the local government was not able or willing to make financial commitments in this field, and still the project attempted to build a permanent institution, which would rely on government funding in the future. Clearly, the project should not have been started.

Chapter 10 – Project cases

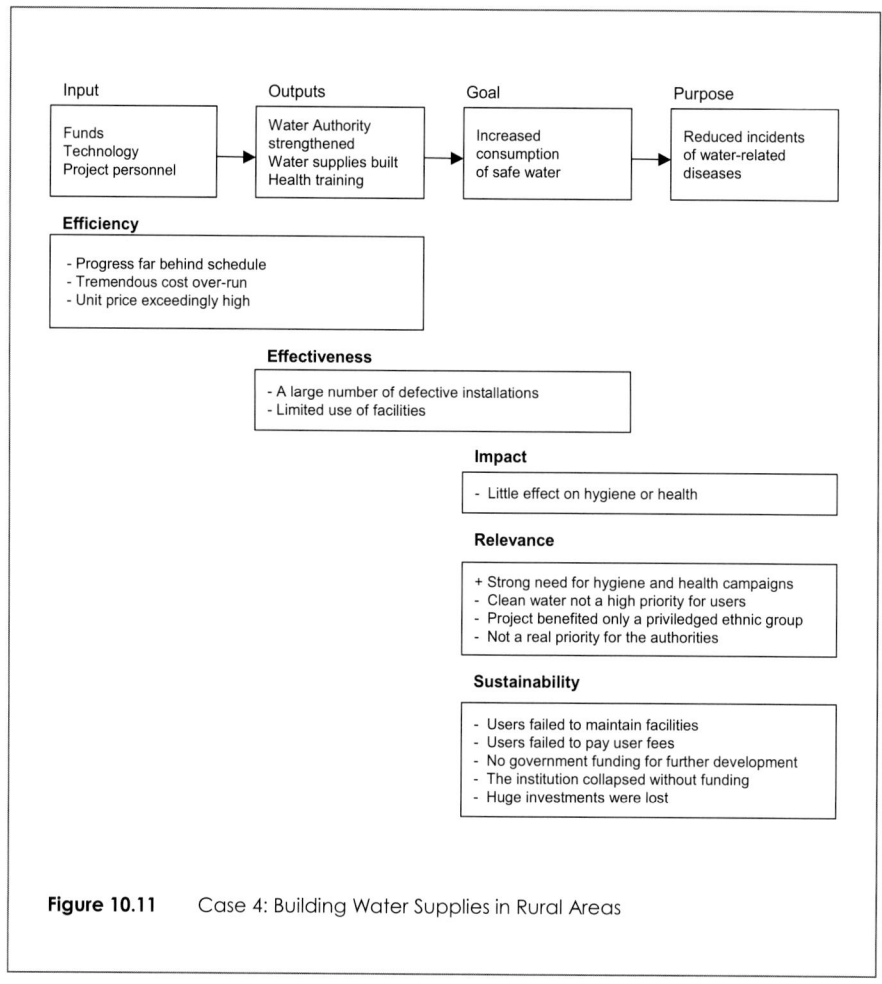

Figure 10.11 Case 4: Building Water Supplies in Rural Areas

Evaluation

This was the wrong type of project under the prevailing conditions, and implemented inappropriately. In terms of *efficiency* it caused tremendous cost and time over-runs in its attempt to turn a government technical department into a construction unit. The lack of the right type of technical expertise resulted in a trial and error approach with a lot of defective water supplies. Because of this, and since the facilities frequently broke down and were not maintained, the project was not *efficient* in providing safe water for the target population. The *impact* of the project was correspondingly limited. The main reason for these failures was that the project was not *relevant* in terms of people's priorities and needs. Since water was easily accessible in the area and people were poor, their needs would rather be to improve agricultural production than improve the quality of domestic water. For the same reason the project was not *sustainable*. People were not able or willing to pay for water, and there were no funds available to repair facilities when they broke down. Government was not willing to provide funds for further construction, and the investments in technical equipment and human resources in the government institution were therefore wasted.

Chapter 10 – Project cases

DISCUSSION

The findings above are summarised in table 10.4. What these four project cases have in common is that they were all based on a realistic design in terms of probabilities: the operational objectives were realistically achievable, and the tactical and strategic objectives were limited technical objectives which one would imagine would be realised under favourable conditions if resources were sufficient. And still, in two cases the strategy did not work: project no. 2: Refugee Entrepreneurs and no. 4: Water Supply. In both cases the priority accorded to the project by governments was low. This goes for part of the target group as well as for the governments. In one of these cases the government had not even been consulted.

	Case no 1 Earthquake Centre	Case no 2 Refugee Entrepr.	Case no 3 Quality Assurance	Case no 4 Water Supply
GENERAL PERFORMANCE				
Adequacy of tactics	+	+	-	-
Adequacy of strategy	+	-	+	-
TACTICS				
Reliance of qualified local staff	+	+	+	-
Clear, but not too detailed agreement	+	+	-	-
Careful monitoring by the client	+	+	-	-
Degree of compliance required by client	+	+	-	-
Use of contractors in implementation	+	+	-	-
STRATEGY				
Realism of project design	+	+	+	+
Priority accorded by government	+	-	+	-
Appraisal before project was planned	+	-	(+)	-
Quality of planning	+	-	+	-
Availability of funds for future operation	+	-	(+)	-

Table 10.4 Summary of project characteristics

In both cases no proper appraisal was done before the projects were designed and initiated. Project no. 2 was based on a rigid detailed plan made at the Headquarters according to a standard scheme but without sufficient information about local conditions. Project no. 4 also suffered from an analysis of fundamental determinants, and was guided by a plan that was very rich in operational details but which lacked an overall perspective to guide the project's interventions in the field. Both projects were therefore planned without taking notice of a few major stumbling stones, which subsequently caused the projects to fail. In both cases this was in terms of a potential ethnic conflict between target groups. It is reasonable to suggest that these major issues could have been detected had comprehensive feasibility studies been made in advance and the projects been adequately appraised before they were planned.

In project no.1: the Earthquake Centre and the no. 3: the Quality Assurance programme the situation was almost exactly the opposite. The projects were accorded a high priority both by the governments and the target groups. Project no. 1 was highly successful and was the result of a very thorough appraisal process which extended over one and a half year, based on a joint feasibility study and three subsequent appraisal missions undertaken by the industrial country to clarify the basic principles that should guide the agreement between the two parties. This process resulted in an agreement, which was brief and focused on the main issues of concern, not on the details. This obviously made it easier for the two parties to monitor and follow up the projects. [8] Project no. 3, the Quality Assurance programme, was designed by a highly specialised company with a unique expertise in the field, and based on a feasibility study with visits to some of the cooperating institutions and target companies.

In terms of tactics, the pattern is consistent in these cases. The projects were implemented using private contractors to a large extent, except for the Water Supply project (no. 4) where the construction was done by a government institution. The two projects that were most successful in tactical terms, no. 1 the Earthquake Centre and no. 2 the Refugee Entrepreneur project, strongly relied on the use of qualified local personnel in key positions, whereas the other two projects were managed almost exclusively by internationally recruited staff. The two successful projects were monitored meticulously by the funding agencies according to an agreed set of performance indicators. In both cases these agencies exerted considerable pressure on the implementing parties to comply with the agreed strategy. In the two other projects the situation was the opposite. There were no agreed reporting formats, and the follow-up by the funding agencies was erratic to the extent that the executing organisation in the quality assurance project was able to choose its own venue, different from the agreed one when the project was implemented. In the case of the water supply project it developed along a trial-and-error path with an abundance of resources made available, and operating under an unclear strategy and with inadequate control by the funding agency.

Two main questions to be answered are whether a better strategy in projects nos. 2 and 4 would have resulted in successful projects and whether improved tactics in projects 3 and 4 would have improved success rates. In the Refugee Entrepreneur project (no. 2) it seems reasonable to suggest that with a more thorough pre-study and appraisal,[9] the refugee target group would have been included in ongoing programmes on equal terms with the country's own residents and the problem been avoided. The project would still be under professional supervision of the UN agency with its specialised expertise, and training would be done by the same competent local institutions. In the Quality Assurance programme (no. 3), the main problem was the coordination and follow-up of the executing company. Since both the funding agency and the local governments were unable to perform adequately, an external coordinator or overseer could have been assigned to the project to control and supervise the implementing organisation. This

---

[8] In case no. 4, the Water Supply project, the situation was entirely different. The main guiding document was a very detailed Plan of Operation which diverted attention from the main issues and could hardly be used as a management instrument by the parties.

[9] In fact, an initial dialogue with the host government would probably be sufficient

would have been a cost-effective solution to focus resources on a more long-term strategy to build local quality assurance capability in the involved countries. In the short term the results in industry might be meagre, but in the long term the strategy could prove to be more cost-effective.

In the water supply project (no. 4) the situation is less obvious. The project was designed to produce a specified number of simple wells. A reasonable suggestion would be to have construction and maintenance done by local contractors answerable to the water authorities. A limited institutional build-up would be necessary to enable the water authorities to control and supervise the contractors. Construction would be done rapidly and at a much lower cost than was the case. A number of technological and institutional questions would be left in the hands of the contractors to solve. But still the problem of the needs of the target groups remains. Ideally, the project should have focused on the disadvantaged ethnic group. In this particular case water was relatively easily available for all people in the area. Since both population groups are relatively poor, it is reasonable to assume that both groups would consider improved water supply a relatively low priority compared with other needs. A thorough feasibility study would have disclosed the priorities and would probably concluded that a water supply project would not be feasible in this particular area.

All projects encountered numerous operational difficulties during implementation that had to be handled if the project should succeed. Most of these were problems associated with the project's operational objectives and related to cost, timing and quality of outputs. This is the main focus of project management and the most common techniques and tools of the trade.

Such tools lay the framework for the tactical performance of the project manager, seen in relation to the project's strategy. At the same time, they tend to limit his focus to the operational perspective. Project failure can be achieved even in a favourable environment if internal factors are unsuccessful. On the other hand, success is difficult to achieve if the external factors are favourable. In the first instance the strategy may be appropriate but tactics may be a failure. In the latter case both tactics and strategy will have to be appropriate.

What the cases above show is that there are a few major issues that are critical in determining success and failure of projects. These are related both to the tactical and strategic objectives. The challenge for the project manager is to apply the appropriate mix between strategic planning to avoid the main stumbling stones while guiding the project in the right direction - at the same time be able to respond tactically to unforeseen events in order to coach the project towards a successful conclusion.

Much of the answer to the problems seems to lie in the quality of information at entry, how this information is interpreted in terms of probabilities and utilities, and how these findings are used to assert the realism of the strategy.

CONCLUSIONS

The assessments of the four projects are summarised in Table 10.5. It demonstrates the significance of the evaluation criteria in assessing success and failure, and furthermore that they are expressions of tactical and strategic performance of a project. Comparing table 10.3 and table 10.5 the pattern is almost exactly the same. This is because *efficiency* is a direct indicator of tactical performance, which is measured for instance in terms of compliance with budgets, time schedule and the realisation of operational objectives quantitatively and qualitatively. *Effectiveness* is to some extent also an indicator of tactical performance as regards whether the outputs produced by the project are sufficient seen in relation to the longer-term fulfilment of the tactical objective. *Impact*, however, is an indicator of the strategy in the sense that the agreed direction of the project has been such that the positive effects outweigh the negative effect by a safe margin. The same goes for *relevance*, which is an indicator on whether objectives are rooted in genuine needs and priorities in society. And finally, *sustainability* is also an indicator of the strategy that will provide the final proof of the impact and relevance of the project as seen in a longer-term perspective.

EVALUATION CRITERIA	Case no 1 Earthquake Centre	Case no 2 Refugee Entrepr.	Case no 3 Quality Assurance	Case no 4 Water Supply	Type of feature measured
EFFICIENCY	+	+/-	-	-	Tactical
EFFECTIVE NESS	+	+/-	+/-	-	
IMPACT	+	-	+	-	
RELEVANCE	+	-	+	-	Strategic
SUSTAIN ABILITY	+	-	+	-	

Table 10.5   Performance of the project cases

From what has been discussed above, the five evaluation criteria can also be used pro-actively to establish design and performance standards that could ensure not only quality at entry, but also guide the tactical performance of projects. Applied systematically in the initial pre-study it could be used to elicit relevant information to improve project design: In order to design a *relevant* and *sustainable* project information must be produced on the needs and priorities that would justify the project both in the short- and long term. This would require studies of the relevant policies, market needs and user capabilities. In order to ensure that the *impact* of the project is essentially positive, information would be needed on what could possibly go wrong, what would be the likely negative effects of the project, how likely these effects would be and how they could be avoided. In order to design an *effective* project a combined analysis would have to be done taking all these aspects into consideration to identify risks and opportunities - as well as the resources available and the time perspective - in the pursuit to define a realistic tactical objective. An finally, in order to ensure an *efficient* project, information would be needed on the institutional setting, logistics, market capacities, technology, etc. to establish operational objectives that are realistically achievable, and also substantial enough to facilitate the realisation of the tactical and strategic objectives.

GLOSSARY OF EVALUATION TERMS ANNEX 1

Accuracy	The extent to which an evaluation is truthful or valid in what it says about a program, project or material.
Achievement	A manifested performance determined by some type of assessment or testing.
Activity	An element of work performed during the course of a project to produce specific outputs. An activity normally has an expected duration, cost, and resource requirements. Activities are often subdivided into tasks.
Appraisal	Assessment of the feasibility and acceptability of a project or program prior to commitment in accordance with established decision criteria. These would commonly include relevance and sustainability. May also relate to the examination of options as part of the project identification process.
Assessment	Often used as a synonym for evaluation. The term is sometimes recommended for restriction to processes that are focused on quantitative and/or testing approaches.
Assumptions	External factors (or risks) which could affect the progress or success of a project or program, but over which the management has no direct control. (Common synonym: external factors). Initial assumptions constitute conditions perceived to be essential for the success of a project or program. Critical assumptions constitute conditions perceived to threaten the implementation of a project/program. (Common synonym: Killing assumption).
Attribution	The estimation of the extent to which an observed phenomenon is caused by another. Example: the extent to which observed change can be attributed to a specific a project or program, in view of the effects of other interventions or confounding factors. (Related terms: causality, incrementatity)
Audit	Verification of the legality and regularity of the implementation of resources. The audit determines whether and to what extent activities and procedures conform to norms and criteria set out in advance, and are adequate to meet stated objectives. The distinction is made between internal audit, where the auditors report to the organization being audited – and external audit, where the auditors report to the organization's owners.

Annex 1 – Glossary of evaluation terms

Bar Chart	A graphic display of schedule-related information. In the typical bar chart, activities or other project elements are listed down the left side of the chart, dates are shown across the top, and activity durations are shown as date-placed horizontal bars. Also called a Gantt chart.
Baseline	Facts about the condition or performance of subjects prior to a project or intervention.
Base-line study	An analysis describing the situation prior to a project, against which progress can be assessed or comparisons made
Benchmark	Reference point or standard against which to compare performance or achievements. The benchmark might refer to what has been achieved in the past, by other comparable organizations, or what could reasonably have been achieved in the circumstances.
Beneficiaries	The individuals that are intended to benefit from the project (the target group) plus others that might benefit
Bias	A consistent alignment with one point of view.
Breadth	Breadth refers to the scope of the measurement's coverage.
Case Study	An intensive, detailed description and analysis of a single project, program, or phenomenon in the context of its environment.
Causal relationship	The logical connection or cause and effect linkage between the achievement of related, interdependent results. Generally the term refers to plausible linkages, and not statistically accurate relationships. Synonyms: vertical logic, narrative summary, results chain
Causality analysis	The study of cause and effect relations, which link a project to its impacts. Related term: attribution
Commissioner	The organization or institution that commissions an evaluation
Comprehensive-ness	Full breadth and depth of coverage on the evaluation issues of interest.
Confidence Level	A statement that the true value of a parameter for a population lies within a specified range of values with a certain level of probability.
Contingency Planning	The development of a management plan that identifies alternative strategies to be used to ensure project success if specified risk events occur.
Control Group	In (quasi)experimental designs, a group of subjects that receives all influences except that of the project in exactly the same way as the target group

Annex 1 – Glossary of evaluation terms

Contract	A contract is a mutually binding agreement which obligates the seller to provide the specified product and obligates the buyer to pay for it. Contracts generally fall into one of three broad categories:

- ❑ Fixed price or lump sum contracts-this category of contract involves a fixed total price for a well-defined product. Fixed price contracts may also include incentives for meeting or exceeding selected project objectives such as schedule targets.

- ❑ Cost reimbursable contracts-this category of contract involves payment (reimbursement) to the contractor for its actual costs. Costs are usually classified as direct costs (costs incurred directly by the project, such as wages for members of the project team) and indirect costs (costs allocated to the project by the performing organization as a cost of doing business, such as salaries for corporate executives). Indirect costs are usually calculated as a percentage of direct costs. Cost reimbursable contracts often include incentives for meeting or exceeding selected project objectives such as schedule targets or total cost.

Corrective Action	Changes made to bring expected future performance of the project into line with the plan.
Correlation	A statistical measure of the degree of relationship between variables.
Cost-benefit analysis	The comparison of investment and operating costs with the direct benefits generated by the investment (using a variety of methods and means of expressing results). Related terms: financial cost-benefit analysis, economic cost-benefit analysis, social cost-benefit analysis
Cost Budgeting	Allocating the cost estimates to individual project components.
Cost Control	Controlling changes to the project budget.
Cost-effectiveness analysis	Comparison of the relative costs of achieving a given output by different means (employed where benefits are difficult to determine).
Cost Estimating	Estimating the cost of the resources needed to complete project activities.
Cost of Quality	The costs incurred to ensure quality. The cost of quality includes quality planning, quality control, quality assurance, and rework.
Data Collection Method	The way facts about a project and its impact are amassed. Data collection methods often used in program evaluations include: literature search, file review, direct observations, surveys, expert opinion and case studies.
Depth	Depth refers to a measurement's degree of accuracy and detail
Design	The process of stipulating the investigatory procedures to be followed in doing a certain evaluation.

Annex 1 – Glossary of evaluation terms

Dissemination	The process of communicating information to specific audiences for the purpose of extending knowledge and, in some cases, with a view to modifying policies and practices.
Effect	A generic term that refers to the changes resulting directly or indirectly from a project or process. Related terms: impact, primary effect, secondary effect, unexpected effect, direct effect, external effect, indirect effect, gross effect, net effect, first round effect
Effectiveness	A measure of the extent to which a project or process has attained its objectives at the goal or purpose level.
Efficiency	A measure of how economically inputs (funds, expertise, time, etc.) are converted to outputs.
Environmental analysis	Examination of the environmental risks and benefits associated with a project. This is a broad term used to describe any form of environmental study, including the full formal environmental impact assessment
Evaluability assessment	Assessment of information requirements and available knowledge in order to determine whether reliable and credible answers can be given to the questions asked.
Evaluation	A systematic examination of an on-going or completed project or program that is undertaken selectively to answer specific management questions. Evaluations commonly aim to determine the efficiency, effectiveness, impact, sustainability and the relevance of objectives.
Evaluation Design	The logical model or conceptual framework used to arrive at conclusions about outcomes.
Evaluation Strategy	The method used to gather evidence about one or more outcomes of a program. An evaluation strategy is made up of an evaluation design, a data collection method and an analysis technique.
Evaluation team	The individuals that perform an evaluation. An evaluation team collects data, carries out analyses and produces the evaluation report. An evaluation team may be internal or external. It may consist of several organizations (consortium) or of one contracting out the work. It may even consist of a single person.
Ex-ante evaluation	Evaluation that is performed before implementation. Related term: appraisal
Ex-post evaluation	Evaluation that recapitulates and judges a project when it is over. Its purpose is to study how well the project performed, and to draw conclusions for similar projects in the future.
External evaluation	Evaluation of a project by people outside the financing or implementing organisations. Synonym: independent evaluation

Annex 1 – Glossary of evaluation terms

Formative evaluation	Evaluation conducted during implementation, intended for managers and direct protagonists of a project or program with the intent to improve performance.
External Validity	The ability to generalize conclusions about a project to future or different conditions. Threats to external validity include: selection and project interaction
File Review	A data collection method involving a review of project files.
Focus group	A group selected for its relevance to an evaluation that is engaged by a trained facilitator in a series of discussions designed for sharing insights, ideas, and observations on a topic of concern.
Formative evaluation	Evaluation designed and used to improve an intervention, especially when it is still being developed.
Generalizability	The extent to which information about a program, project, or phenomenon in one setting can be used to reach a valid judgment about how it will perform in other settings.
Goal	The higher-order program or sector objective to which a project contributes. Common synonym: strategic objective
Immediate objective	See: Purpose
Impact	The positive and negative changes produced by a program or project, directly or indirectly, intended or unintended.
Impact evaluation	An evaluation focused on outcomes or pay-off.
Indicator	Quantitative or qualitative variable that provides a simple and reliable basis for assessing achievement, change or performance.
Input	The financial, human and material resources that are necessary to produce the intended outputs of a project or program.
Internal evaluation	Evaluation of a project by people belonging to the financing or implementing organisations.
Internal Validity	The ability to assert that a project has caused measured results (to a certain degree), in the face of plausible potential alternative explanations. The most common threats to internal validity are history, maturation, mortality, selection bias, regression artefacts, diffusion or imitation of treatment and testing.
Interview Guide	A list of issues or questions to be raised in the course of the interview.

Annex 1 – Glossary of evaluation terms

Lessons learned	Learning from experience that is applicable to a generic situation rather than to a specific circumstance. Related term: feedback, experience
Longitudinal Data	Data collected over a period of time, sometimes involving a stream of data for particular persons or entities over time.
Logical Framework	Management tool used to improve the design of projects, programs and strategies. It helps to identify strategic elements (inputs, outputs, purpose, goal) and their causal relationships, and the external assumptions (risks) that may influence success and failure. It thus facilitates planning, execution and evaluation of a program or project. An LFA matrix is the analytic framework used to present the results of a logical framework analysis.
Long-term Objective	See: Goal
Measurement	Determination of the magnitude of a quantity.
Measurement Validity	A measurement is valid to the extent that it represents what it is intended and presumed to represent. Valid measures have no systematic bias.
Meta-evaluation	Evaluation of evaluations, usually for the purpose either to aggregate findings from a series of evaluations, or to judge the quality of evaluations.
Mid-term evaluation	Evaluation performed towards the middle of the period of implementation of the project. Its principal aim is to draw conclusions for administering a project or program. Related term: on-going evaluation
Monitoring	A continuing function that uses methodical collection of data to provide management and the main stakeholders of an ongoing project or program with early indications of progress and achievement of objectives
Needs assessment	Using a diagnostic definition, need is anything essential for a satisfactory mode of existence or level of performance. The essential point of a needs assessment for evaluation is the identification of performance needs.
Nominal data	Data which consist of categories only without order to these categories (i.e., region of the country, courses offered by an instructional program).
Objective Data	Observations that do not involve personal feelings and are based on observable facts. Objective data can be quantitatively or qualitatively measured.
Objectivity	Evidence and conclusions that are capable of being verified by someone other than the original authors.
Observation	The process of direct sensory inspection involving trained observers.
Outputs	The tangible immediate and intended results to be produced through sound management of the agreed inputs. Examples of outputs include

Annex 1 – Glossary of evaluation terms

	goods, services or infrastructure produced by a project, meant to help realize its purpose. Synonyms: results, deliverables, operational objectives
Participatory evaluation	A broad term for the involvement or primary and other stakeholders in evaluation. The primary focus may be the information needs of stakeholders rather than the financing party.
Performance	The degree to which a project, program or institution operates according to specific criteria or quality standards.
Performance indicator	A variable that allows the verification of changes in the project or results relative to fixed targets. Related terms: performance target, target
Performance measurement	Review activities undertaken by line management to assess performance of projects, programs, and operations. Performance measurement includes such activities as performance monitoring, self-assessments, and operational reviews. Related terms: performance assessment, performance review, performance monitoring
Policy	Clear and concise mandate, rule, or regulation that is required for organizations to perform. Policies are often accumulated incrementally through the years. A policy level evaluation focuses on the implementation of a specific policy.
Population	The set of units to which the results of a survey apply.
Portfolio	The sum of programs or projects being managed by an agency or organisation.
Primary Data	Data collected by an evaluation team specifically for the evaluation study.
Probability Sampling	The selection of units from a population based on the principle of randomisation. Every unit of the population has a calculable (non-zero) probability of being selected.
Process evaluation	An evaluation aimed at setting out and understanding the internal dynamics of a project, program or institution. Related term: formative evaluation
Program	A group of related projects managed in a coordinated way Programs usually include an element of ongoing activity Programme evaluation. Evaluation of several individual projects, which converge to attain the same goal.
Project	A temporary endeavour undertaken to create a unique product or service. A project consists of a set of planned, interrelated activities designed to achieve defined objectives within a given budget and a specified period of time.
Project Cost Management	A subset of project management that includes the processes required to ensure that the project is completed within the approved budget. It

Annex 1 – Glossary of evaluation terms

	consists of resource planning, cost estimating, cost budgeting, and cost control.
Project Cycle Management	A tool for understanding the tasks and management functions to be performed in the course of a project or program's lifetime. This commonly includes the stages of identification, preparation, appraisal, implementation/supervision, evaluation, completion and lesson learning.
Project evaluation	Evaluation of an individually planned project designed to achieve specific objectives within a given budget and time period.
Project Life Cycle	A collection of generally sequential project phases whose name and number are determined by the control needs of the organization or organizations involved in the project.
Project Management (PM)	The application of knowledge, skills, tools, and techniques to project activities in order to meet or exceed stakeholder needs and expectations from a project.
Project Management Team	The members of the project team who are directly involved in project management activities. On some smaller projects, the project management team may include virtually all of the project team members.
Project Manager (PM)	The individual responsible for managing a project.
Project Phase	A collection of logically related project activities, usually culminating in the completion of a major deliverable.
Project Plan	A formal, approved document used to guide both project execution and project control. The primary uses of the project plan are to document planning assumptions and decisions, to facilitate communication among stakeholders, and to document approved scope, cost, and schedule baselines. A project plan may be summary or detailed.
Project Planning	The development and maintenance of the project plan.
Project Risk Management	A subset of project management that includes the processes concerned with identifying, analysing, and responding to project risk. It consists of risk identification, risk quantification, risk response development, and risk response control.
Project Schedule	The planned dates for performing activities and the planned dates for meeting milestones.
Project Team Members	The people who report either directly or indirectly to the project manager.
Project Time Management	A subset of project management that includes the processes required to ensure timely completion of the project. It consists of activity definition, activity sequencing, activity duration estimating, schedule development,

Annex 1 – Glossary of evaluation terms

	and schedule control.
Purpose	The positive improved situation which a project or program is expected to contribute significantly to if completed successfully and on time. The purpose is the central objective expressed in terms of benefits to be achieved by the target group. It does not refer to the services provided by the project/program (these are outputs), but to the benefits, which beneficiaries derive as a result of using these services.
Qualitative Data	Observations that are categorical rather than numerical, and often involve attitudes, perceptions and intentions.
Qualitative evaluation	The part of the evaluation that is primarily descriptive and interpretative, and may or may not lend itself to quantitative treatment.
Quality assurance (QA)	The process of evaluating overall project performance on a regular basis to provide confidence that the project will satisfy the relevant quality standards.
Quality Control (QC)	The process of monitoring specific project results to determine if they comply with relevant quality standards and identifying ways to eliminate causes of unsatisfactory performance.
Quantitative Data	Observations that are numerical.
Quantitative evaluation	An approach involving the use of numerical measurement and data analysis based on statistical methods.
Random	Affected by chance.
Random sampling	Drawing a number of items of any sort from a larger group or population so that every individual item has a specified probability of being chosen.
Reliability	Consistence or dependability of data, with reference to the quality of the instrument or procedure used to collect evaluation data. Information is reliable when repeated observations using the same instrument under identical conditions produce similar results.
Research	The general field of disciplined investigation.
Reserve	A provision in the project plan to mitigate cost and/or schedule risk. Often used with a modifier (e.g., management reserve, contingency reserve) to provide further detail on what types of risk are meant to be mitigated. The specific meaning of the modified term varies by application area.
Response bias	Error due to incorrect answers.
Results	A measurable change resulting from a cause-and-effect relationship. Related terms: output, outcome, effect

Annex 1 – Glossary of evaluation terms

Results Based Management	A broad management strategy aimed at achieving important changes in the way government agencies operate, with improving performance as the central orientation. Results based management provides a coherent framework for strategic planning and management based on learning and accountability in a decentralized environment.
Results framework	Reflects the RBM framework - from inputs to outputs, to ultimate impacts. Related terms: vertical logic, narrative summary, causal relationship, strategic framework, result chain
Review	An assessment of the performance of a project or programme, periodically or on an as-needs basis. A review is more extensive than monitoring, but less than evaluation. An evaluation is more comprehensive, and places greater emphasis on impact, relevance and sustainability.
Risk Event	A discrete occurrence that may affect the project for better or worse.
Risk Identification	Determining which risk events are likely to affect the project.
Risk Quantification	Evaluating the probability of risk event occurrence and effect.
Risk Response Control	Responding to changes in risk over the course of the project.
Sample	A part of a population.
Sample bias	Error due to non-response or incomplete response from selected sample subjects.
Sampling error	Error due to using a sample instead of entire population from which sample is drawn.
Secondary Data	Data collected and recorded by another (usually earlier) person or organization, usually for different purposes than the current evaluation.
Sector	A specific area of activities. such as Health, Industry, Education, Agriculture, Transport etc.
Sector evaluation	Evaluations of a selection of projects or programs, all of which are located in the same economic sector.
Selection Bias	The experimental and comparison groups involved in the program are initially statistically unequal in terms of one or more of the factors of interest. This a threat to internal validity.
Sensitivity analysis	Analysis of how changes in the assumed values of key variables might affect outcomes of a project.
Stakeholder	An agency, organization, group or individual who has a direct or indirect interest in the project/program, or who affects or is affected positively or

Annex 1 – Glossary of evaluation terms

	negatively by the implementation and outcome of it.
Standard Deviation	The standard deviation of a set of numerical measurements (on an "interval scale") indicates how closely individual measurements cluster around the expected measurement.
Statistic	A summary number that is typically used to describe a characteristic of a sample.
Statistical Analysis	The manipulation of numerical or categorical data in order to predict phenomena, to draw conclusions about relationships among variables, or to generalize results.
Statistical Model	A model that is normally based on previous research and permits transformation of a specific impact measure into another specific impact measure, one specific impact measure into a range on another impact, or a range on an impact measure into a range on another impact.
Statistically Significant Effects	Effects that are observed and are unlikely to result solely from chance variation. They can be assessed through the use of statistical tests.
Strategy	A strategy constitutes a framework of objectives and priorities for a project or process drawn up and used to steer investments. Synonyms: strategy, strategic framework
Subjective Data	Observations that involve personal feelings, attitudes and perceptions. Subjective data can be quantitatively or qualitatively measured.
Summative evaluation	Evaluation designed to present conclusions about the merit or worth of an intervention and recommendations about whether it should be retained, altered, or eliminated.
Surveys	A data collection method that involves a planned effort to collect needed data from a sample (or a complete census) of the relevant population. The relevant population consists of people or
Summative evaluation	Evaluation to justify a project or program. It is usually conducted at the end of implementation and with external evaluators.
Sustainability	The likelihood that the positive effects of a project, (such as assets, skills, facilities or improved services), will persist for an extended period after the project is completed.
SWOT analysis	Analysis of the Strengths and Weaknesses associated with a project or program, and the Opportunities and Threats that it faces. A tool used for project appraisal.
Target group	The specific group for whose benefit the project or program is undertaken.
Terms of	An action plan used to explain the motives behind an evaluation, define

Annex 1 – Glossary of evaluation terms

Reference	the scope of work to be carried out by the evaluation team, and the time schedule. Related term: mandate
Thematic Evaluation	Evaluation of selected aspects or cross-cutting issues in different types of projects (poverty, environment, choice of technology, gender aspects, sustainability, etc.)
Time series study	A study in which periodic measurements are obtained prior to, during, and following the introduction of an intervention or treatment in order to reach conclusions about the effect of the intervention.
Triangulation	The use of several sources of information, methods or analysts to verify information. In an evaluation, it is an attempt to get a fix on a phenomenon or measurement by approaching it via several independent routes. This effort provides redundant measurement and help to overcome the bias that comes from single informants, single-methods, single observers or single theory studies.
Validity	The extent to which the information measure what it is intended to measure. Validity can often be improved by using several different measures, information sources or methods for the same phenomenon, see triangulation

LITERATURE ANNEX 2

Bemelmans-Videc, Made-Louise, Ray C. Rist and Evert Vedung, *Carrots, Sticks and Sermons: Policy instruments and their evaluation.*, Transaction publishers, 1998.

Boer, F. Peter, The Real Options Solution: Finding Total Value in a High-Risk World, Wiley 2002

Boulmetis, John, and Dutwin, Phyllis, *The ABC of Evaluation. Timeless Techniques for Program and Poject Managers*, Jossey-Bass, CA: 2000

Carlsson, Jerker, Gunnar Köhlin and Anders Ekbom, *The Political Economy of Evaluation: International Aid Agencies and the Effectiveness of Aid*, St. Martin's Press 1994.

Chelimski, Eleanor, and William R. Shadish Eds., *Evaluation for the 21st century, a handbook*, Sage Publications 1997.

Clarke, Alan and Ruth Dawson, *Evaluation Research*, Sage Publications 1999.

Compton Donald W., Baizerman Michael, Stockdill Stacey H., *The Art, Craft, and Science of Evaluation Capacity Building*, New Directions for Evaluation, Jossey-Bass, 2002

Cook, T. D. & Campbell, D. T. *Quasi-experimentation: Design and Analysis Issues or Field.* Settings, Chicago, IL: Rand McNally. 1979.

Cracknell, Basil E., *Evaluating Development Aid*, Sage Publications, 2000

Danish Ministry of Foreign Affairs: *Evaluation Guidelines, 1999*. Available in fulltext at *www.um.dk/udenrikspolitik/udviklingspolitik/evaluering*

Denzin, Norman K., Yvonna S. Lincoln, *Handbook of Qualitative Resesarch*, Sage publications, 1994.

Douglas, M. and A. Wildavsky (1982) Risk and Culture: An Essay on the Selection of Technological and Environmental Dangers. Berkeley, CA: University of California Press.

Eisner, E. W, *The Enlightened Eye: Qualitative Inquiry and the Enhancement of Educational Practice.* (2nd ed.) New York: Merrill, 1997

European Commission: *Evaluating socio-economic programmes: Evaluation design and management* MEANS collection Volume 1, European Commission, 1999.

European Commission: *Evaluating socio-economic programmes: Principal evaluation techniques and tools.* MEANS collection Volume 3, European Commission, 1999.

Annex 2 - Literature

European Commission: *Evaluating socio-economic programmes: Selection and use of indicators for monitoring and evaluation.* MEANS collection Volume 2, European Commission, 1999.

Fink, Arlene, *Evaluation Fundamentals Guiding Health Programmes, Research and Policy*, Sage Publications, 1993

Fitz-Gibbon, C. T. & Morris, L. L. *How to Design a Program Evaluation.* Newbury Park, CA: Sage, 1987

Fowler, F. J., *Survey Research Methods.* Newbury Park, CA: Sage, 1987

Friedlob George T., Plewa Jr. Franklin J., *Understanding Return on Investment,* Wiley InterScience, 1996

Gray, S. T. *Evaluation with Power.* San Francisco: Jossey-Bass, 1998.

Guba, Egon G., Yvonna S. Lincoln, *Fourth Generation Evaluation*, Sage Publications, 1990.

Harper, Malcolm and Gerry Finnegan, *Value for money? The impact of small enterprise development.*, Intermediate Technology Publications, 1998.

Herman, J. L., Morris, L. L., & Fitz-Gibbon, C. T. *Evaluators Handbook.* Newbury Park, CA: Sage 1987

Love, A. J. (ed.). *Evaluation Methods Sourcebook.* Ottawa, Canada: Canadian Evaluation Society, 1991

Light Richard J., *Evaluation Findings That Surprise,* New Directions for Evaluation, Jossey Bass, 2001

Madaus, G. F, Scriven, M., and Stufflebeam, D. L. (eds.). *Evaluation Models: Viewpoints on Educational and Human Services Evaluation.* Boston: Kluwer-Nijhoff, 1983.

March, J. G. and H. A. Simon, *Organizations.* New York: John Wiley, 1958.

Mark, Melvin M., Henry Gary T., Julnes George, *Evaluation: An Integrated Framework for Understanding, Guiding, and Improving Policies and Programs,* Jossey-Bass, 2000

Mintzberg, H. (1994) *The Rise and Fall of Strategic Planning.* New York: The Free Press.

Morris, L. L., Fitz-Gibbon, C. T., & Lindheim, E. (1987). How To Measure Performance and Use Tests. Newbury Park, CA: Sage.

Morris, P. W. G. and G. H. Hough, *The Anatomy of Major Projects: A Study of the Reality of Project Management.* Chichester: John Wiley and Sons, 1991

Norwegian Agency for Development Cooperation (NORAD): *The Logical Framework Approach (LFA): Handbook for objectives-oriented planning.* 4th ed., 1999.

Oakley, Peter, Brian Pratt and Andrew Clayton, *Outcomes and Impact - Evaluating Change in Social Development*, INTRAC, 1998

Patton, Michael Quinn, *Practical Evaluation*, Sage Publications, 1982.

Patton, Michael Quinn, *Qualitative Research and Evaluation Methods, 3rd ed.*, Sage Publications, 2001.

Picciotto, Robert and Eduardo Wiesner, *Evaluation and Development: The institutional dimension,* Transaction Publishers for the Word Bank, 1998

Quick James A., Carter Cheryl, *Grant Winner's Toolkit: Project Management and Evaluation,* Wiley InterScience, 2000

Rog Debra J., Fournier Deborah, *Progress and Future Directions in Evaluation: Perspectives on Theory, Practice, and Methods,* Jossey-Bass, 1997

Rossi, Peter H., Howard E. Freeman, Mark W. Lipsey, *Evaluation: A systematic approach, 6th ed.*, Sage Publications, 1998

Samset, Knut, *Evaluation of Development Assistance, Handbook for Evaluators and Managers,* Royal Norweian Ministry of Foreign Affairs, Oslo, 1993

Samset, Knut, *'Project Management in a High Uncertainty Situation',* Trondheim, The Norwegian University of Science and Technology. 1998

Scriven, Michael, *Evaluation Thesaurus, 4th edition,* Sage Publications, 1991.

Shadish, William R. Jr, Thomas D. Cook and Laura C. Leviton, *Foundations of Program Evaluation: Theories of Practice,* Sage Publications 1991.

Stecher, Brian M. and W. Alan Davis, *How to Focus an Evaluation,* Sage Publications, 1987.

Stewart, P. W. & Shamdasani, P. N., *Focus Groups.* Newbury Park, CA: Sage, 1990

Thomas, Alan, Joanna Chataway and Marc Wuyts, *Finding out Fast, Investigative Skills for Policy and Development,* Sage Publications 1998.

Torres Rosalie T., Preshill Hallie S., Piotek Mary E., *Evaluation Strategies for Communicating and Reporting. Enhancing Learning in Organisations.* Sage Publications, 1996.

Weiss, Carol H., Improving the use of Evaluations: Whose Job is it Anyway?, in *Advances in Educational Productivity,* Vol. 7, 1998 p. 263 - 276.

Weiss, Carol H., The Interface between Evaluation and Public Policy, in *Evaluation,* Vol. 5(4) 1999 pp. 468-486.

Whitmore Elizabeth, *Understanding and Practicing Participatory Evaluation,* New Directions for Evaluation, Jossey-Bass,1998

Wholey Joseph S. , Hatry Harry P., Newcomer Kathryn E. (Eds.), *Handbook of Practical Program Evaluation,* Jossey-Bass, 1994

Worthen, Blaine R. et al. *Program Evaluation: Alternative Approaches and Practical Guidelines,* 2nd ed. Addison-Wesley, 1996

Yin, R.., *Case Study Research.* Newbury Park, CA: Sage 1989

EVALUATION SITES AND SOURCES ANNEX 3

Organisations

American Evaluation Association AEA
   http://www.eval.org/

Candian Evaluation Society
   http://www.evaluationcanada.ca/

European Evaluation Society
   http://www.europeanevaluation.org/

Evaluation in the European Commission
   http://europe.eu.int/comm/budget/index.htm

The Evaluation Cooperation Group
   http://www.ecgnet.org/

Journals

Evaluation. The International Journal of Theory, Research and Practice, Sage Publications
   http://www.sagepub.co.uk/

The American journal of evaluation, Elsevier Science publishing
Evaluation and Program Planning, Elsevier Science publishing
   http://www.elsevier.nl/

New directions for evaluation, Wiley InterScience Publications
   http://www.wiley.com/

Other

OECD database of evaluation report abstracts
   http://www.dac-evaluations-cad.org/

INDEX

A
Acceptable attribution   117
Accuracy   155, 166, 200
Accuracy standards   168
After study with control group   121
After study without control group   122
Appraisal   38, 196,
Attribution   114 - 117
Audit   34, 46

B
Before and after study   121

C
Case study   144
Commisioner   56
Commissioning party   55, 61, 176, 177
Conclusions   118, 119
Contextual setting   41
Contextual uncertainty   9, 19, 22
Cost effectiveness   49, 99
Cost of evaluations   49
Cost-benefit analysis   99
Counterfactual question   116
Credibility   48, 124, 160
Crosscutting issues   93

D
Data analysis   65
Data collection   65, 129 - 149
Decision to evaluate   58 - 60
Deductive research   111
Direct measurement   136
Direct observation   131, 138
Direct use   39
Distributional analysis   101
Documentation   34 - 36

E
Economic analysis   98
Economic and financial aspects   93
Effectiveness   73, 77, 81 - 83
Efficiency   73 - 80
End evaluation   32, 38
Environmental impact   94, 103
Evaluability assessment   50, 53
Evaluation criteria   77, 118, 120
Evaluation design   111
Evaluation ethics   167
Evaluation instruments   117 - 120, 158
Evaluation questions   65, 118 - 120
Evaluation report   67, 157, 167, 173 - 180

Evaluation team   58, 63 - 65
Evaluation work plan   63
Evaluations of individual projects   32
Evaluator   55
Evidence   153
Ex post evaluation   32, 38
Expert's assessment   153
Extensive observation   131, 146
External evaluators   36
External validity   159

F
Feasibility   155, 167
Feedback   176 - 178
Finalisation   69
Financial analysis   98
Financial sustainability   98 - 100
Financing party   11 - 17, 55
Focus group interviews   140 - 142
Follow-up   69
Formal methods   129
Formal surveys   148
Formative evaluations   32, 35
Front-end phase   16, 60

G
Generalisability   42
Goal model   44

I
Impact   83
Impartiality   48, 160
Implementation phase   18
Independence   48
Indirect use   39
Inductive research   111
Informal methods   129
Informal survey   142
Information process   118, 132
Inputs   98
Institutional aspects   94, 105
Interim evaluation   32, 38
Internal evaluators   161
Internal factors   105
Internal validity   158
Intuition   153

K
Key informant interviews   131, 134
Knowledge   153

Annex 3 – Sites and sources

L
Learning 179
Legislative environment 97
Limited attribution 117

M
Main parties to an evaluation 55
Managers' assessment 153
Mandate 58, 61
Measurement validity 158
Measures of success 25, 73
Monitoring 38

N
Non-participant observation 146

O
Objectivity 146, 160
Observer bias 138
Operational level 47
Operational perspective 25
Operational phase 16
Operational uncertainty 9
Operator 11 - 14
Opportunity 7
Outputs 98

P
Performance management 37
Policy support 93, 96
Preparatory phase 118
Preparatory work 61 - 63
Pre-study 66
Process model 44
Productivity 79
Program level evaluations 32
Project 5, 105
Project design 19
Project goal 16, 19 - 21, 96
Project life cycle 37
Project purpose 16, 19 - 21
Project strategy 16, 22, 116
Project structure 19
Project success 26
Propriety 155
Propriety standards 168
Purpose of evaluation 46, 62

Q
Qualitative analysis 123 - 125
Quality of evaluations 48
Quality of information 155
Quality standard for evaluations 156
Quantitative analysis 123 - 125

R
Rapid assessment methods 129
recommendations;119
Relevance 74 - 78
Reliability 157 - 159
Replicability 41 - 43
Reports 173
Resources 165

Risk 7

S
Science 153
Scope of evaluation 31, 111
Sector or company level evaluations 32
Socio-economic aspects 93, 101
Stakeholders 11, 55
Stakeholder's commitment 93
Strategic perspective 26
Study design 121 - 123
Successful projects 25
Summative evaluations 32
Sustainability 62, 75 - 78, 88, 93, 98
Sustainable development 103

T
Tactical level 47
Tactical perspective 25, 73, 77
Team leader 63, 67
Technology 94, 107
Time-series study 122
Triangulation 153, 162 - 164

U
Uncertainty 7 - 10
Use of evaluation 176 - 179
Users 14, 55
Users' assessment 153
Utility 155
Utility standards 167

V
Validity 156 - 159